Get **more** out of libraries

Please return or renew this item by the last date shown.

You can renew online at www.hants.gov.uk/library

Or by phoning   0345 603 5631

Hampshire
County Council

C015648350

From Hitler's U-Boats to Khrushchev's Spy Flights

From Hitler's U-Boats to Khrushchev's Spy Flights

Twenty-Five Years with Flight Lieutenant Thomas Buchanan Clark, RAF

Chris Clark

Pen & Sword
AVIATION

First published in Great Britain in 2013 by
Pen & Sword Military
an imprint of
Pen & Sword Books Ltd
47 Church Street
Barnsley
South Yorkshire
S70 2AS

Copyright © Chris Clark 2013

ISBN 978 1 78159 054 6

Typeset in Ehrhardt by
Mac Style, Driffield, East Yorkshire
Printed and bound in the UK by CPI Group (UK) Ltd, Croydon,
CRO 4YY

Pen & Sword Books Ltd incorporates the Imprints of Pen & Sword
Aviation, Pen & Sword Maritime, Pen & Sword Military, Wharncliffe
Local History, Pen and Sword Select, Pen and Sword Military
Classics, Leo Cooper, The Praetorian Press, Remember When,
Seaforth Publishing and Frontline Publishing.

For a complete list of Pen & Sword titles please contact
PEN & SWORD BOOKS LIMITED
47 Church Street, Barnsley, South Yorkshire, S70 2AS, England
E-mail: enquiries@pen-and-sword.co.uk
Website: www.pen-and-sword.co.uk

Contents

Dedication

This book is dedicated to the memory of my late Father, Tom Clark. Also to the memory of Peter Coles, Aviation Commissioning Editor Pen & Sword Publishers, who sadly died whilst in the process of reviewing it for a second time. Without his continued professional interest, belief and support in its contents it would not be presented to you now.

Prologue

Tom's long and varied journey took him over four Continents and many seas during his twenty-five years service with the RAF. From Britain to France during 1940, with an Army Cooperation Squadron flying Lysanders, and the British Expeditionary Force artillery, as a Ground Signaller.

Then with two Coastal Command Squadrons, firstly to Scotland, the Shetland Isles, the North Atlantic, Iceland, Greenland and Canada in 1941, with a Sunderland Flying Boat Squadron on an anti U-boat and convoy patrol squadron, and the North Atlantic Ferry Service bringing Catalinas to the UK. Then secondly, around the coastal areas of Britain, covering the North Sea, English Channel, Western Approaches, and the Western Isles of Scotland on an Air-Sea Rescue Squadron, flying Hudsons from Bircham Newton.

Then on to Bomber Command, from Norfolk to Egypt and the Western Desert Countries of Libya, Cyrenaica, Tripolitania, and Tunisia, and the Middle East area during 1943 in an offensive instructor role on light bombers, flying various aircraft of 75 Operational Training Unit (O.T.U.), and during 1944 joining a Baltimore Squadron in Italy.

During 1945 and 1946 he travelled from Britain to India and Europe with a Transport Command Squadron flying Dakotas. In 1947 he flew Vikings of the Royal Flight from Britain to the sub-continent of South Africa, Rhodesia (now Zimbabwe) and the Mediterranean.

As a volunteer he flew innumerable missions to the beleaguered city of Berlin during the 'Berlin Airlift'. From 1949 to 1952 he travelled from Britain to Europe and the Mediterranean, again, with Transport Command Squadrons, flying the Valetta on V.I.P. flights and a second tour on the Royal Flight. During 1953 and 1954, he went to the Far East, including Hong Kong, Singapore, Korea, Taiwan, China, Japan, and Indonesia, and on to Australia with a V.I.P. Transport Wing flying Valettas.

From 1955 to 1957 he was a Signals Instructor and Examiner. From 1958 to 1962, he was attached to Signals Command Squadrons and flew Comets, carrying out Electronic Intelligence (ELINT) and Signal Intelligence (SIGINT) flights over Denmark, Sweden, Norway, Finland and the Arctic Circle bordering the northern Soviet Union. Also to Cyprus, Turkey, and the rest of the Middle East, including Syria, Iraq, Iran, Jordan, Saudi Arabia, Oman, the Red Sea, and the countries bordering the southern Soviet Union, including the Black Sea.

Foreword

Foreword by Air Marshal Richard Frank (Dick) Garwood, CB, CBE, DFC, MA, RAF; Deputy Commander-in-Chief Operations, RAF Air Command, High Wycombe:

"I first met Tom Clark when I was at school as he worked with my father at the Council Depot in Hunstanton. Tom was not a man who would state his many achievements, but offered me quiet encouragement and always showed interest as he followed my career into the RAF. Tom Clark was clearly a remarkable man. His career reads like a work of fiction because it is so varied in location, aircraft and event. To have survived the war as an Air Gunner, despite being shot down behind enemy lines and successfully evading capture, is a feat few achieved. He also lived through a catastrophic crash that killed many of his fellow crewmen that would have shaken the nerve of many a brave man.

Even after the war, he did not take the quiet easy route through life; spending years escorting the Royal Family, and then flying on missions high in the rarefied upper air, where being shot down or baling out could have meant instant death. His career and those of his colleagues makes fascinating reading.

Whilst it is vital that the RAF looks to the future, it is also essential that in doing so, we draw on lessons and inspirations from the past. Tom Clark's incredible career spanned twenty-five years and four continents and is captured in this extraordinary book in context so that the account is both personal and extensive.

Those serving in today's armed forces would do well to read this book and apply many of the same principles to current tactics and strategy, to learn from the successes and failures from Air-Sea Rescue to Close Air Support, from the vital bombing runs in the Second World War, to the tactics of deception and adaptation in the Cold War. More than this though, personnel today should learn from the man – Tom Clark was clearly determined, professional and spirited, yet he was also brave, calm and the humblest of men. I am proud to have known Tom Clark and I hope in turn that he would be pleased with where my RAF career has taken me."

Dick Garwood, February 2011

A senior officer who has been at the forefront, and at "the sharp end" of the armed forces, Air Marshal Richard "Dick" Garwood joined the Royal Air Force in 1979, completing his officer and pilot training at the Royal Air Force College Cranwell. During 1982 he was posted to No. 41 (Fighter) Squadron and flew the Jaguar in the ground attack and reconnaissance roles.

He later instructed on the Hawk and became a Qualified Weapons Instructor. During 1987 he flew the Phantom RF-4C as an exchange officer with the United States Air Force. He converted to the Tornado GR1 and rose steadily through the ranks; firstly as Squadron Leader to No. 11 (Army Co-operation) Squadron based in Germany, which shortly afterwards was deployed to Saudi Arabia where he saw active service during the Gulf War of 1991. During "Operation Desert Storm" he flew nineteen night low-level reconnaissance sorties and was awarded the Distinguished Flying Cross.

During 1995 he was promoted to Wing Commander and took command of No. 11 (Army Co-operation) Squadron based at RAF Marham in Norfolk – the squadron had moved there in December 1991 – and led his squadron on many operational detachments to patrol the Iraqi No-Fly Zones. After further roles he was posted back to RAF Marham, this time as Station Commander, taking command in 2000. Ten years on, and after many other personal achievements, he is currently Deputy Commander-in-Chief Operations on promotion to the rank of Air Marshal.

Summary

Tom, my Dad, was a "dark horse", and it is only since his death aged eighty-three during March 2005 that I have been able to piece together his illustrious RAF career, which he had all but managed to keep to himself. Not having access to his personal flight logs caused me to have to research his career from a basic skeleton, his Personnel Record, and I built it from there to the complete article presented before you.

He joined the Royal Air Force at age seventeen and a half – some two and a half months before the outbreak of the Second World War – as an Aircraftsman 2, and after "square bashing" and initial training at RAF Cardington, went to RAF Yatesbury. There, he trained as a Wireless Operator before joining 16 Squadron as a Signaller in January 1940, at RAF Old Sarum. He soon moved with the squadron, firstly to RAF Hawkinge, on the south coast of England, and then on to Bertangles near Amiens in Northern France, in April 1940 during the "Phoney War". There his main task was to liaise with the artillery battery commanders of the British Expeditionary Force on the ground and the "spotter" Lysander aircraft, who would forward the coordinates of where the German guns were located. Tom would relay the messages from the pilots to the army battery commanders so that fire could be directed onto the enemy positions.

His stay in France was, however, short-lived, as on the 10 May 1940, the "Real War" started when the Germans released their "Blitzkrieg" and the Allied Forces were driven out of Belgium and France to Dunkirk, where there was a mass troop evacuation. Northern France was quickly sealed off by the enemy. However, Tom's unit managed to escape by going south to Cherbourg and boarding a freighter back to Southampton.

Wanting to give "The Hun" something back, he left 16 Squadron in July 1940, and during August, trained at RAF Manby in Lincolnshire as an Air Gunner. At the end of August 1940, he passed out as a Flight Sergeant Air Gunner/Wireless Operator, and the following month trained at RAF Stranraer in Wig Bay, Western Scotland, on the Flying Boat Training Squadron. He then joined 201 Squadron at Sullom Voe, in The Shetlands, as a Wireless Operator/Air Gunner (WAG) on the recently acquired Short Sunderland Flying Boat, as part of Coastal Command's general reconnaissance, anti-submarine and shipping patrol of the North Atlantic and northern North Sea.

The squadron role was the protection of Merchant and Royal Navy convoys, bringing vital equipment and supplies from the United States of America to a beleaguered Britain, which were running the gauntlet of German U-boats and battleships. As well as accounting for a number of U-boats, the squadron was also involved in the hunt for the German battleships "*Bismarck*" and "*Prinz Eugen*" during the last week of May 1941. During the spring of 1941, Tom was also involved in the ferrying of Catalina and other aircraft from Canada to the UK, before returning to 201 Squadron.

During August that year, Tom was involved in a fatal flying accident involving a Sunderland which crashed into the sea, where five of his colleagues perished, and he survived along with six others. After being patched up by Surgeon Daniel Lamont, Lord Norman Lamont's father, and a spell in a Shetland Hospital, Tom was moved firstly to Stracathro Hospital near Brechin, and then to RAF Hospital Dingwall, to convalesce until the 22 October 1941. Tom, on returning fit for duty, found that his squadron had moved to County Fermanagh, in Northern Ireland, on 1 September 1940.

Number 279 Squadron was formed at Bircham Newton in north-west Norfolk during November 1940 and Tom joined them on the 12 December as a rear dorsal gunner on the Lockheed Hudson Mk 1. The squadron role was the increasing task of air-sea rescue (ASR) of RAF bomber and fighter crews shot down or ditched in the southern North Sea/English Channel or Western Approaches; en route back from missions in enemy Europe. They would locate a stricken crew and drop the Lindholme Dinghy and emergency supplies to them.

During 1942 this also applied to many of the USAF 8th Air Force, as by then, America had joined the war effort. Tom had detachments from the squadron to Thorney Island in Hampshire, St Eval in Cornwall, and the Isle of Benbecula in the Western Highlands of Scotland. The squadron held monthly dances on the Bircham Newton Air Base and it was at one of these that Tom met and later courted his future wife, and my mother, Stella Stringer, a local woman from the village of Stanhoe in West Norfolk. Despite the war intervening for a further three years, they would eventually marry in August 1945, and I, a by-product of their intense relationship, would be born that December.

During his stay with 279 Squadron, Tom ditched in one of the ASR Hudson's, and after he came to he found himself floating on one of the plane's doors which had a mattress attachment. The crew he had been with from the formation of the squadron was involved in a near fatal shoot-up on 30 November 1942, with a pair of German Fokker Wulf 190s. The rear gunner replacing Tom was wounded in the head and hospitalized. At the time, Tom was on a Gunnery Leaders Course at Sutton Bridge, before being posted to Egypt in January 1943. Then on 4 February 1943, Tom's close friend and former Polish crew member colleague, Flight Sergeant "Slug" Slugoski, was lost in a ditched ASR Hudson in the North Sea off Happisburgh, near Cromer in Norfolk.

Tom was trained at 75 Operational Training Unit (OTU) in Egypt during February 1943, before joining them on an emergency commission as a Flying Officer Gunnery Instructor during May 1943. His role was teaching new Air Gunners and Wireless Operators before they joined squadrons of the Desert Air Force. In January 1944, he joined 55 Squadron of the Desert Air Force as a dorsal gunner, and a flying Gunnery Leader with the Commanding Officer, Wing Commander "Cookie" Leon, in the Martin Baltimore. Their role was supporting the allied armies during the Italy Campaign. This included strafing enemy road supply convoys, trains and munitions dumps along the length of the Italian mainland.

Tom flew many missions with his various crews of colleagues, but his luck finally ran out some three weeks after "D Day" and the Normandy landing – the Allied Invasion of Europe. During the evening of the 26 June 1944, whilst attacking enemy convoy targets on the Pistoia to Bologna roads north-east of Florence, his Baltimore was brought down by enemy aircraft after evading "ack-ack" artillery fire from the ground. The crew of four had to bale out behind the enemy's recently erected "Gothic Line". Tom landed alone in farmland and hid in a field of maize, eventually being located by Italian peasants who took him to a "safe house" in an enemy held town, and there he was reunited with one of his crew, who was injured.

Both were posted as missing by the Air Ministry and believed either killed in action or captured by the Germans. However, they were being well looked after by the – now allied – local population, and they were moved on again at the start of July in disguise and under the gaze of German troops to another "safe house", situated in a district of Florence, where both stayed for some six weeks before being repatriated with the advancing Allies and taken to Naples for treatment, debriefing, and rest, before returning to his squadron. To his delight Tom was reunited with his other two crew members who he thought had been captured after baling out. Tom was nominated for a gallantry medal by the Commanding Officer of 55 Squadron, and later received a "Mention in Despatches" for his service during the Italy Campaign. He continued with 55 Squadron until his overseas tour expired in December 1944.

In early 1945, the squadron re-equipped with Bostons in Northern Italy, until the Germans were pushed out, they then moved on to Greece in September 1945, where they received Mosquitos, before being disbanded in 1946. Meanwhile, during March and April 1945, Tom had gone on a Training and Re-crewing Course for Wireless Operator/Air. He then joined 271 Squadron as a Signals Leader Wireless Operator, flying the Douglas Dakota to India, and later Europe, collecting time-expired troops, repatriated prisoners of war, and resupplying fresh troops.

During 1946 The King's Flight was re-formed at RAF Benson, with its role of flying the monarch HM King George V1, HM Queen Elizabeth, HRH Princess

Elizabeth, HRH Prince Philip, and HRH Princess Margaret within the British Isles and overseas, and four Vickers Vikings were purchased. Tom, by now a Flight Lieutenant, was chosen as one of the Wireless Operator/Signallers. He would receive his permanent commission on 4 December 1953 from the new Queen.

The flight's first task, once organized, was to ready itself for the forthcoming Royal Tour of South Africa in 1947. The four Viking aircraft flew the long journey to Cape Town, whilst the Royal party travelled by sea on HMS *Valiant*. Tom was involved with flying members of the Royal Family around various countries in the south of Africa, including the former Rhodesia (now Zimbabwe), where he briefly met his brother James, who had settled in Salisbury (Pretoria) after the war. During the tour HRH Princess Elizabeth (now HM The Queen Elizabeth II) celebrated her twenty-first birthday in Cape Town. In November of that year HRH Princess Elizabeth and HRH Prince Philip were married, and she took over many of the royal duties which her ill father was unable to perform.

Tom was involved with flying the heir to the throne, and her husband, to various official engagements, until the forthcoming scheduled 1948 Royal Tour of East Africa. Australia and New Zealand was cancelled due to HM The King's ill health. Tom, together with others, was "time expired" and he left the Royal Air Force on the 9 March 1948. He later volunteered his services with 47 Squadron at RAF Topcliffe during the Berlin Airlift.

During 1948 and 1949 the "Cold War" escalated, and the Soviets blockaded East Berlin, this resulted in many RAF and USAF flights to the beleaguered city of Berlin; taking coal, food, clothing, etc.

During September 1949, Tom was recalled to the RAF with his short service commission and went onto 10 Squadron as a Signals Leader, flying V.I.P. flights out of Waterbeach for four months; this squadron was disbanded on the 20 February 1950, and on the 27 February 1950 he joined 24 Squadron which also ran V.I.P. flights at Waterbeach, and within days the squadron moved to nearby Bassingbourn, where he remained for a further four months.

From June 1950 and up until the end of October 1952, Tom was again with The King's Flight as a Signaller, flying The Royal Family to various locations, including Prince Philip to and from Malta, where he was then stationed as a naval lieutenant and lived there with Princess Elizabeth from 1949 until 1951. Upon the death of King George VI in February 1952, and Queen Elizabeth II's accession to the throne; Tom was still involved with royal duties and the flight was renamed The Queen's Flight during that autumn.

From November 1952 until May 1955, Tom was posted to the Far East Air Force (FEAF) Transport Wing, as a Flying Qualified Signals Leader in mainly Valetta aircraft. He was also attached to V.I.P. Flight, ferrying the commander-in-chief of FEAF and other high ranking officers around the Far East. He was also involved in supporting, and supplying, ground troops during the end of The Korean War, from RAF Kaitak, Hong Kong, and into The Malayan Emergency, then stationed at Changi in Singapore, where the supply was to SAS and other specialized troops. As a highly qualified Signals Leader he was also involved in the Far East Communications Squadron psychological warfare "voice aircraft".

Following the death of his father-in-law, John Stringer in April 1955, he was posted back to Britain. In June he was an examiner in the Air Signallers School, at Swanton Morley in Norfolk, this was later renamed Air Electronics School.

During the continuation of the "Cold War", in April 1956, Tom was at RAF Marham when the Soviet Leader Nikolai Bulganin, together with Nikita Khrushchev, the Soviet leader in waiting, visited the station under the guise of a "goodwill tour". This came four days after the M16 "Buster" Crabb and the Soviet cruiser "*Ordzhonikidze*" affair, where Crabb, a former naval frogman was recruited to find out what technological advances the Soviet fleet had. Crabb disappeared and was assumed murdered by Soviet special forces. Tom had been hand picked for this visit by Air Chief Marshall Sir Lewis Hodges, a former Second World War SOE pilot, and pioneer of the British "V" Bomber Force, a nuclear weapon carrying aircraft. Tom was to monitor the activities of the party whilst they were inspecting the base.

At that time Marham had just taken delivery of the Vickers Valiant B1's as part of Britain's Independent Nuclear Deterrent Programme. The Russian party included the Soviet nuclear scientist Mr Ivan V. Kurbachov, and the Russian aircraft designer Mr Andrei N. Tupolev. At that time the Soviets did not have an aircraft capable of delivering a nuclear bomb, but were extending their rocket and missile programme under the cover of space exploration in a race with the Americans, and they urgently needed to see Britain's nuclear aircraft capability up close. Tupolev was also copying and cloning various aircraft, including the Comet, for his newer civil and military aircraft designs. He later designed a Russian equivalent of a Comet, named Tu-104 and a Concorde ("Concordski"), a Tu–144, which again was a "clone" of the French/British version.

During 1958 Tom was at RAF Hullavington as an Air Electronics Officer on a Signals Category Flight. In November that year he moved to RAF Watton Central Signals Establishment as a Qualified Signals Leader, and became involved with special operations on 51 Squadron, where he was a "front end" signaller. The secret squadron was flying a De Havilland Comet, in tandem with, but high above, an English Electric Canberra. They flew along Soviet Bloc corridors in the Baltic, Arctic Ocean and the Middle East, under the guise of weather reconnaissance flights, but in reality they were "ferret" missions of Signal Intelligence (SIGINT) and Electronic Intelligence (ELINT).

These flights sought out the newly built Soviet radar and surface-to-air missile installations. They listened in to Soviet radio bands and tested their mettle, when the Soviets were locking onto the Canberra's position. The intelligence from these flights was passed to GCHQ and the CIA, then U2 spy planes – including the one piloted by Gary Powers, who was at Watton at the time – would overfly the USSR and photograph the newly reported installations. During the next few years Watton had various visitors based there; the USAF Lockheed U2 spy plane, "Bloodhound" Surface-to-Air missiles (SAM), and "Thor" Intermediate Range Ballistic Missiles (IRBM), the forerunner of the Intercontinental Ballistic Missile (ICBM). The SIGINT, ELINT, and U-2 flights continued right up until October 1962 and "The Cuban Crisis", when John Fitzgerald Kennedy, the President of the USA, ordered the Soviet Leader Khrushchev to stop his nuclear capability missiles from entering Cuba and averted a probable Third World War.

During 1960 Tom's left eyesight was fading rapidly due to injuries brought on by the wartime Sunderland Flying Boat crash and flak flashes. During February 1961 he had a delicate eye operation at Royal Air Force Hospital Ely, in Cambridgeshire, and for some time thereafter he wore an eye patch, and later thick lens spectacles. During September of that year he was at RAF Thorney Island as an Air Electronics Officer Instructor, before moving back to Hullavington and Watton. He returned to operational flying during December 1962. Tom recommenced flying as a Qualified Signals Leader with Development Squadron, renamed 151 Squadron, on Lincoln and Canberra aircraft up until March 1963, when 51 Squadron moved to Wyton; and 151 Squadron was renamed 97 Squadron.

For the last year of his twenty-five year loyal service he became the families' officer at RAF West Raynham, which involved organizing service personnel postings, movements, housing, welfare, etc. Having become "desk bound" and swapping a flight deck for an office, he decided to take retirement on his forty-third birthday.

Upon retirement he commuted part of his pension into a greenhouse complex, together with horticulture paraphernalia, and a Bedford Dormobile van. He unsuccessfully tried, due to the economic climate of Britain, to become a mobile garden centre; which at that time was a pioneering venture before garden centres became the norm. Tom then joined the local council parks department as a landscape gardener and was promoted to foreman, where he stayed until his retirement in 1985. Upon retirement he maintained a number of allotments and kept his, by now extended family, well supplied with fruit and vegetables. He became well established in the local and national horticultural events, including Kew and Chelsea. He also attended the various RAF Squadron Association reunions of the squadrons he had served in.

During the last eight years of his life Tom also devoted himself to being a full-time carer for Stella, my mother, who was completely bedridden following a number of major strokes. In the twilight of his life, during June 2004, obviously knowing that he did not have long with us, Tom retraced his boyhood and youth of the mid-twenties and thirties on a journey that took him to the border areas of Scotland, Northumberland and Newcastle. During the winter of that year and into 2005, the "Big C" riddled his body and he slipped away on the 22 March 2005, with Stella also dying exactly three months later on the 22 June.

Rest in Peace.

Chapter One

"A Colonial Scot Childhood and Getting the Right Signal"

Birth And Childhood

Thomas Buchanan Clark entered the world on the 2 November 1921, in Peterborough, some thirty miles east of Toronto and twenty miles north of Lake Ontario, Canada, to Scottish parents, Charles James Clark and Elizabeth, formerly Buchanan. Although both had been born outside of Scotland they were of direct Scots ancestry; Charles was born in Danbury, Connecticut, USA, during December 1886 and Elizabeth at Wellington Barracks, Coonoor, South West India, in September 1890.

Charles' father, David Reekie Clark, was a master painter who embossed wallpaper in posh Victorian houses, he also painted scenery in water colours. His mother was Agnes Renton Wares, who was English by birth, and employed in the

Elizabeth Buchanan 1890–1930.   Charles James Clark 1886–1939.

herring fishery industry, her father and ancestors hailed from Wick in the North of Scotland. Charles, as a young boy, came with his family to live in the borders area of Scotland, at Melrose and Galashiels.

Elizabeth's father, Thomas Buchanan, was a corporal and later a sergeant PTI with the 2nd Battalion King's Own Scottish Borderer Regiment and her mother was Annie Begg, who had previously been married under the name of Blackhall. Elizabeth's family journey was via India, and Mandalay in Burma, to Glasgow, Scotland; and it eventually took her to Canada where she was naturalized just before the outbreak of the First World War.

It is believed that Charles and Elizabeth both met in Flanders, he a soldier with the Lothian and Border Horse, who was mustard gassed in the trenches, and she a nurse. They married on the 5 July 1920 at Saint Andrew's Church, Cobham, Surrey, England, and emigrated to Canada on the 6 August 1920. Tom was born the following year in Peterborough, Ontario, Canada.

Nearly three years later, James Wares Clark, Tom's brother, was born on the 5 September 1924, at Woodstock in Ontario; he would later be called Wares, his paternal grandmother's maiden name.

It would appear that the first four years of Tom's life were of an enjoyable family existence, judging by early photographs of the group. However, shortly after James birth, the marriage between Charles and Elizabeth deteriorated, him being an alcoholic and her most probably suffering from post-natal depression, a condition not recognized then. There are no surviving photographs of either boy taken with their mother after this period, and it would appear that the couple split up. Charles returning to Galashiels in Scotland together with the boys, and Elizabeth on her own, moving to Edinburgh. Charles' father, David Clark had also been an alcoholic, and eventually this would also take a hold on Tom and he would only free himself from it in his latter years and fling off the shackles which had chained at least three generations of Clark.

Tom's great-grandfather Charles Clerk, had been a papermaker and importer of fine china during the mid 1880s, then his grandfather David Clark came along, and the Scottish enumerator changed the family name to what it is now. David would become

Tom aged about four years old.

a master painter, and paint and print wallpaper during the late Victorian period, he also painted watercolour landscapes (four of these paintings by my great-grandfather have since been left to me by dad's cousin, Irene Henderson, who passed away in December 2008, and also one painted by my grandfather, Charles Clark).

When Tom's father Charles James Clark was a young man he became an apprentice with Messrs A. Walker & Sons, Printers and Stationers, Galashiels, moving on to printer and eventually works manager for John McQueen & Son of Galashiels, either side of the First World War; until he left to emigrate to Canada and to marry. In his younger days he was a keen rugby player, and was a former captain of Gala Rugby Club, for which he played for several seasons as a forward. During the First World War he was a trooper with the Lothian and Border Horse and fought in Flanders where he contracted mustard gas from the trenches.

From about 1925 onwards, Charles James Clark was a printer's travelling salesman for stationary firms in Edinburgh and Glasgow. Tom was sent to live some forty miles away from Galashiels in Edinburgh with his Uncle William and Aunt Mamie; William being Charles younger brother. William and Mamie had a son called Kenneth during 1929 and he and Tom were brought up together until 1933. Meanwhile, Tom's brother James lived with his grandmother Agnes (formerly Wares), at 146 Wood Street, Galashiels, who, with his two maiden Aunts, Grace and Agnes, raised him. Tom and James only saw their mother on rare occasions, and sadly the breakdown of the family and her separation from her boys was too much for her to bear, and on the evening of the 1 May 1930 she

The Eildon Hills from Bemersyde.

committed suicide by swallowing a poison. Tom was eight and James four. They were told by their father at the funeral, which they both attended, that "their mother was a bad woman."

From 1933 to 1935, both boys then lived together in Galashiels, with Tom going to Galashiels Academy School, joining the Church of Scotland there, and serving as an altar boy and in the choir. After a while he found unnatural things going on there and he was abused by certain adults of the church. This led to him becoming an agnostic and he did not have any of his later children baptized. Tom told me that on a Sunday he would accompany his father Charles – who would have paper, paints and easel – and together they would climb the central peak of the three hills known as the Eildon Hills near Melrose, rising to 1,385feet (422metres); and there, his father would paint the scenery in watercolours, whilst Tom played.

Eventually their father sought employment with Remington, a Newcastle based firm, and around 1935 they moved with him to 4 Benton Park Road, South Gosforth, Newcastle-upon-Tyne, and Tom went to Heaton Grammar School at High Heaton, Newcastle-upon-Tyne, where he learnt French Language, with James following sometime around 1936. Tom left school during 1937, and from January 1938 at age sixteen years and two months, he went to work for a Mr H. Lewis (Printers), of Shields Road, Newcastle-upon-Tyne, as an apprentice lithographer (printer to you and me), so carrying on the Clark genes of his father and forebears. He was also part of the Northumbria Racing Cycle Team and they would cycle over a hundred miles a day! At some stage their father, Charles Clark, met in Tom's words, "a rather unpleasant lady" called Essie Scott Richardson, a spinster, and teacher from Galashiels, and they married on the 2 December 1938 at Dryburgh Abbey Hotel (previously painted in water colours by his father during the 1870's). Some four months later on the 27 March 1939, Charles Clark died from diabetes and pneumonia at age fifty-three years. The very next day the stepmother, Essie, cleared the house of any valuables and destroyed precious memories of the former family.

Due to a combination of being separated from his mother and her untimely death, his experience in the Scottish Church, his father's sudden death and his stepmother's attitude, Tom, being an unhappy teenager of some seventeen years old, abandoned his roots for the best part of sixty years. He left his printing occupation in March 1939; and signed on to join the Royal Air Force on the 13 June 1939, nearly three months before the outbreak of the Second World War. When he enlisted as an Aircraftsman 2, his service number was 647790; he cited his next-of-kin as Mr W.J. Clark of 146 Wood Street, Galashiels, and relationship, brother.

James Wares left school just before he turned fifteen and joined the Scottish Post Office; eventually joining the Royal Corp of Signals in March 1943 and in December of that year joined the Royal Navy, where he saw war service during

1944 in the Mediterranean. It's strange that both became signallers independently of each other and that both were in a similar theatre of war.

A Thought For The Quiet Hour by Patience Strong:
Hymn For The RAF

"Lord, hold them in thy mighty hand
Above the ocean and the land
Like wings of eagles mounting high
Along the pathways of the sky
Immortal is the name they bear
And high the honour that they share
Until a thousand years have rolled
Their deeds of valour shall be told
In dark of night and light of day
God speed and bless them on their way
And homeward safely guide each one
With glory gained and duty done"

Chapter Two

"World War Two Begins"

On the 4 September 1939, one day after war was declared, the Royal Air Force received this message from His Majesty King George V1. "The Royal Air Force has behind it a tradition no less inspiring than those of older services…you will have to shoulder far greater responsibilities than those which your service had to shoulder in the last war; one of the greatest of them will be the safeguarding of these islands from the menace from the air. I can assure all ranks of the Air Force of my supreme confidence in their skill and courage and their ability to meet whatever calls will be made on them".

In the meantime Tom, a seventeen and a half year old teenager, had joined the RAF on the 13 June 1939 as an Aircraftsman and Wireless Operator, and completed his basic training and "square bashing" at RAF Cardington.

Tom then trained as a Wireless Operator and Signaller at No 2 Electrical and Wireless School, at RAF Yatesbury, near Calne in Wiltshire, arriving on the 25 August 1939, and on the 21 September he was made acting corporal whilst on the

Initial Training at Cardington, Tom in middle row fourth from right.

Number 2 Radio School RAF Yatesbury Motto "Celer Et Vigilans" "Swift and Watchful".

No 16 Squadron Mottos "Operta Aperta" meaning "Hidden Things Are Revealed".

Coastal Command Crest.

course. On the 31 December 1939, he was an Aircraftsman 2, Aircraft hand/ Wireless Operator, untrained.

During the Second World War, RAF Yatesbury, together with RAF Compton Bassett was a major radio and radar training school. Tom received the princely sum of three shillings a day (30p) as an Aircraftsman 2nd class whilst training as a Wireless Operator. The signals school was run like a college, in accordance with its pre-war ethos, so there was no marching about; school hours were worked, with weekends off unless there was something special on. The trainees learnt electrical and radio theory and aircraft recognition. Radio telephony was learnt and "Harwell Boxes" were used. These contraptions were mock-ups, made to look and feel like an aircraft radio cubicle, from which messages could be exchanged with the instructor; they were nicknamed "coffins" by those who would not be at risk flying in real combat situations.

Tom received his first posting on the 20 January 1940 to Coastal Command.

When Tom joined 16 Squadron on 6 February 1940, he was an ex-mustered Wireless Operator and partly trained in telephone communications. The squadron, was at that time established at Old Sarum in Wiltshire, some two miles NNE of Salisbury; at the outbreak of war the appearance of the station had changed little from when the squadron had moved in during April 1924. Its line of hangars still looked out onto the grass flying field; while the old Roman road still formed the northern border of the airfield. The squadron continued to be primarily engaged in training and developing ground support techniques. The Officer Commanding (OC) of 16 Squadron was Wing Commander Humble.

Thus, 16 Squadron was an Army Cooperation Squadron operating Westland Lysanders and had been the first squadron to receive these aircraft in May 1938; the aircraft would be used for spotting German held positions in enemy held terroritory. During 1939, sixty-six Lysander MK 1's were completed, and of those 16 Squadron received fourteen.

A Short Stay In France

At the outbreak of war there were seven Lysander Squadrons. With 4 Squadron and 13 Squadron, 16 Squadron formed the 50 Army Cooperation Wing, under the command of Group Captain A.R. Churchman. Its HQ was in Athies and they flew the Westland Lysander Mk 2 with Squadron Code UG.

Tom was a ground wireless operator in the signals section of 16 Squadron, which meant relaying messages between the Lysanders and their army colleagues' batteries on the ground, and was later based with the British Expeditionary Force (BEF). The squadron became part of The British Advanced Striking Force (BASF) and moved to RAF Hawkinge, north of Folkestone in Kent, between the 16 February and the 13 April 1940, to hone up its skills before crossing the English Channel.

When they did, the Lysanders firstly landed at Glissy near Amiens but moved the following day, the 14 April, to Bertangles, some fifteen minutes flying time to the north-east. The ground crew staff, including Tom, had earlier crossed by ferry from Folkestone to Cherbourg, then by train, and the contingent tried to prepare the empty airfield and purchase rented accommodation. The signallers worked in pairs, often away from the airfield, and also in close conjunction with their allotted battery. Tom enjoyed "the phoney war" for a few weeks, visiting local towns and even Paris. Here he describes this period of his life in his own words, submitted to 16 Squadron News Brief, Issue 18, in April 2001.

Recollections of 16 Squadron in 1940, by 647790 AC2 Thomas B. Clark, Wireless Operator

"I joined 16 Squadron at RAF Old Sarum on 20 January 1940, just out of training at RAF Yatesbury. My main memories of the station are of watching Hawker Audaxes cavorting about; of drinking cider in the NAFFI and seeing a tall sturdy figure, in black leather flying boots and sporting a brass 'flying bullet' on his arm (the insignia then of an Air Gunner), enter the room straight from flying in one of these contraptions; and of a Warrant Officer of the old school, who was Irish.

"In April, we moved en masse by troop-train to Folkestone, where the flying was set up at RAF Hawkinge, and we were billeted out in the town. After about a week, we embarked for France and duly arrived in Cherbourg after a calm Channel crossing. Off again, this time by train and we fetched up eventually at Glissy, an airfield south of Amiens. This was a short stay and we found ourselves at Bertangles, north-east of Amiens and reputedly a First World War airfield and the scene of Baron Von Richtofen's demise.

"There were about sixty of us in the Signals Section, and our main task was to liaise on the ground with the artillery in the field, by relaying messages to the battery commanders from our Lysanders, which were 'spotting' for the guns. So we were set up in pairs and issued with bivouacs, a .45 Colt automatic but no ammunition, and a wireless receiver known as 'the wayside three' because it had three valves. I have only vague memories of actual operations, but I know that some teams got as far as Belgium with their batteries.

"The Signals Section was very efficiently run by Warrant Officer Corden, a highly trained communications expert, who was also an active pilot flying frequent sorties in the Lysanders. Some of the officer pilots seemed to have commission in both the Army and the RAF, as I remember seeing one or two in khaki one day and RAF blue the next. Although names are always a bugbear with me, I do remember some of my immediate colleagues such as Adams, Powell, 'Taff' Jones and Emmanuel, also Bert Hawkins DFM, who was the aforementioned W/Op AG I had seen in Old Sarum NAFFI.

"While the so called 'phoney war' was in progress, we availed ourselves generously of what the local area had to offer, including visiting Amiens by 'liberty bus' and frequenting the various *estaminets*. We were amazingly affluent, as I remember the French franc was 148 to the £ sterling and, even on an 'erks' pay, I was 'quid's in', as it were. A trip to Paris was organized, and we had a memorable day at the Parc des Princes seeing the RAF rugby team beat the Armee de l'air and then touring the city before catching a late train back to Amiens".

(Author's Note: During 2000, Tom submitted this article to 16 Squadron Association News Brief, together with a copy of the photograph reproduced overleaf. As a result ex Flight Lieutenant J.M.R. "Taff" Jones was very pleased

LAC Tom Clark and friends in the 16 Squadron Signals Section at Amiens April 1940
(1-r) Emmanuel(?) Adams Powell Clark Jones (all Welsh except Tom)
Photo: Tom Clark

to recognize himself in the photograph of five "sprogs" of the 16 Squadron Signals Section at Amiens in 1940. This resulted in a long telephone conversation between them, their first contact for sixty years. They discovered that, after the war, Tom was in 47 Squadron at RAF Topcliffe when "Taff" was Wing Signals Officer there, and they were both with Transport Command during the Berlin Airlift.)

We will now leave Tom's story to fill in the gaps. During April 1940 Germany invaded Norway and Denmark, leaving Sweden, who had declared neutrality like Switzerland. It unleashed on these countries its "Blitzkrieg", or Lightning War. It was a surprise attack using Stuka JU87 dive-bombers to strafe ground positions with bomb and cannon fire, and immediately in the aftermath send in tanks of the Panzer Division to clear the area. On the 10 May the real war started in earnest when the Germans loosed their "Blitzkrieg" on Holland, Belgium, France and the Allied Armies, driving back and surrounding the British at the port of Dunkirk; ironically on the same day Winston Churchill took over as Prime Minister from Neville Chamberlain. As the German attack began, No 4 Squadron moved to Belgium, but such was the fury of the onslaught that eleven Lysanders were lost between the 10 May and 23 May, some being eliminated on the ground. One of the squadron's Lysander crews destroyed a Bf 110 during a running battle with six Messerschmitts and managed to return to base.

Going back to Tom's first hand account:

"This rather idyllic existence continued until, one day in early May, we heard unfamiliar aero–engine noises and looked up to see formations of

Dorniers and Stukas making for Amiens and beyond. Some of our Lysanders were dispatched, and some did not return. I remember seeing Glissy being bombed by masses of Stukas, and great clouds of black smoke indicated the damage they had inflicted. After that, things went from bad to worse and it seemed that our aircraft and crews went like fierce lambs to the slaughter, as our losses were considerable. I remember a visit we had from the AOC, Air Chief Marshall Sir Arthur Barratt, who addressed the assembled squadron on the airfield; but it made little difference to morale, and we eventually received the order to abandon ship.

"The fuel dump and the few remaining unserviceable Lysanders were set alight and the bomb dump was bombed out of existence, while we destroyed our tents and equipment, retaining the minimum kit to take away. We were loaded onto a small fleet of 3-ton Crossleys and set off south-west with our tails between our legs. I remember when we stopped briefly in Amiens, a rumour circulated that the Mayor had been shot as a leading member of the Fifth Column. We had a huge problem negotiating the unending columns of refugees, which delayed our progress considerably, and I can still see people spitting at us and shouting 'A bas les Anglais!' while gesturing with their thumbs down and fingers up.

"We halted at Rouen for an hour while the convoy leader requested further instructions, and heard that we had left Amiens just in time and that any possible escape to Dunkirk had been cut off. We carried on west and eventually arrived in Cherbourg, somewhat the worse for wear after two days on the road. Off the truck, we found ourselves in the docks and were herded straight onto a medium-sized freighter, which was already loaded to the gunwales. I finished up topside and found a small space near the funnel, where I proceeded to flake out. I woke up just as we entered Southampton, so I missed the trip. We offloaded straight onto a troop train, which soon set off – we knew not where! After getting under way, we were issued with standard tin mugs, which were then half filled with Navy rum. In about ten minutes the whole train was roaring drunk, and in about half-an-hour everything went quiet. I woke up again and we were in Folkestone, back where we had started!

"The last word goes to a W/Op named Medlock, who was up-country with the artillery when the floodgates opened to the Germans. He purloined a motorcycle in the confusion and set off, as it turned out, north. Nobody stopped him and he soon found himself in Zeebrugge, where he managed to get aboard a coaster, one of the last to leave. I think he came back via Lowestoft, but he was in England days before the rest of us!"

This is what a former member of 16 Squadron wrote:

Flight Lieutenant H.J.S. "Jimmy" Taylor, ex Second World War 16 Squadron Pilot, and Secretary of 16 Squadron Association:

"Although I served on 16 Squadron as a pilot in 1944, I never knew Tom during the war, as he joined the squadron as a Wireless Operator in January 1940 and, after an exciting time on the ground in France in May, left it in July of the same year, to train as an Air Gunner.

"His wartime career after this was extremely varied, including an adventurous two months with the Partisans in Italy. But Tom was extraordinarily modest, and never discussed his war with anyone. He was equally reticent about his rank in the RAF. In the group of wartime survivors that I organized as '16 Squadron 1939–1945', I gave him the rank of Leading Aircraftsman (LAC), and only after his death discovered that he had been commissioned at some time and reached the rank of Flight Lieutenant. He was a Wireless Operator on the King's Flight, which in itself was a tribute to his skill and reliability. Again he did not tell me about this until near the end of his life. He was truly a strong, silent man.

"But Tom was more than this: He was also a great gentleman, kind, polite and self-effacing, yet ready to step forward if the need arose. Although he served in many other squadrons, he was particularly proud of having belonged to 16 Squadron, even for a short but critical time. 16 Squadron, in its turn, was proud of having a man like Tom serving in its ranks. His life, which he shielded so carefully from public gaze, is now revealed in these pages as having been of considerable interest, well worth putting on record and well worth reading."

Jimmy Taylor, 28 May 2010.

Chapter Three

"Gunning For Them Flying Boats and Lame Ducks"

The advent of the "new" generation of bombers in the RAF in the mid-1930s led to the first regular inclusion of a "distinct" Air Gunner in each crew; hitherto the back-seat man was all too often simply regarded as a mere passenger, or ballast. Air Gunner, as a distinct aircrew category or "trade", was not fully recognized until the beginning of 1939 in the RAF; when Air Ministry Order (AMO) A17/1939 dated 19 January 1939, finally laid down official policy and conditions of service et al for "Aircraft Crews other than Pilots". Previously, gunners in the RAF were virtually in two categories; Air Gunner (AG) and Wireless Operator (W/Op); the qualification as an Aerial Gunner had been recognized by a special arm badge, officially termed "Winged Bullet", worn on the upper arm of the right sleeve; they were employed only on a part-time basis, with a nominal daily few pence added to an airman's pay when he was actually engaged in official flying duties in that capacity.

The AMO placed all Air Gunners on a full-time employment basis, albeit in the aircrew category of Wireless Operator, on satisfactory completion of a gunnery course of instruction. At the same time existing Aerial Gunners, except those in Flying Boat Squadrons, were expected to take the Wireless Operator's Training Course. Prospects of further upgrading in aircrew status, and rank, were restricted by the same AMO to the possibility of selection for training as an Air Observer. If selected, the airman underwent a sixteen week course in navigation and bombing, on successful completion of which he would receive an acting rank as a sergeant; and after six months duty as an "Acting Observer" would be confirmed in rank and crew category, and authorized to wear the winged "O" flying badge of an Air Observer above his left tunic pocket. His daily rate of pay went up from nine shillings to twelve shillings (an increase of twenty five per cent); and an eventual rise to commissioned rank was envisaged.

On the 12 December 1939, AMO A.552 finally introduced the now-familiar "AG" cloth badge for wearing by Air Gunners, and the "Winged Bullet" was declared obsolete. All Air Gunners, when qualified, were in future to be of at least the rank of sergeant; while commissioned ranks were provided for, but only in rough proportion of one-to-three of Navigators or Pilots.

Air Observer; Wireless/Air Gunner; Rear Air Gunner; Air Gunner insignia.

The years 1939 to 1945 can truly be regarded as the "golden era" of the Air Gunner (AG). Never before, or since, were gunners employed in such large numbers, or given the official recognition and status befitting their onerous responsibilities. As the potential of aerial bombing began to be realized in practical terms – and particularly by 1943 as the awesome strength and striking power of the bombers emerged – Air Gunners had established themselves vital roles in several contexts and were indispensable. The lot of the Air Gunner in each case was not an enviable one, though issued with the full contemporary flying clothing for every aircrew, he had little provision for any heating to combat the freezing temperatures of winter and upper air night flying, and despite attempts to improve conditions later in the war, it remained the coldest job on every crew.

During the first two years of operations, most AG resorted to layer upon layer of woollen and silk clothing to protect hands, feet and trunk; while exposed faces were liberally coated in some form of lanolin-based grease to ward off frostbite. His tools of trade, guns and ammunition, became severely iced up and the AG sometimes suffered frostbite. The medical standards required of any potential aircrew in the RAF had always been exceptionally high, but sheer stamina and fortitude were needed, in particular by the AG. Sitting almost immobile in the cramped panoply of a metal and Perspex cupola for sometimes six, eight, ten, or even more hours, constantly vigilant, yet unable to relieve cramped legs, arms and back, called for frequent extraordinary feats of physical endurance. At high altitude, when oxygen became a necessity, much depended on the type of aircraft an AG was in. On long, high altitude flights, lack of oxygen resulted in anoxia and, quickly, euphoria.

Undoubtedly the greatest hazard, after direct wounding by enemy aircraft or ground-fire, and certainly the most feared, was fire in the aircraft. The turret gunner, surrounded by alloy metal framework and Perspex only inches away from every part of his body; was in the midst of a conglomeration of highly explosive ammunition, hydraulic pipelines, and electrical wiring. Behind him, in the case of the tail and dorsal gunner, was the hollow tunnel of the fuselage stretching forward to the nose compartment. In the event of any damage to almost any section of the fuselage, with any consequent outbreak of fuel fire, he was at the receiving end of a slipstream driven furnace, promoted by the venturi effect through the fuselage tube. Normally, too, the tail or dorsal position AG parachute pack was stowed inside the fuselage, behind his turret doors; any damage or heat-buckling to his turret doors meant that he was automatically cut off from his only safe means of abandoning a stricken aircraft.

In the Baltimore, Boston, and Mitchell, the situation was to some extent, even more immediate if any fire broke out. With relatively less fuselage space in which to manoeuvre, the AG, usually in mid-upper or possibly prone ventral location had to act immediately, if he was to avoid being "fried" or going down with the aircraft. Baling out by parachute from such twin-engine "medium" bombers was never an easy prospect (as Tom would later realize on the 26 June 1944).

That young men, from all walks of life and widely varying backgrounds, cheerfully accepted such built-in odds against ultimate survival, day in, day out, night in, night out, as a volunteer; is a measure of the quality and courage of all aircrews during those fateful years. Only the unimaginative failed to know fear before each take-off; while each succeeding mission merely accentuated that inner terror, as experience taught early recognition of every potentially deadly circumstance.

By 1942 every member of an operational aircrew was initially expected to undertake a tour of approximately thirty sorties before being "rested" in a non-operational sphere. However, it was not uncommon for a complete crew, on finishing their first tour, to undertake a second tour. Many individual Air Gunners remained on operations well beyond the second tour "cut off" point, by tagging onto any aircrew short of a gunner. Various statistics have been published in the past to illustrate the hair thin chances of any individual actually surviving a first tour, and then a second or even third. It was calculated that a man's chance of achieving a first full tour was scarcely one-in-three, to tempt providence by volunteering for further tours could only reduce such thin odds. However, for the AG and other aircrew of the RAF during the period 1939-1941, there was no set "tour"; operations continued to be flown until local commanders considered it propitious to "rest" any man.

In terms of his "ironmongery", the RAF Air Gunner of 1939-1941 was ill-served for the purposes of a modern air war. Though protected to some extent from the elements in some form of cupola or gun turret, his personal discomfort was hardly assuaged. Lack of adequate heating, life-saving oxygen equipment, and clothing to protect him against bullets or shell damage, often eroded the 100 per cent concentration so necessary for his role. While the numbing effect of squatting on a small metal seat for hours might be ignored by the more stoic, the prospect of permanent crippling of fingers and toes as a result of agonizing frostbite hardly enhanced the efficiency. Armour plating to resist attacks from German fighters was unknown, except for individual fitments near the pilot in certain aircraft. In the case of gunners who operated single or twin hand-operated machine guns, sighting remained only a modification of decades-old ring and bead sight; leaving the gunner to calculate the deflection angles when firing at a moving target. Tracer ammunition, though useful as a very rough guide to the trajectory of his bullets, was not accurate enough visually to verify aim. Where gunners had the benefit of a power-operated battery of two or four .303 Browning guns, sighting was by means of the early Marks, or Reflector Sight. This provided an illuminated circle via optical lenses directly in line with the gunner's eye-line.

Whether Tom knew any or all of the pitfalls of at least being in an aircrew, and more acutely as an Air Gunner, we don't know, but he still applied for the role.

Sergeant Wireless Operator/Air Gunner

Tom was recommended for training as an Air Gunner on the 2 July 1940, and on the 21 July he left 16 Squadron at Oakhampton to train as an Air Gunner at 1 Air Armament School, at RAF Manby, some four miles east of Louth in Lincolnshire; and on the 10 August he was made a temporary sergeant. The syllabus covered not only basic armament, gunnery and Morse code, but also navigation, mathematics, RAF Law, administration, and several other subjects which embryo gunners found great difficulty in associating with their eventual trade; there were also cross–country runs and other physical training.

Classroom Gunnery Training.

There was live ground firing at "Bulls-Eye" targets from a cupola mounted on a trailer, and then firing at a mock-up of an aircraft pulled along the ground on a railway track at speeds up to 30mph.

Live ground firing at targets.

Mock-up aircraft target.

Eventually, AG pupils flew in tired Whitley bombers, practising their trade by shooting at canvas drogues towed by ancient Westland Lysanders. Tom passed out as a Wireless Operator/Air Gunner and was awarded his AG (Air Gunner's badge), having attained 82.4per cent, on the 7 September, just over one year after joining, aged eighteen and a half.

Poem "Air Gunner" by John Pudney:

"The eye behind this gun made peace
With a boy's eye which doubted, trembled,
Guileless in the mocking light
Of frontiers where death assembled.
Peace was as single as the dawn,
Flew straight as the birds migrating,
Timeless in tune with time,
Purposeful, uncalculating.
So boyish doubt was put away,
The man's eyes and the boy's were one.
Mockery and death retreat
Before the eye behind this gun"

Flying Boats

On the 7 September 1940, the same day as the London "Blitz" started, Tom joined the Flying Boat Training Squadron as a temporary sergeant, trained Air Gunner, and untrained aircrew. Tom did his flying boat training as an Air Gunner at RAF Stranraer (Wig Bay), in Loch Ryan, on Scotland's west Atlantic coast.

Tom in the summer of 1940 looking like he should still be at school.

Sergeant Taylor and Sergeant Clark, Flying Boat Training Squadron, RAF Stranraer 1940.

An Air Gunner handling a pair of .303 Browning machine guns mounted in one of the blister gun-turrets of a Consolidated Catalina on Loch Ryan.

Poem "If I Must Be A Gunner"

By Corporal George Harding RCAF

"If I must be a gunner,
Then please Lord grant me grace,
That I may leave this station
With a smile upon my face.
I wished to be a pilot,
And you along with me,
But if we all were pilots
Where would the Air Force be?
It takes guts to be a gunner
To sit out in the tail
When the Messerschmitts are coming
And the slugs begin to wail.
The pilot's just a chauffer,
It's his job to fly the plane;
But its we who do the fighting,
Though we may not get the fame.
If we all must all be gunners,
Then let us make this bet.
We'll be the best damn gunners
That left this station yet"

RAF Stranraer was the Flying Boat Training Squadron from the 24 June 1940 to the 16 March 1941. Tom would become a "Tail End Charlie" for the Sunderland aircraft, and dorsal "mid-fuselage" for subsequent ones, whilst an Air Gunner. Life expectancy for him was less than the other aircrew, due to its vulnerable exposed position giving enemy fighters a clear target. Tom flew in both Sunderland and Catalina Flying Boats, the latter as part of the RAF Ferry Organization (later RAF Ferry Command), before going to join 201 Squadron at Sullom Voe.

The Battle of the Atlantic and the U-boat menace

While war was raging on land in the bitter cold of the eastern front and the harsh heat of the North African deserts, war was also raging at sea. One of the mainstays of the German Navy was its U-boats, at the outbreak of war in September 1939 their navy had twenty-one U-boats ready for action. But, the German Navy had faced an uphill struggle to be ready for combat duty due to the limitations posed on the country by the Treaty of Versailles, following Germany's defeat in the First World War. Although rearmament was inevitable some twenty years later, the fleet amassed by the Germans was still not on a par with those of the Allies. Of the original twenty-one U-boats, nine were sunk in the first four months of the war. However, U-boats had already caused a great deal of damage and loss of life by wiping out the "*Athenia*", the aircraft carrier "*Courageous*" and the battleship "*Royal Oak*". British merchant vessels were under the greatest threat from the German U-boats as the German Navy sought to cut-off and obliterate British trade links.

As a result, merchant ships were organized into convoys to help repel attacks; but in the summer of 1940 Allied shipping had suffered tremendous losses and the power of the U-boats was recognized globally. These were helped by further attacks from long-range Fokke-Wulf Condor aircraft. By the end of 1940 the Allies had lost more than one thousand vessels; another three hundred were lost in 1941, and a further three hundred during 1942. American destroyers were leased to the Allies in 1941 but, even with their involvement, numbers rose as escort vessels remained few and far between. They also suffered with the lack of long-range aircraft which could meet oncoming convoys, until the Sunderland Flying Boat and the Liberator bomber became part of the naval setup. But, the earlier lack of air cover had meant that convoys travelling via the Arctic route to Murmansk in Russia suffered severe losses. Those that made it travelled through severe cold, ice, and storms, as well as constant attacks from Germany.

From 1941, U-boats were deployed in "packs" to shadow convoys. Known as the "wolf-pack" tactic, the groups of U-boats would attack the convoy on the surface at night. However, the wolf-packs increased radio transmission, and codes were broken at Bletchley Park, which gave away their movements to the

Allies. U–boats were quickly subjected to bombing and gunfire on the surface, as well as depth charges when submerged. As a result, shipping losses began to fall and "team tactics" were employed to give the Allies a better chance against their enemy.

Sullom Voe

Located on the barren, windswept shores of Shetland, Sullom Voe, the most northerly wartime air station in Britain, and only 200 miles from the Norwegian coast (which by the late spring of 1940 was in German hands), RAF Sullom Voe became operational in the summer of 1939 when SS *Manela* and Saro London flying boats arrived on the 27 June, shortly after Tom joined up. There was little to indicate the existence of RAF Shetland, its first official title, apart from some Saro London flying boats moored in Garth's Voe and the support ship SS *Manela* anchored off Calback Ness; Voe was the Shetlands word for coastal inlet.

All the operational support for 201 Squadron's London aircraft, and for the newly formed 100 Group, was provided by the former P&O ship, as work had not begun on any shore installations. Therefore the station took its name from the expanse of coastal water used for taking off and landing, and not from any shore location. Conditions on-board *Manela* were crowded and work soon began on shore facilities; initially a slipway and maintenance base was built at Sellaness. Offices and quarters were erected on the hillside at Graven; in the meantime

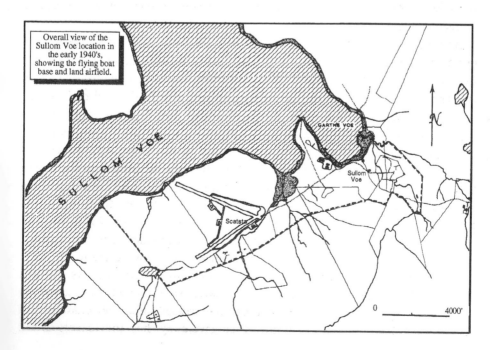

Overall view of the Sullom Voe location in the early 1940's, showing the flying boat base and land airfield.

201 Squadron Motto "Hic Et Ubique"
"Here And Everywhere".

a few isolated buildings were pressed into service. Eventually, hangars and maintenance aprons, workshops, offices and living quarters covered Sellaness and Graven. Another anchorage was established at Voxter Voe and a subsidiary airfield with two runways and its own hangar was built; this latter became RAF Scatsta, a fighter station to protect the flying boats. On the 15 April 1940 the first officers moved into shore accommodation with the major move on the 17 April; SS *Manela's* work was done and it sailed on the 23 April.

By the outbreak of war in September 1939, some forty Sunderlands had gone into service with the RAF Coastal Command. Based at Pembroke Dock, 228 Squadron, together with 210 Squadron, had begun re-equipping with the new boats some ten months earlier and by April 1939 it had eight Sunderlands on strength, 204 Squadron started to re-equip with them in June 1939, and by the end of July that year, it too had a complement of eight boats. In July 1939, No 10 Squadron of The Royal Australian Air Force arrived in Britain to take delivery of their Sunderlands and ended up staying here for the rest of the war. As hostilities got underway the Sunderland began to perform the operational role to which it was best suited, the large and tiring maritime patrol. When Hitler invaded Norway in April 1940, the extent of enemy North Sea coastal waters was extended dramatically.

With new bases from which to operate, the German U-boats became an even bigger threat to British convoys travelling from North America across the North Atlantic. The Sunderland at this time had no technology with which to locate these U-boats, or other shipping, other than by visual sightings. The Sunderland's armament and skill of its Air Gunners was to prove effective during one escort flight which occurred on 3 April 1940. A Sunderland attached to 204 Squadron was attacked by six Junkers JU88s of the Luftwaffe. In the ensuing air battle, one of the German aircraft was shot down, a second was forced to land in Norway, and the other four were driven off.

At the outbreak of war, 201 Squadron was equipped with Saro London Mk2 Flying Boats and operated from the depot ship "*Manela*" at Sullom Voe. During 1939 squadron crews located several damaged vessels; thus began the search and rescue role, which continued throughout the squadron's peacetime history. The squadron began to re-equip with Short Sunderlands in early 1940, and despite losing several aircraft in accidents, it proved to be the mainstay of Coastal Command. Convoy escort and anti-submarine patrols were the main tasks throughout the war, operating from Sullom Voe (Shetland Islands), Castle Archdale (Lough Erne, Northern Ireland), and Pembroke Dock (Wales).

In January 1940 the known squadron strength of Sunderlands were V K5258; W K5259; X K5260; Y K5257; Z K5262; and an unknown lettered K6929; and by February these were supplemented by R L7040. In March an unknown lettered K6930 had joined the ranks, followed in April by a replacement R P9606; a new S L5800; U L5802; and a new V N6138; and in May a replacement Z L2168. In June came a new replacement for Y N6133, this aircraft failed to return on 8 July 1940, and the crew were reported missing believed dead.

On 25 September 1940, a Sunderland on escort duty was proceeding to base after carrying out an anti-submarine patrol round a convoy. After some time its crew sighted a lifeboat in the sea and flying lower, the captain saw that some of the people on board were children. One of them, a small boy, slowly began to wave a white rag, spelling out the letters "City of ---------." The captain knew the rest, this was a lifeboat of the "City of Benares," a liner which had been torpedoed eight days before; it had been carrying children from the UK to Canada. The Sunderland turned back towards the convoy which it had left, and signalled the details to the relief Sunderland, and then, petrol being low, returned to base. The other Sunderland flew fifty miles to a warship and led it to the boat. Forty-six survivors were picked up.

On 12 October 1940, Tom joined 201 Squadron, which was a Flying Boat Squadron and it was part of Coastal Command's General Reconnaissance Group, as a satisfactorily trained Wireless Operator/Air Gunner. Just three days earlier, on 9 October 1940, 201 had lost a Sunderland Mk1 – P9621 Code ZM – when it force-landed in bad weather whilst on anti-submarine patrol and ran aground at Scalasaig Bay, Colonsay, whilst being piloted by Flight Lieutenant E. J. Brooks.

When Tom joined 201 at Sullom Voe as a temporary sergeant he was established within a crew of normally eleven or twelve personnel on the Short Sunderland Flying Boat, the largest flying aircraft of its time.

No further changes of aircraft came about until October 1940 when W was replaced by P9622 and X by P9621. In October, a new P W3988 entered squadron strength; this lost a float on landing in the sea near Carrowmore Point. On 9 October, 9621 ran into rocks in a forced landing at Scalasaig Bay, Colonsay, and on 28 October, 9622 crashed south-east of Wick.

Little has been said of the perils encountered by the aircraft of Coastal Command engaged in their long and unremitting task, and it was a temptation to take them for granted, as did the pilots and crew. The chief of them was not flak nor fighters, but the weather. However skilful the Met forecasters, they were not infallible. When they erred, or rather, when they did not foresee everything, an aircraft or flying boat may not have returned. Here is a graphic illustration of how terrifying life could be aboard a Sunderland Flying Boat caught up in the mercy of the weather.

On 20 October 1940, a Sunderland (squadron and number unknown) set out at 1700 hours from a Scottish base on a special mission connected with the Battle of the Atlantic. Two hours later a magnetic storm of the first magnitude developed. This put the wireless set partially out of action and gravely affected the compass. After seven and a half hours the Sunderland succeeded in making a signal saying that it was returning to base. It received none of the replies sent in return. Five hours later an SOS, followed by a request for bearings, was picked up at base and group headquarters. By then it was 0600 hours, but still dark. The Sunderland, its compass unserviceable, was lost and had no fuel left. The captain decided to alight onto the Atlantic Ocean. The gale was now blowing at eighty miles an hour and the navigator judged the waves to be more than twenty feet high (a normal house height!). Three flame-floats were dropped, but they did not burn, and the direction of the wind was gauged by a parachute flare. The captain brought the flying boat down in the trough between two waves. It was lifted up by one wave that was so large and powerful that it took all flying speed away from the boat, which came to a halt with both wing tip floats intact. The crew were at once prostrate with violent seasickness and this endured for many hours. The wireless operator began to send out signals, not knowing if any would be received. One was, and they presently picked up a message telling them that a warship would arrive in eight hours. The Sunderland continued to drift in tumultuous seas at a speed of about eight miles an hour.

How long she would endure the buffeting was hard to say. The wireless was dismantled, repaired and reassembled. The signals subsequently made were picked up by the warship HMAS "*Australia*"; faint at first, but strong after midday. At 1420 hours, the Sunderland signalled "Hurry, cracking up." Fifteen minutes later she was sighted and the lookout on the bridge of the warship read the word "hurry" flashed by the Sunderland's lamp. At that moment, as the crew caught sight of the warship, a wave larger than the rest struck the Sunderland head on. She began to break up and the crew of thirteen were flung into the water.

The captain of the warship HMAS "*Australia*", manoeuvred her so as to approach the wreckage of the flying boat from the lee quarter. He took the way off his ship as the Sunderland crew swept past abreast of, and almost as high as, his bridge. A naval commander and twelve ratings with lines secured to them went over the side and pulled on board nine of the crew, who had then been fifty minutes in the sea; the other four were lost. The Sunderland had remained afloat in a full gale for not quite nine hours before she sank.

On 29 October, Sunderland P9620, attached to 201 Squadron, ditched in rough sea in the Atlantic; some 200 miles N.N.W. of Cape Wrath, four of the crew were killed and nine were rescued by ship. No. 18 Group gave orders for aircraft to search for the Sunderland; the weather conditions were exceptionally bad, with a southerly gale of 70knots and an estimated swell of 60 to 70 feet. The search proved fruitless and at 1700 hours, Flying Officer Field, in command of Sunderland Mk1 P9622 Code ZM-W, decided to make for Invergordon. Trouble started when the wireless went unserviceable, but, by skilful navigation, landfall on the Butt of Lewis was made an hour later. At this point the weather closed right in and Field decided to climb to 6,000 feet and set course for Invergordon. At his ETA (estimated time of arrival), he descended to 2,000 feet, only to find, with the aid of his landing-light, the land and trees dimly discernable through mist. The Sunderland was again taken up to a safe height of 6,000 feet. By now the wireless was working once more and a fix was obtained; it put the Sunderland fourteen miles west of Wick!

Meanwhile, the ground defences of what later turned out to be Scapa Flow opened up. The shooting, however, was not good and the "friendly fire" proved in the circumstances to be "a minor annoyance". Plotting the fix, Field set course due east and after flying for twenty minutes, decided to descend. At 800 feet the landing light showed water (actually a lake), and a few seconds later there was a bump which brought some of the aircrew to their knees and shook off a depth charge. Boost controls full rich, airscrews in fine pitch, throttles open against the stops – but still the Sunderland lost height – then suddenly, the ground loomed up, giving the captain just enough time to pull back the stick before the inevitable crash at Dunnet Head, Caithness, a hill about twenty-eight miles south-west of Wick. The impact broke the Sunderland in two just aft of the trailing edge; the front part skating on for several hundred yards over the marshes and the tail-end of the Sunderland caught fire. From the crew of eleven: four were killed, five were injured and two were safe. The crew consisted of Pilot Officers Field; Rabou; and Cooper; Sergeants R. Laude (killed); Corbin; J. L. Carson (killed); R.W.J. Phelps (killed); Ault; and Anderson; Corporal Wells; AC1 G.A. Nangle (killed). The survivors spent the night under the wing with a gale raging about them, and Field walked four miles over the marsh to get help. That same night, 201 Squadron Flying Boat "R" captained by Flying Officer Fleming, "E" captained by Squadron Leader Cummins, and "Y" captained by Flight Lieutenant Lindsay, were also despatched on this search. "E" force-landed near Thurso and "Y" got safely down at Sullom Voe; "R" was the only aircraft to get back to Invergordon.

Flight Lieutenant Lindsay was soon to have another adventure on Sunderland "Y". During November 1940, while he was on patrol some 150 miles west of Oban, an enemy aircraft was sighted. On closer acquaintance it turned out to be a Fokker Wulf Fw200. The two aircraft approached each other head on, turning away at the last moment. This manoeuvre gave the Sunderland front gunner an opportunity to get in a burst; no reply came from the Fw200. After the two big machines had circled several times in an elephantine sparring-match, during which the Sunderland's front and midship gunners got in another burst each, the Fw200 veered off. Later the Admiralty reported that an Fw200 had been seen in the sea off the Dutch coast. In the light of this, and the fact that no other engagement with an enemy aircraft of that type had been reported, it was assumed that "Y" was the cause of this loss. This more than made up for Lindsay's embarrassment of some two years previous, when on 22 November 1939, he had been a flying officer on board a Saro London Flying Boat L7042 moored at Sullom Voe when six German bombers raided the area and set fire to the Saro London. Lindsay and the crew had to be rescued from the stricken aircraft by the destroyer H.M.S. "*Imperial*".

At that time Sullom Voe was also host to 204 Sunderland Squadron, and 700 Fleet Air Arm (FAA) Walrus Squadron. 201 Squadron had originally been at RAF Calshot on the south coast where it had Southampton Flying Boats until 1936, when it was re-equipped with Saro Londons. From September 1938 until the outbreak of war it moved to Invergordon, at Cromarty Firth, on the east coast of Scotland. Then, from September 1939 until November 1939, it was at Sullom Voe on the Shetland Isles, before going back to Invergordon from November 1939 until May 1940; then it was back to Sullom Voe. Its role at this time was anti U–boat and enemy shipping patrol, and its defined area was much of the North Atlantic and the North Sea between the Shetland Isles, Iceland and the Norwegian Coast.

During November unknown lettered N9021 and L5865 were added to the squadron, and in December N9021; P9622 and P9621 were awaiting "writing off."

Crew List; December 1940, some names are repetitive:

Sqn Ldr Cecil-Wright, Fg Off Alexander, Plt Off Mountford, Sgt Martin, Sgt Conduit, Sgt Sweet, Sgt Hammett, LAC Douglas, LAC Biggs, AC1 Doncaster.

Plt Off Fletcher, Plt Off George, Plt Off Parsons, Sgt Walker, Sgt Gibbon, Sgt Lodge, Sgt Abbott, LAC Hamilton.

Flt Lt Lindsay, Fg Off Smith, Plt Off Spink, Sgt Simmons, Sgt McVittee, Sgt Holwill, Sgt Foubister, Sgt Hogan, Sgt Heard, Sgt Clark, LAC White, LAC Drummond, LAC Lax.

Flt Lt Rea, Fg Off Scrutton, Plt Off George, Sgt Briden, Sgt Brown, Sgt Parkes, Sgt James, Sgt Corless, LAC Currie, LAC Lowry, AC Trott.

Wg Cdr Riccards, Fg Off Smith, Flt Lt Lindsay, Plt Off Spink, Sgt Simmons, Sgt McVittee, Sgt Foubister, Sgt Holwill, Sgt Heard, Sgt Hogan, LAC Drummond, LAC White, LAC Lax.

Here is a snapshot of 201 Squadron's coastal war diary for the month of December 1940:

2/12/40 Sullom Voe (Detachment) 1 Sunderland 1 on Cold Snap Patrol, 0910 to 1640.

3/12/40 Sullom Voe (Detachment) 1 Sunderland 1 on Transit to Oban in Argyll, 1050 to 1720.

5/12/40 Sullom Voe (Detachment) 1 Sunderland 1 on Reconnaissance to Narvik in Norway, 0240 to 1030.

6/12/40 Sullom Voe (Detachment) 1 Sunderland 1 on Escort Duty, 0830 to 1615.

8/12/40 Invergordon 1 Sunderland I on Reconnaissance to Sullom Voe, Shetland, 1115 to 1350.

10/12/40 Sullom Voe (Detachment) 1 Sunderland 1 on Cold Snap Patrol, 0905 to 1615, and 1 Sunderland 1 on Muggy Patrol, 0855 to 1550.

11/12/40 Sullom Voe (Detachment) 1 Sunderland 1 on Muggy Patrol, 0845 to 1620.

On 11 December a Short Sunderland Flying Boat, "V" N9046 of 204 Squadron, was destroyed by fire at its moorings in Sullom Voe.

12/12/40 Sullom Voe (Detachment) 1 Sunderland 1 on a Square Search of HQST 5840, 0845 to 1910, and 1 Sunderland 1 on Muggy Patrol, 0850 to 1555.

13/12/40 Sullom Voe (Detachment) 1 Sunderland 1 on Cento Patrol, 0855 to 1305.

15/12/40 Sullom Voe (Detachment) 1 Sunderland 1 on Cento Patrol, 0930 to 1450 and 1 Sunderland 1 on Escort Duty, 0815 to 1930. Crashed on Landing at Invergordon, Cromarty. The full extract of this incident follows:

On 15 December 1940, Sunderland Mk1 N9021, ZM-P on escort duty, took off from Sullom Voe at 0815 hours tasked with escorting convoy HX93 and was ordered to land at Invergordon, and whilst doing so, stalled from fifteen feet and collapsed a float at 1930 hours. The aircraft turned turtle a quarter of a mile from the slipway and sank in ten fathoms, but without injury to the crew who had managed to escape and were rescued by launch and landed safely on the quay. The crew consisted of Flying Officer D.J. Fletcher; Pilot Officers George and Parsons; Sergeants Walker; Gibbon; Lodge and Abbot; L.A.Cs Hamilton and Thompson; Aircraftsmen 1 W.M. Kinnish and AC Todd. On this occasion Abbott and Kinnish survived, but some eight months later they would be part of a crew of twelve, who together with Tom, crashed on 11 August 1941. Again, Abbott would cheat death, but Kinnish would perish along with four others.

16/12/40 Sullom Voe (Detachment) 1 Sunderland 1 on ASR Patrol to Invergordon, Cromarty, 1400 to 1630.

23/12/40 Sullom Voe (Detachment) 1 Sunderland 1 On Night Patrol, 0220 to 0915.

25/12/40 Sullom Voe (Detachment) 1 Sunderland 1 on ASR Search, 0900 to 1600.

26/12/40 Sullom Voe (Detachment) 1 Sunderland 1 on Shipping Search, 0750 to 1540.

27/12/40 Sullom Voe (Detachment) 1 Sunderland 1 on Enemy Force Search, 0720 to 1620.

28/12/40 1 Sunderland 1 on ASR Search from Helensburgh to Sullom Voe.

29/12/40 Sullom Voe (Detachment) 1 Sunderland on Shipping Patrol, 0755 to 1525.

In January 1941, unknown lettered T9049 came on squadron strength, followed by T9074 in February, and during March L5798 and a replacement Y T9077. In July came a replacement W W3982, and a replacement X W3981. This formation was complemented by Tom's ill-fated W3978 in August, this aircraft crashed at Sullom Voe on 11 August 1941.

The MK1 attained a speed of 210 mph with a ceiling of 17,900 feet (about three miles or five kilometres), and a range of 2110 miles flying (about 3,000 kilometres). Its maximum flying endurance was thirteen and a half hours. It carried a .303 inch machine gun in the nose turret and a cluster of four .303 inch Browning machine guns in the tail turret, where Tom would be positioned; the aircraft carried a maximum bomb load of 4960lbs. Altogether these aircraft accounted for fifty-eight German U-boats sunk, or badly damaged, throughout the duration of the war, and in May 1941 were involved in the search for the enemy battleships "*Bismarck*" and "*Prince Eugen*" during

The great size of the Sunderland is apparent in this picture; note the sting in the tail, the four hooded guns in the rear turret.

the "Battle of the Denmark Straits" in the North Atlantic. (More on this in chronological date order.) Originally, the Sunderlands had carried 250lb bombs, and later, naval depth charges, for anti submarine operations. These were used with an ingenious device called "Mickey Mouse", which automatically set the depth charges to be released at varying depths. These ranged from 10 feet; 20 feet; 50 feet; and so on, so that when a U-boat was spotted and it went into action stations and crash dived, the charges were released on its last known projected course and hopefully scored an underwater hit upon its hull. Later the German U-boat commanders were ordered to remain on the surface and fire up at the poorly defended underside of the Sunderland, whose weapons were forward, rear, and side facing for aerial battle.

Offensively the Sunderland was able to carry a load of 2000lbs, made up of bombs, depth charges, or mines. Two motorized tracks were mounted underneath the wings and when the aircraft went into action; its payload of weapons could be trundled out on sliding carriers through large holes situated in the fuselage. Behind the engineer's compartment, the rear end of the flight deck carried a variety of smoke markers, reconnaissance flares and flame markers. Further behind and below, in the deep rear fuselage deck, the Sunderland carried a mixture of other equipment, including distress flares, a reconnaissance camera, a dinghy, emergency rations, and three spare propeller blades. At the end of the plane was a canvas doorway giving access to the fin and tailplane mountings and the rear gun turret, which was Tom's position, protecting the rear of the large aircraft. In the forward part of the hull, beneath the flight deck, was the bomb aimer's position, and behind that the dinghy and anchor storage area. The nose turret above this area was rail mounted so that when the flying boat was moored at sea, the whole turret could be winched back and allowed the large anchor to be passed through the "bowers nest". Immediately under the flight deck was a toilet compartment, a connecting stairway, and the forward wardroom and sleeping area.

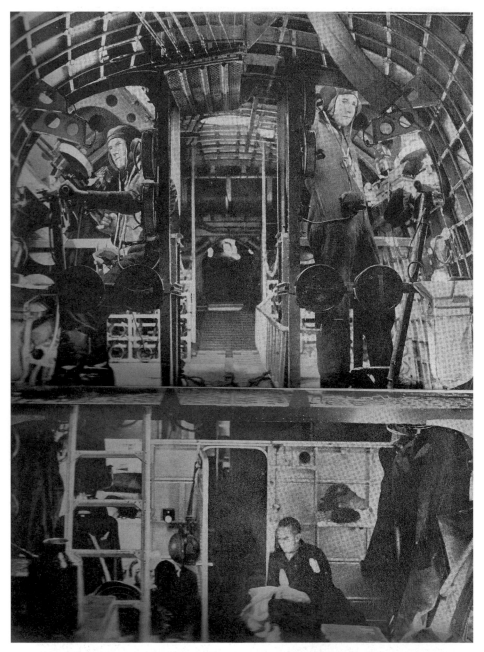

Internal layout of a Sunderland Flying Boat on patrol, the midship gunners are alert at their stations, below is the crew's quarters, and the "watch off" takes it easy.

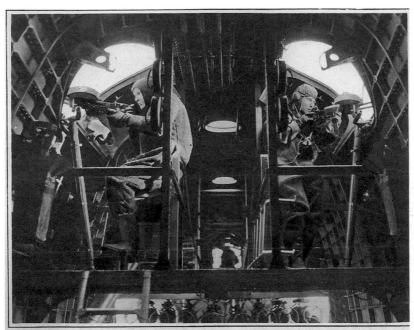

INSIDE A "SUNDERLAND" FLYING-BOAT: AIR-GUNNERS IN THE PORT AND STARBOARD GUN HATCHES, WHICH ARE SITUATED ON THE TOP OF THE HULL AND JUST AFT OF THE WINGS. IN THE CENTRE IS THE WALKWAY

Below the Air Gunners position a Sergeant Navigator plots the craft's course.

THE PILOT AND AN OBSERVER AT THEIR PLACES IN THE DUAL-CONTROL CABIN OF A "SUNDERLAND" DURING RECONNAISSANCE FLIGHT. THESE CRAFT ARE SOMETIMES ON PATROL FOR TEN TO FOURTEEN HOURS AT A STRETCH.

Below the cockpit and right in the nose of the aircraft; the Bomb–Aimer adjusts his sights.

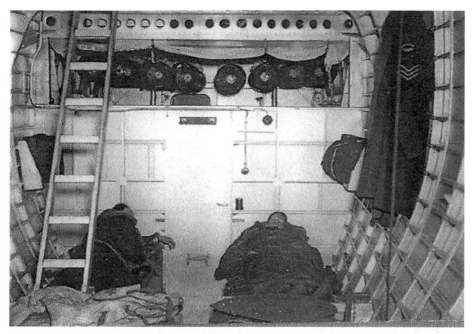

Sleeping quarters.

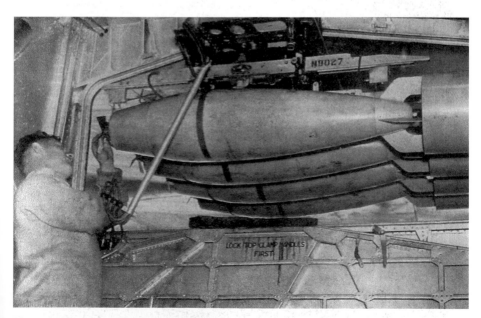

Heavy bombs being placed in the bomb bay of a Short Sunderland.

By the end of October 1940, British losses of all of its aircraft totalled over 900, with the German losses being almost double; the Royal Air Force had dented Hitler's faith in his air force, The Luftwaffe.

Poem: Children Of The Night:

Jim Davis Ex 90 and 7 Squadrons

"The sun is slowly setting, and as it slips away,
A changing pattern of colour around one lies.
We feel so very humble as we watch the closing day,
And onward soars our plane across the skies.
This silent world of wonder means everything to me,
The storm and cloud, with winds and rainbow ring.
Round us there's a feeling, in our hearts that we
Are in the presence of the King of Kings.
The evening's velvet mantle gathers dark around us,
We feel like children in the night
As men the fear of darkness has not found us,
Still we seek comfort in the stars so bright.
As endless as the sky seems the long and weary night,
We laugh and talk though nerves are tightly drawn
And quietly we pray that he will guide our homeward flight,
And we will live to see the beauty of the dawn"

Ocean Rendezvous

In the early days of the war, our Atlantic convoys were covered by Coastal Command, either when approaching these shores or when sailing coastwise. The first to meet the convoys were the Catalina, they did so many hundreds of miles out in the Atlantic; the normal duration of their patrol was, in summer eighteen hours, and in winter fourteen hours, and it was possible for them to remain airborne for considerably more than twenty-four hours. Close behind them came the Liberators and Sunderland Flying Boats, followed by Whitley, Wellington, Hudson, Blenheim and Beaufort.

Tail-sting; a FN13 four .303mg rear turret in an early Sunderland.

Crew List for 1941 not all aircraft and crew are listed, but other names are again repetitive:

L5802: Fg Off Vaughan, Fg Off Evill, Plt Off Cooper, Sgt Veale, Sgt Haggar, Sgt Martyn, Sgt Hancox, Sgt Archer, Sgt Fairbairn, Sgt Holroyd, Cpl Gratton, LAC Richard, LAC Stephen, LAC Thompson.

L2168: Sqn Ldr Fraser, Plt Off Parsons, Plt Off Champion, Sgt Anderson, Sgt Benton, Sgt Devereux, Sgt Griffiths, Sgt Beach, Sgt Lewis, Sgt Lowth, Sgt Adams, LAC McRobb, AC Ramsey.

Interior view of a FN20 rear gun turret.

T9076: Flt Lt Fletcher, Plt Off Westcott, Plt Off Paton, F/Sgt Mitchell, Sgt Penny, Sgt Orr, Cpl Lutley, LAC White, LAC Wallace.

P9606: Fg Off Alexander, Plt Off George, Plt Off Mountford, Plt Off Kitchin, Sgt Martin, Sgt Harritt, Sgt Sweet, Sgt Hannett, Sgt Conduit, LAC Biggs, AC Doncaster, AC Rimmer.

T9074: Flt Off Field, Plt Off Day, Plt Off Balfour, Plt Off Champion, Sgt Brown, Sgt Lodge, Sgt Penny, Sgt Abbott, Sgt Paton, LAC Currie, LAC Todd, AC Cheetham.

W3977: Flt Lt Field, Plt Off Balfour, Plt Off Day, Sgt Brown, Sgt Lodge, Sgt Ault, Sgt Penny, **Sgt Clark**, LAC Todd, AC Gordon, AC Cheetham.

L5805: Flt Lt Lindsay, Fg Off Raban, Plt Off Spink, Sgt Simmons, Sgt Heard, Sgt Ince, Sgt McVittee, Sgt Holwill, Sgt Foubister, LAC Lax, LAC White, AC Wallace.

T9077: Flt Lt Lindsay, Plt Off Spink, Sgt Simmons, Sgt Collins, Sgt Fairbairn, Sgt Foubister, Sgt Conduit, Cpl Hussey, LAC Patterson, AC Neeve, AC Buckley.

W3981: Fg Off Raban, Plt Off Day, Plt Off Fairlough, Plt Off Cox, Sgt Webster, Sgt Louth, Sgt Anderson, Sgt Dyson, Sgt McSherry, Sgt Briden, Sgt Louth, LAC Lyons, LAC Thompson.

Group photo of 201 Squadron Spring 1941 at Sullom Voe. Tom is absent away on Atlantic Ferry Service duties.

By the start of 1941 the Battle of the Atlantic was beginning in earnest with the first of the great and bloody convoy battles across the ocean. The Fokke Wulf FW200 Condor was used as a long-range reconnaissance aircraft to spot the convoys and send sighting reports for the U-boats. Flight Lieutenant Lindsay met one in January between Iceland and the Faeroes. The crew jettisoned the depth charges to gain speed and closed for the attack; Ray Heard, a guest navigator on the crew remembered the fight vividly:

"We were ordered to action stations; I took up my position in the front turret, clamped a magazine onto the single VGO gun, switched on the reflector sight and waited, with some trepidation, for the action to begin. Someone in the astrodome was giving range estimates as the Condor turned towards us for a pass along the port side. We dropped almost to sea level and the Condor continued closing. By the time its silhouette more than filled my gun sight I opened fire, anticipating the controller's order by a second or two. While I could see my tracers arcing towards the target, I did not see any hits, and at our approach speed the entire action was over in seconds. I could hear the two dorsal guns blasting away but the surprising thing to all of us was the lack of return fire from the Condor, which banked hard away from us and escaped. At this point the Captain sent a chill through us all, shouting 'The port tanks! The port tanks!' We all thought they had been hit but it turned out that someone had forgotten to switch over fuel tanks and one engine was beginning to cough; and all this close to the sea in pursuit of the Condor. When we returned to Bowmore, on Islay, the Skipper berated us all for our abysmal marksmanship, with the warning that a lot of gunnery practice was in the offing, only to discover the following day that the Condor had put out a distress call and crashed into the Bay of Biscay!"

The conditions under which the squadron operated at this time are shown in the loss of 201 Sunderland "O", which was the first Sunderland to be equipped with long-range A.S.V. and Loran approach equipment. With Squadron Leader Cecil Wright as Captain, it departed on its eventful first operation – a reconnaissance of Narvik, Namsos and Trondheim on 21 January 1941. Starting out from Sullom Voe at 0230 hours, the Sunderland made its first landfall at Trondheim at 0745 hours; it then flew up the Norwegian coast to Narvik, which was reached at 1050 hours. On the approach to the town it was able to surprise a parade of German soldiers by using a general purpose bomb; the ground defences were disconcertingly accurate, the first burst put both power–operated turrets out of action, another hit the tailplane. The remaining bombs were dropped on a barracks, a motor convoy and a 6,000 ton ship, and at 1105 hours the Sunderland headed for home. Despite an outside temperature of -20° Centigrade, weather conditions were good until 1645 hours, when landfall was made on Muckle Flugga.

Here, with approximately two-and-a-half hours' fuel left, heavy snowstorms were encountered. Finding no way through or round them, Squadron Leader Wright decided to try putting down on the sea near Woodwick. A twelve foot swell was running at that time, and the port wing-tip float hit a crest; the wing was submerged up to the port outer engine, but after what seemed an age the flying boat righted itself. The crew resigned itself to a night on the ocean. At 1930 hours the anchor was dropped, but held only for a few minutes. The engines had to be restarted and the flying boat taxied into the lee of a cliff, where the anchor was dropped again. This process of restarting engines when the anchor dragged was repeated at least thirty times – and then the anchor broke. At 0430 hours, deciding to run the Sunderland aground, Squadron Leader Wright taxied to a rock and made fast with the anchor chain; shortly after, the aircraft swung round and went aground. Meanwhile, the lighthouse keeper at Muckle Flugga had seen the crew's distress signals and help came at dawn. Despite its battering the Sunderland was still in a fit state to be towed to Culli Voe, where minor repairs were made before returning to Sullom Voe.

Flight Lieutenant Vaughan spent several anxious hours one February night holding off over the Moray Firth while waiting for snow storms to clear. The aircraft was then struck by lightning. On the ground a loud explosion was reported which led to "Air Raid Purple" sounding and a separate report of a Sunderland crashing into the sea off Burghead; in fact they landed, quite safely, later on.

A Sunderland crew boarding their aircraft.

Ferrying Catalinas

Atlantic Ferry Organization November 1940; Ferry Command 20 July 1941 to 25 March 1943

The Atlantic Ferry Organization was an allied transatlantic air ferry service which, from November 1940, to July 1941, flew United States built combat aircraft to the United Kingdom. Delivery then became the responsibility of RAF Ferry Command from 20 July 1941 until 25 March 1943 when it became part of Transport Command. It was initiated by Lord Beaverbrook and organized by the Canadian Pacific Railway. During the war about 10,000 US built aircraft were delivered to the UK in this way.

A job which came the way to some of 201 Squadron's pilots early in 1941 was the Ferrying of Catalinas from America to Britain, via Montreal, Canada and Bermuda, USA. On 4 January 1941, Tom was at the Personnel Despatch Centre Headquarters at Uxbridge. From there he would be involved for a while as a Wireless Operator/Air Gunner flying Catalinas on the Atlantic Ferry Organization (ATFERO), later named the Ferry Boat Command. In the early days of the war, whilst the USA was still a neutral country, American built aircraft such as the Consolidated PBY Catalina Flying Boat, a smaller cousin to the Short Sunderland; these could not be flown into Canada and had to be hauled across its border on their wheels by teams of horses. On the arrival of these craft on Canadian territory, it was necessary to have an organization to handle them. The

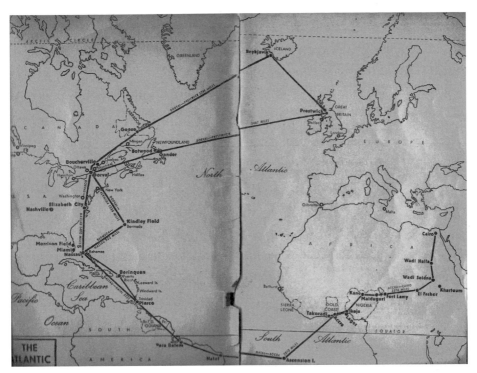

Atlantic Ferry Organization Routes.

British and Canadian Governments collaborated; a flow of pilots and aircrews came from Canada, the USA, Australia, New Zealand, Free French/Dutch and RAF Coastal Command, the latter provided from Hudson and Catalina crews fresh from flying training. A headquarters was established at the Canadian Pacific Railways Windsor Station and Railways Exchange in Montreal, and RCAF St Hubert was the airfield used.

During February 1941, twenty-four complete RAF crews were sent specially to Montreal in order to undertake the ferrying of aircraft from there to Britain; and during March, Bermuda delivered fifteen flying boats.

From May to August 1941 United States service pilots of the Air Corps Ferrying Command were allowed by the USA Government to deliver them to Montreal.

Ferry Command was formed on 20 July 1941, by the raising of the RAF Atlantic Ferry Service to Command status. Its commander for the whole of its existence was Air Chief Marshal Sir Frederick Bowhill, and he was also the first commander of Ferry Command's successor, Transport Command. The Ferry Command's operational area remained the North Atlantic, and its responsibility was to bring the larger aircraft that had the range to do the trip over the ocean from American and Canadian factories to the RAF home Commands. Gander Airport, formerly Newfoundland Airport, was the base of transatlantic operations. This was pioneering work; before Ferry Command, the RAF Atlantic Ferry Service, in nearly eight months of existence, only had about one hundred aircraft attempt a North Atlantic crossing in good weather, and only about half had made it. (I remember years ago Tom (Dad) talking about when he was one of a few people who had made a non-stop Atlantic crossing, presaging the inauguration of scheduled commercial air transport services after the war.)

Even this apparently dull job, compared to anti-submarine patrol, had its excitements. Flight Lieutenant Fleming, DFC, on his first trip from Bermuda, had his automatic pilot jam at 18,000 feet, putting the Catalina in a spin from which he was able to recover only 400 feet above sea level. Both

Tom and AN Other shopping in Montreal, Spring 1941.

ailerons were wrenched off and the Catalina completed the final 1,000 miles of its journey in six hours, with no lateral control at all.

The Catalina, with an extreme range of 4,000 miles, first saw active service with RAF Coastal Command, before the United States entered the Second World War, but it was never present in Britain in large numbers. Seven squadrons operated the PBY named "Catalina" from Britain, and two briefly from Iceland, giving the often quoted total of nine Coastal Command squadrons. However, of these, six used the Catalina with Coastal Command for less than a year, and only 210 Squadron retained the Catalina in Britain from its introduction in 1941 until the end of the war. At no point were there more than three squadrons operating the Catalina from Britain; and it had a limited level of use. An order for thirty-seven PBY Catalina Flying Boats was placed with the American firm Consolidated in November 1940, and the first one was delivered to No. 240 Squadron at Stranraer, on Scotland's south-west coast on 5 March 1941. Despite the limited level of use, the Catalina did produce some noteworthy achievements with Coastal Command; one, the sighting of "*Bismarck*" on 26 May 1941.

By the Spring of 1941 "The Blitz" of London had come to an end, and it proved a great morale booster for the British people, they had taken everything that Germany had thrown at them and come back fighting. Britain became increasingly dependent on the United States of America for the production of armament and aircraft. Under the "Lending Scheme" authorized by President

Roosevelt and the Constitution, the USA could provide arms for the defence of any nation vital to her own (US) security. As the USA fulfilled its role as the arsenal of democracy, its convoys of supply ships crossed the Atlantic to Britain; running a fearsome gauntlet of German U-boats, battleships and Luftwaffe aircraft. Early in 1941 the loss of merchant vessels had prompted Churchill to declare "That the battle of the Atlantic must take precedence over every other theatre of conflict". The guarding of convoy ships was a frustrating affair for Coastal Command and U-boats simply stayed submerged until they were out of range of our aircraft; this left a wide expanse of mid Atlantic Ocean where no air cover could be provided. The RAF also carried out bombing raids on the U-boat bases and factories where they were built, but with minimal success, due to the formidable defences of these installations. From the air merchant convoys were attacked by the Luftwaffe's four engined ME Condor, which far outstripped in distance any Royal Air Force fighter.

Against the German battleships, the RAF had greater success, although its corresponding casualties were high. Up to the end of 1941, 8.1 million tons of allied and merchant shipping would be lost to the Germans in the Atlantic alone. I remember a friend of mine in Wisbech, when I was working for "Age Concern", Paulo Mikalov, a little Maltese man who gave his age as seventy-nine; he served as an engineer with the Royal Navy in the war. When recalling one incident he was in, he said, "Chris, I was on a convoy of fifty-one ships which we were protecting, all were lost but ours, which was of a flat bottom design and they couldn't sink us. They dropped a bomb through the funnel which blew up the engine room and there was a shout for everyone to get on deck; I realized that my mate was missing and went back down below. I swam in about six feet of complete black oily water and located an arm; I recognized it belonging to my mate by the feel of the watch; as I felt further up the arm for him that was all that was left of him." The horrors of war! He had also been involved with the Royal Navy in helping Norway. We worked out Paulo's age from his birth certificate, for an attendance allowance claim due to him suffering from severe breathing difficulties brought on by the engine room saga. We found out that he was actually aged eighty and had lied when he joined up – he was only fifteen! A brave little man who never made the slightest fuss or moaned about his lot in life; God bless you Paulo.

Another brave young man was my wife Jeanne's Dad, Bill Twigden, who was an electrician by trade, and only three months older than Tom; he had joined the Royal Navy in March 1941, and after initial training at Chatham became a wireman on board various minesweepers, sweeping the Channel and North Sea ports from Lowestoft for German laid mines, and keeping shipping lanes open for convoys. At one stage he went to Brooklyn in North America to study the USA Naval Gyroscope.

On 11 March 1941, ZM L 2168 of 201 Squadron based at Sullom Voe; overshot upon landing and ran aground and was repaired on site.

Some five months before Tom's serious flying boat accident, which occurred on 11 August 1941, another very similar one occurred off the west coast of Scotland in the Firth of Lorne at Oban, home of 210 Squadron Sunderland Flying Boats. A patrol had been out on an Atlantic convoy escort duty on 13 March 1941, it had been purely a routine trip, with no incidents. This night convoy Sunderland arrived back between 0300 hours and 0400 hours on 14 March and was immediately put on standby duty for a strike boat. This meant that the crew could not go off

Bill Twigden.

duty and the Sunderland had to be refuelled, and restocked of bombs, ammunition, provisions etc. The captain, navigator and pilot grabbed what sleep they could on a rota basis, on a camp bed situated in the operations room, and at 1600 hours they were called out to patrol the coast of Iceland; which was a journey time of four hours to and from base. At this time the British were able to intercept enemy radio transmissions and decipher them by use of the "Enigma Code" machine. A U-boat had been identified as operating in these waters and the Sunderland had been despatched to seek and destroy. No trace of the craft was discovered however; as the Sunderlands were not fitted with radar at this time; and sighting was purely visual. After a fruitless search the Sunderland crew made their way back to Oban, the landing area had thick fog and the sea surface was flat calm like a mirror; this gave a distorted picture for a smooth landing.

Subsequently the plane crashed headlong into the sea and sank, together with its crew of twelve. Six died and six survived, including the pilot, twenty-one year old Flight Lieutenant (later Wing Commander) Derek Martin, OBE. When his rescuers found him he heard one of them say, "This one's dead"; his left eye was hanging out of the torn socket and his scalp had been ripped off, so that it was attached to his head by only an inch of skin, and he was covered with a blanket. Derek was quite pleased about this because he couldn't close his eyes and the bright lights were hurting them. He remembered coming round in hospital and asking his sister when he could fly again! He had to have intensive care treatment and pioneering plastic surgery; and remarkably, a year later he was again flying Sunderlands!

For her crews, the Sunderland was very much a home and, aside from the dangers to be faced on ops, there was always the possibility of domestic catastrophe. Around this time, 201 Squadron shared a life at Sullom Voe with 204 Squadron, and inter-squadron rivalry no doubt abounded, especially when 204 lost at least one aircraft through a galley fire which got completely out of hand.

Also during March 1941, Flight Lieutenant Alexander, flying 201 Sunderland "R", which rejoiced in the nickname of "Reilly Ffoull", tried conclusions with a Fokke-Wulf Fw200 and a Junkers Ju88, both caught in the act of attacking S.S. "*Staffordshire*". At the beginning of the action the Fw200 was approaching at 1,000 feet out of the sun, about five miles distant from the Sunderland, which was at an altitude of only 100 feet. The German made a dive attack on the ship's starboard bow, dropping four bombs — one or two of which were direct hits. While the enemy aircraft circled in one direction to continue the attack, the Sunderland went the other way round in order to intercept it. This it failed to do, owing to the lack of sufficient speed, but in the second enemy attack a near miss was the best that the Fw200 could manage. At this stage of the scrap the Ju88 put in its appearance. The newcomer dropped a stick of four bombs, which fell short of the ship's port side; then, on his second run, he was intercepted by the Sunderland; he steered off and was not seen again. Flight Lieutenant Alexander then turned up-run to be in an advantageous position should further attacks develop. Almost immediately, the Fw200 was seen approaching head-on. It opened fire at 600 yards, but fortunately the shooting was bad and the shells went wide, as did those fired a few seconds later from the rearward-facing guns in the ventral gunner's position. The Sunderland used its front gun — the third burst of which was seen to hit the Fw200's nose — both midships guns, and the tail turret. The enemy disappeared into low cloud and was not seen again. Sunderland ZM "R" scarcely deserved its uncomplimentary nickname, for in the twelve months from May 1940 to May 1941 it put in 1,100 flying hours — a performance which 201 Squadron claimed to be a record for any one aircraft in the service. On 12 May 1941, Sunderland "Z" L57798 was deployed to RAF Flying Boat Base, Reykjavik in Iceland.

During the greater part of 1941, Coastal Command had been striving to develop, with the assistance of the Operational Research Unit (ORU), tactics which would improve the effectiveness of the anti-submarine aircraft. Some procedures and tactics had to be devised on a trial and error basis, to counter problems that were entirely new in the field of warfare. Such was the content of tactical Instruction No. 15. The work of the ORU had shown that once the U-boat was sighted, the approach had to be made direct, and as fast as possible, since it only took about half a minute for an alerted U-boat to submerge. The direction of attack relative to the course of the U-boat did not matter at this point in the battle. Later on, when the submarines began to stay on the surface and engage the attacking aircraft with a formidable array of anti-aircraft cannon and machine guns, it became more prudent to attack by flying along the target's track when making an attack, so reducing the number of guns that the U-boat could use. The instruction made it clear that the attack had to be made from below 100 feet to achieve the desired accuracy and that all the depth charges on the aircraft should be dropped in one stick, spaced at a 60 foot interval, and set to explode at a depth of 50 feet.

Hunt The Bismarck

The big excitement for Tom and the squadron in 1941 was the sighting and pursuit of the German battleship *"Bismarck"*.

"I give you the hunter's toast; Good hunting and a good bag". With these words German Admiral Lutjens ended his speech to the ship's company of the *"Bismarck"*. They were heard throughout the vessel, those who could not be on deck listened to them through the loudspeakers situated throughout the battleship. The hour was a few minutes past noon on Monday, 19 May 1941. That evening the *"Bismarck"* weighed anchor and put to sea, taking a northerly course from Kiel Bay. It was the intention of Admiral Lutjens to raid commerce in the Atlantic. He had done so earlier in the year, flying his flag on the *"Gneisenau"*, which together with the *"Scharnhorst"*, had sunk twenty-two British and Allied ships, including the *"Jervis Bay"*. The *"Gneisenau"* and *"Scharnhorst"* were now in Brest and had already suffered damage from an attack made on them by aircraft of Bomber and Coastal Commands. If Germany was to obtain a decision in the Battle of the Atlantic, other units of her navy must be sent to sea. The *"Bismarck"* and *"Prinz Eugen"* were chosen; for the *"Bismarck"* it was to be her first and last voyage.

"Bismarck" German Battleship 1940–1941.

"Bismarck" a 41,673 ton battleship was built at Hamburg in Germany. First of a class of two heavy ships, with *"Tirpitz"* being the second; she was commissioned in August 1940 and spent the rest of that year running trials and continuing her outfitting. In the wake of the successful cruise of the Battleships *"Scharnhorst"* and *"Gneisenau"* against Allied Shipping in January to March 1941, when they sank naval ships and seriously threatened British seaborne supply lines in the Atlantic, another German raiding expedition was undertaken employing the newly built battleship *"Bismarck"* and heavy cruiser *"Prinz Eugen"*. After many delays these ships left the Baltic Sea on 19 May and 20 May 1941, briefly stopping near Bergen in Norway where they were photographed by an RAF Reconnaissance Spitfire; analysis of the photographs showed fuel tankers alongside which suggested that they were preparing for a long voyage.

Returning from patrol on 21 May, in their 201 Squadron Sunderland Flying Boat, Flight Lieutenant Field, with Pilot Officer Balfour and Pilot Officer Day, as his second and third pilots, reported seeing the battleship with its attendant

The photograph that sank a battleship. The "Bismarck" caught by reconnaissance aircraft in Dobric Fjord.

cruiser "*Prince Eugen*" at Narvik. To clear up any doubts as to the identity of the ships a further five aircraft were sent to investigate. By this time, however, the weather had clamped down in the north and they returned without success. HMS "*Hood*" and HMS "*Prince of Wales*" sailed from Scapa Flow.

The next day there was total cloud cover down to 75 feet which meant that the photographic Spitfire could see nothing. However, a Fleet Air Arm target-towing Maryland did manage to reach Bergen and discover that the "*Bismarck*" had sailed; they then headed north-west, planning to enter the shipping zone by way of the Denmark Strait, situated between Iceland and Greenland. Once the RAF intelligence of "*Bismarck*" reached the Allied Chief of Staff, Air Chief Marshal Sir Frederick Bowhill, the Royal Navy was ordered out to sea in an effort to intercept the enemy and keep them from attacking the vital convoys. RAF aircraft, including Sunderlands from 201 Squadron, in which Tom was rear tail gunner in Sunderland "Z" L5798; were sent out on enemy shipping patrol.

British cruisers located them by radar in the Denmark Strait about sixty nautical miles off Iceland's north-west coast. All available Coastal Command aircraft in the area were put on high alert. At 1836 hours on 24 May, HMS "*Norfolk*" signalled that a battleship and cruiser were in the position already mentioned off Iceland's north-west "claw", and Sunderland "Z" L5798 of 201 Squadron, piloted by Flying Officer Vaughan, with Tom on board, took off at 2025 hours to patrol the Denmark Strait and locate the enemy force.

The weather conditions in the area were extremely unfavourable, with cloud ceiling only 300-500 feet, frequent showers and poor visibility (ASV could only be used occasionally owing to the necessity of keeping frequent W/T watches). The search was commenced at 2140 hours, but not until six hours and fifteen minutes later were the enemy ships located when gun flashes were seen ahead at 633N 3200NW. By this time the weather had improved, the conditions were ideal, and the allied aircraft and ships began to shadow the small German convoy. At about 0530 hours on 24 May 1941, whilst west of Iceland, the German vessels encountered the Battleship Cruiser HMS "*Hood*" and the Battleship HMS "*Prince of Wales*". In the ensuing battle off the Denmark Strait, the "*Hood*" blew up and sank, and the seriously damaged "*Prince of Wales*" was forced to break off contact. The engagement was over within ten minutes of the Sunderland's arrival, the "*Bismarck*" was observed emitting a lot of smoke, which subsequently ceased, and also losing a large quantity of oil.

Flight Lieutenant Vaughan, Flying Officer Evill and crew, including Tom, in Sunderland "Z" L5798 ("Zachariah of the Long Whiskers"), whilst on a search from Reykjavik, witnessed the action between the German force and H.M.S. "*Hood*" and "*Prince of Wales*". Vaughan approached within five miles of the enemy ships on the starboard beam at an altitude of 2,500 feet and identified them as the "*Bismarck*" and "*Scheer*". The Sunderland remained on the scene, shadowing the enemy force for about three hours, signalling the course and speed to the other British ships converging on the coordinates from afar, before setting course for base, where the aircraft landed at 1003 hours, having been airborne for thirteen hours and thirty-eight minutes.

Here is the report from Vaughan; three days after the initial sighting by Flight Lieutenant Field:

Eyewitness Account from Flight Lieutenant R.J. Vaughan of Sunderland Z/201, attached to 100 Wing, RAF Station Sullom Voe

Report on the sighting of the *Bismarck* and the sinking of HMS *Hood*:
"At 0537 hours on 24 May 1941 a County Class Cruiser was sighted steering a course of 240°T at an estimated speed of 28 knots and at the same time gunfire

was seen well ahead. As we closed, two columns, each of two ships in line ahead, were steering on parallel courses at an estimated range of twelve miles between columns. Heavy gunfire was being exchanged and the leading ship of the port hand column was on fire in two places, one being at the base of the bridge superstructure and the other further aft. In spite of these large conflagrations she appeared to be firing from at least one turret forward and aft. (This ship was found afterwards to be "*Hood*".) At this juncture, no engaged ships had been identified and I instructed the pilot to proceed towards the starboard column of ships. The second ship of this line ("*Bismarck*") was making a considerable amount of smoke, which appeared to come from near the mainmast on the port side. Oil was also escaping and leaving a broad streak in the water behind her.

"As we approached the two ships were identified as enemy and a first sighting report was made at 0610 hours. Immediately prior to this an explosion was noticed on the burning ship of the port column ("*Hood*") and at the same time we came under A.A. fire from the enemy, and were forced to take cloud cover at 2500ft. On emerging from cloud some five minutes later, the "*Hood*" had almost completely disappeared and only part of the bow was showing. The second ship of this line then fired a salvo which fell short and slightly ahead of the second enemy ship and immediately afterwards reversed course after having laid a light smoke screen. The second enemy ("*Bismarck*") then fired a salvo at the ship which had reversed course (later identified as "*Prince of Wales*") and this was a very near miss, with perhaps one hit near the stern. This was the most accurate I had observed during the action, the previous bursts from the enemy appearing to be well ahead, but with range correct, those from our units seemed to be either under or over, although in most cases line appeared to be good. The leading ship ("*Prinz Eugen*") of the enemy line had also been firing and the salvos also fell well ahead of our leading ship but range again appeared to be correct. After emerging from cloud we flew over the wreckage of the sunken warship ("*Hood*"), observing one large red raft and a considerable amount of wreckage amidst a huge patch of oil. From the height we were flying, no survivors could actually be seen".

Flight Lieutenant Vaughan remained in the vicinity of the German vessels, shadowing them and reporting changes of course until lack of fuel forced him to return to base. Soon after this episode Flying Officer Evill lost his life when Sunderland "V", of which he became captain, was shot down while on patrol.

On 25 May, Sunderland, Catalina and Hudson aircraft carried out patrols to search for the enemy; again on the 26 May, two Sunderland aircraft from 201 Squadron, L5798 and P9606, and two of 240 Squadron continued to search without success. No. 201 Squadron flew from Sullom Voe to the RAF flying boat base at Reykjavik.

The Commander-in-Chief of Coastal Command, Air Chief Marshal Bowhill, had served as a merchant seaman before joining the Royal Naval Air Service and the Royal Air Force. His knowledge of navigation stood him in good stead. He argued that after his voyage the "*Bismarck's*" captain would not risk blundering headlong into the dangerous French Biscay coast, but would make a landfall further south and sail up the coast. Bowhill therefore extended his patrols further south than the Admiralty plan. During 25 May all available flying boats searched the huge expanse of the North Atlantic for the crippled ship, but no sightings were made until just after 1000 hours on 26 May when Bowhill's foresight was rewarded that morning when the Catalina aircraft Z for Zebra sighted "*Bismarck*" in the southernmost patrol area.

Winston Churchill ordered that "*Bismarck*" must be sunk at all cost and the Royal Navy vectored its ships to attempt to sink "*Bismarck*" before she could reach the protection of Luftwaffe aircraft from France. Later that day, planes from the aircraft carrier "*Ark Royal*" scored at least two torpedo hits, one of which crippled "*Bismarck's*" rudder. Unable to maintain course for France and still out of range of friendly airpower, "*Bismarck*" was now at the mercy of her enemies. Torpedo attacks by destroyer on 26 and 27 May achieved no success, but on the morning of 27 May two Royal Navy battleships, HMS "*Rodney*" and HMS "*King George V*" and two heavy cruisers arrived. Firing began before 0900 hours with German gunfire accuracy degrading to ineffectiveness. British fourteen and sixteen inch shells gradually smashed "*Bismarck's*" main guns, superstructure, hull and armour and reduced her to a wreck. Prompted by torpedoes and scuttling charges the German battleship rolled over and sank somewhat after 1030 hours that day, 27 May 1941, bringing to an end the most serious challenge those German warships would make to British ocean supremacy. The majority of the 2,300 crew of "*Bismarck*" were lost, save for 110 who survived.

About this time 201 Squadron took delivery of its first MkII Sunderland, although even with the new aircraft, the crews saw little action against the U-boats during the summer of 1941. The reason for this is that the U-boats were concentrating their savaging of the convoys in the Atlantic Gap, beyond the range of the Sunderland. The Operational Record Book for the squadron during June 1941 contains an account of one crew's experience with an armed trawler, the "*Vascama*," in the Shetlands-Faeroes Gap, which might sound rather familiar to those operating in a more modern context. The aircraft had been specifically tasked to cooperate with the trawler, and their conversation, signalled by Aldis lamp, is recorded:

Aircraft:	"Have you seen anything?"
Vascama:	"No, but I am in contact with U-boat."
Aircraft:	"Shall we carry on the search?"
Vascama:	"Stay; submarine in close vicinity."
Aircraft:	"What position?"
Vascama:	"Contact seven hundred yards ahead."

The trawler then attacked, using her last depth charges in the process. The exchange continued:

Aircraft:	"We have three depth charges aboard; shall we drop them on your instructions?"
Vascama:	"Yes, I will bring contact in direct line ahead at one hundred and fifty yards."
Aircraft:	"What depth settings?"
Vascama:	"Suggest stagger 150, 250, 350 feet."

A few minutes later the boat reported the submarine contact in line ahead of her at 150 yards and the Sunderland swept in to deliver the attack. That it failed to produce obvious destruction is in this instance not the point; significant though, is the procedure itself and the date of its inception.

In June 1941, The President of the USA, Theodore D. Roosevelt, required a firsthand report of the fighting in the Soviet Union and a personal assessment of Josef Stalin. To this end, shortly after the Germans invaded the Soviet Union, the President's personal envoy, Harry Hopkins, was flown to Moscow for a critical meeting with Stalin. The man chosen to fly the envoy was Flight Lieutenant (later Air Vice-Marshal) David McKinley, one of RAF Coastal Command's more experienced flying boat captains, who had served with 228 Squadron and 210 Squadron flying Sunderlands. He then joined the North Atlantic Ferry Organization and delivered numbers of the Catalina flying boats to the RAF. Hopkins landed first in Britain and walking with Winston Churchill – who had made the necessary arrangements for the visit – in the grounds at "Chequers", the Prime Minister's official country home, Churchill briefed Hopkins. He said "Tell him (Stalin) Britain has but one ambition today, but one desire – to crush Hitler. Tell him that he can depend on us. Goodbye – God Bless You, Harry". McKinley then flew Hopkins to Moscow from Invergordon in a fully loaded Catalina; more than twenty hours later they landed on the White Sea. The return journey took twenty-four hours, taking off late in the afternoon of 1 August 1941, landing at Scapa Flow. Roosevelt, through Hopkins, had earlier informed Winston Churchill, that he was prepared to help us by flying all of the aircraft destined for Britain from the factories on the west coast of the USA to Montreal or any other airport in Canada and on 20 July of that year RAF Ferry Command (Later RAF Transport Command) was formed in Montreal. The route for the aircraft was from North Carolina flown by US pilots to the seaplane base at Boucherville on the St Lawrence River near Montreal, where it would be taken over by the RAF and flown onward to Great Britain via Labrador, Newfoundland, or Greenland over Iceland and to the Shetland Isles. In winter, when the St Lawrence River froze over, the route was via Florida to Bermuda where it was collected by the RAF.

In the meantime, Tom and 201 Squadron were going about their missions in the North Atlantic, sometimes long and boring, and at other times life threatening. Wakened, say, at midnight on a night patrol, or 0630 hours on a day patrol, the

A galley photo.

twelve man crew consisting of a Captain, two Pilots, an Observer-Navigator, a Fitter, a Flight Engineer, three Riggers, and three Wireless Operators who double as Air Gunners; breakfast twenty minutes later.

One of the Riggers serves breakfast, if possible a married man, for married men make the better cooks. It is the first of four main meals that are eaten during the course of the long patrol. To maintain concentration and avoid fatigue and air sickness on long sorties, it was discovered that a full and balanced diet, supplemented by chocolate and barley sugar and copious drinks of cocoa, tea, or coffee, helped to overcome these problems. The crew would eat or drink something every two hours on a long patrol and a typical menu for one sortie would be:

Breakfast
Cereal, Bacon and Sausage, Bread and Butter or Margarine, Tea.

Lunch
Soup, half the quantity of Steak carried cubed and stewed, Potatoes and Vegetables, Dried Fruit, Orange.

Tea
Poached or Scrambled Egg, Bread and Butter, Tea.

Supper
Remainder Steak, Fried Potatoes and Vegetables, Bread and Butter and Cheese.

While the Captain, Navigator and Senior Wireless Operator went for briefing to the Operations Room the rest of the crew collected the rations, got on board by launch and prepared for departure. At the briefing, which was to give anti-submarine escort to an Atlantic Convoy made up of around forty-nine merchant ships, particulars of the accompanying naval escort are given and the position at which it should be found. A quarter of an hour after the captain and his companions had come on board, the rigger prepared to let go of the moorings. One of the fitters started the engines, each in turn, by means of an auxiliary power unit which filled the flying boat with fumes and these would disperse once she was airborne. The engines were warmed up one after the other, so that the flying boat turned in circles, first one way and then the other; like a mayfly in the eddy of a stream. All hatches were closed, take-off began, and as the pilot took her out of the water the navigator gave the course to be steered. One fitter would then keep the First Engineer's watch, his eyes on the instrument panel, and rectify any problem that occurred, such as falling oil pressure. If the conditions were favourable and the aircraft was given a steady course, the pilot would relax and throw in the automatic pilot; handing over to "George" as it was called; each of the gun positions would be constantly manned.

Here is an excerpt of a wartime memory from a former Wellington Bomber air gunner who joined 201 Squadron in 1941, and flew with Flight Lieutenant Fleming. "After a fourteen hour fifteen minute patrol in Sunderland ZM9606 we finished very tired at Invergordon. As a newcomer to the crew I had been trying to make myself 'fit in' by doing the odd chore aboard the boat. On this occasion, I went forward with Biggs, who did the mooring up to the fixed heavy anchored buoy. Winding back the front turret, Biggs positioned the aircraft's front bollards on the side and hung the short shaped ladder over the port side. The system used by this crew was for the pilot to approach the buoy keeping it on his port side, as slowly as possible, with inner engines shut down. When the aircraft nudged the large buoy, Biggs would put out a short ladder, shaped with a central hook to fit the socket on the forward side. Biggs would go over the side onto the ladder, and, hanging on by the right hand, he would push a slip-rope through the wire loop on top of the bollard.

"The assistant would then lean over the bow to take the loose end and make a hitch on the bollard. Not an 'advised' procedure, especially when the guy on the ladder falls into the water because he had not fixed the ladder securely! However, Biggs had the foresight to have a safety rope attached to the ladder. I pulled until

I could grab the top of the ladder; Biggs then climbed the ladder and me, taking a grip of my clothes, hair, arms, legs, back and then over me into the aircraft. Back in the 'saloon' he stood shivering, much to the amusement of the three hands. The pilot, Flight Lieutenant Fleming, had his head out of the side window wondering what was going on as it was difficult to keep the aircraft nudged up to the buoy with the tide running out of the Firth. I fastened the ladder down quickly, passed the slide-rope through the loop, caught the loose end, went up the ladder and took a hitch around the aircraft bollard, then used the boat hook to snag the mooring pendant attached to the buoy, dropping the grommet over the bollard. Thumbs-up to Flight Lieutenant Fleming and he shut down the outer engines. The rest of the mooring could wait until the 'swimmer' returned to his duty. All this panic seemed to last a long time but could have only been a few minutes. I looked down at my watch – What watch! Biggs had held my wrist on his way".

This is how the squadron log is drawn up for the second week of August 1941:

9.8.41. W3978. F/Lt Vaughan; Flying Officer Champion. Sgts Simmonds; Briden; Butler; Abbott; Parkes; Clark. LACs Cutchie; Richard. AC Kinnish. A/S Patrol. 1815 to 2143. Aircraft was detailed to carry out A/S Patrol of VOE C. Having set course for patrol area aircraft sighted seven trawlers in position 60°56'N 02°03'W at 1837. Aircraft commenced patrol at 1856. At 2010 aircraft sent message to base "Returning owing to oil leak ETA 2040." Aircraft completed last leg of patrol at 2044 and set course for base.

10.8.41. W3978. S/Ldr Fraser; Flying Officer Champion; P/O Powell. Sgts Briden; Butler; Abbott; Parkes; Clark. LACs Walker; Cutchie. AC Kinnish. A/S Patrol. 1722 to 1907. Aircraft was detailed to carry out A/S Patrol VOE C. Aircraft commenced patrol at 1757, but in position 61°46'N 02°42'W at 1810, patrol was abandoned owing to weather conditions, and aircraft set course for base.

11.8.41. W3978. S/Ldr Fraser; Flying Officer Champion; P/O Powell. Sgts Briden; Owen; Abbott; Butler; Clark; Parkes. LACs Walker; Cutchie. AC Kinnish. A/S Patrol. 1906 to 2221. Aircraft was detailed to carry out A/S Patrol of NOSE 1. Aircraft originally airborne at 1251, but returned at 1257 owing to the weather. After being airborne again at 1906 and on patrol, aircraft crashed on landing at 2221, and records were lost.

A Shetland Second World War crash log covering the incident is endorsed as follows: "On 11 August 1941, a Sunderland 2, Registration W3978 attached to 201 (Z) Squadron took off at 1906 hours on anti-submarine patrol and at

2221 hours, due to worsening weather, it was coming in to land at night on the waters of Sullom Voe. Just as it was about to touch down the pilot switched on the flap light and was blinded by the green indicator lamp. Both pilots leaned forward to cover the lamp with their hands, and the pilot inadvertently pushed the control column forward. The aircraft struck the water and sank, but the crew were able to escape." Tom's good luck had nearly ran dry, but he, along with six others, survived the terrible crash and impact, although the cold waters of the North Atlantic claimed the lives of five of his close friends and colleagues. The squadron diary entry is endorsed thus:

201 Squadron Report Crash of "Z" (W3978)

"At dusk on the evening of 11 August 1941, Z/201, Captain; S/Ldr B.A. Fraser, with pilots Flying Officer B.R. Champion and P/O A.S. Powell, crashed on landing at Sullom Voe. Conditions for landing were very poor. There was little light remaining and the surface of the Voe was glassy. "Z" was seen to make a normal daylight approach and then went straight in from the glide. Marine craft section picked up seven survivors, none of whom were seriously injured. We regret that five members of the crew lost their lives in this crash. They were: Sgt P.J. Butler, WOp/AG; AC1 W.M. Kinnish, F/Mech (E); AC1 J.W. Cutchie, F/Mech (A); Sgt D.J. Owen, A/Obs; and Sgt H.J. Parkes, AG."

Despite the wording of the above report, Tom was seriously injured, and sent to the Gilbert Bain Hospital in a smashed up state, including both of his legs broken. He was operated on by the Chief Consultant Surgeon Mr Daniel Lamont a former World War One medical student (The father of Norman, Lord Lamont).

Tom stayed at the Gilbert Bain Hospital until 13 August and was then transferred to Stracathro Hospital by Brechin in Angus. This had been built during 1939 as one of seven Emergency Medical Services (EMS) hospitals at the start of the Second World War. It had 1,000 beds and its first patients had been soldiers and airmen who were injured during an air raid on Montrose air station on 26 October 1940.

Tom's dead crewmates were interned and rest as follows: Sgt Owen in Bebington Cemetery, Cheshire; AC1 Kinnish in Everton Cemetery; Sgt Parkes in St Giles Churchyard and Extension, Willenhall, Staffordshire; AC1 Cutchie locally in Lerwick New Cemetery, Shetland and Sgt Butler in Rothley Cemetery, Leicestershire.

Author's note: Daniel Lamont MA, BD, was a Captain in the 1st King's Own Scottish Borderers during the First World War (the same regiment as Tom's maternal grandfather Thomas Buchanan had been in some twenty-five years previously) and during the Second World War was the Chief Surgeon at the

Old Gilbert Bain Hospital for a number of years. He is the author of "*Sea-Girt Citadel*", published in 1973 by Soldridge Books Ltd, of Scotland; Number 1427.

On 21 August 1941, Sunderland 2, "V" ZM W3982 took off from Sullom Voe at 1107 hours on anti-submarine patrol of area Fate 3. They signalled that they had been attacked by an enemy aircraft and ditched NNW of the Shetlands. No trace of the aircraft or crew of thirteen was ever found. The crew comprised of: Flying Officer A.G. Evill (pilot), Pilot Officer F.W. Selfe, Sergeants Simmons, Barraclough, King, Devereux, Adams, Newman, and Hancox, Flight Sergeant Gange and Leading Aircraftsmen Gordon, Richard and Mills.

On 23 August 1941, Tom was moved on a Hospital Rehabilitation Programme and then admitted to RAF Air Hospital Dingwall on Cromarty Firth, not far from Invergordon, from where he was discharged on 22 October 1941.

In the meantime, 201 Squadron went about its business, and by far the major part of its work consisted of dreary long-range anti-submarine patrols, but variety was always cropping up. On one occasion, Sunderland 'O' was ordered to lead two Catalinas, with an escort of six Blenheims, to a position thirty miles west of the Naze, in Southern Norway, to alight if possible and rescue the crew of the disabled Free French submarine "*Rubis*".

The flying-boats left Invergordon and met the Blenheims at Kinnaird Head. When the aircraft arrived over the prescribed area the submarine was not to be seen, and a square search had to be curtailed owing to the shorter range of the Blenheims. The "*Rubis*" was later found a long way south of the given position and towed into Dundee by naval vessels.

One day in early September 1941, Sunderland 'O', which Squadron Leader Wright had had to beach at Muckle Flugga, Woodwick, was involved in another incident off the east coast. Flight Lieutenant Raban and Pilot Officer Champion (the latter, one of Tom's former crew members on the ill-fated Sunderland W3978) were given the job of taking the flying-boat, stripped of all guns, radio and intercom, down to Felixstowe. Off Flamborough Head it was challenged by a Messerschmitt Me110 – and only had two tommy-guns on board against the enemy's two cannon and five machine-guns. Here is a quote from the squadron diary: "With Raban at the controls pushing everything forward at once, old 'O' did 170kt, while Champion acted as intercom by dashing back and forth with enemy amplifying reports and fresh orders between the tommy-gun posts amidships and the bridge. The Me110 made one straight attack from astern without doing any damage and then broke off the engagement. Several of the crew claimed that they heard a sharp clattering aboard during the attack, but this was probably Raban putting on his tin hat! Sunderland "O" got safely through; the tommy-guns shooting must have been good!"

In September 1941, 201 Squadron and 204 Squadron had been at Sullom Voe, as companions, for over two years. Tom was still convalescing from his injuries sustained in the fatal flying boat accident

It was therefore a relief to all concerned when orders came, on 18 September 1941, for a move to Castle Archdale on Lough Erne, in Northern Ireland. 204 Squadron had already gone to Iceland. A month after the move, 201 Squadron was visited by Air Commodore H.R.H. Prince George, the Duke of Kent, who was killed a year later while flying in a Sunderland flying boat from Scotland to Iceland, to inspect the British forces there. The officers were quartered in the Charter School at Kesh, where accommodation was primitive to the extreme. No light was laid on and one bath had to serve between forty and fifty officers – if, and when, water (fetched by lorry from Lough Erne) was available. Every morning there was a seven-mile journey down to Castle Archdale, where the moorings and squadron offices were situated. Gradually, however, things improved; a mobile generator was obtained and the walls of the anteroom were dormitory decorated by appropriate paintings by "Rembrandt", the squadron artist. Rabbit shooting was organized and a "local" established. Unfortunately, when the time came to go the following April, to a Nissen hut camp near the moorings, all were sorry to leave.

201 Squadron, flying Nimrods, were stationed at RAF Kinloss, they were disbanded during 2011 because of government defence cutbacks. This is what Flight Lieutenant Oliver (Olly) Jackson, one of its serving officers and squadron historian sent to me:

"The vast history of conflict is routinely, neatly reduced to easily described, dramatic significant events, and with it the dedicated and selfless acts performed by individuals is easily overlooked. This document is the result of considerable research across a multitude of areas and serves to reinvigorate the personal story that must never be forgotten. Indeed, the numerous accounts and experiences recounted here clearly demonstrates the varied input that a single individual brings to the overall effort. The subsequent collective effect is only a result of individual ability and these stories must be told in order to really understand and appreciate the realities of war. This account of Tom Clark, documented with utter respect and intrigue, by his son Chris, is a vivid and thorough chronology of such a story. It without doubt, is a clear reminder of how the individual is the key to overall success." Olly Jackson 6 October 2010.

"RAF Sullom Voe War Memorial"

The RAF Sullom Voe war memorial looks out over the bay, rectangular in shape and built of local stone, on the top is a plaque commemorating RAF Sullom Voe. The caption on top of the plaque reads:

ROYAL AIR FORCE STATION
SULLOM VOE

From these waters of Sullom Voe, British, Norwegian, Canadian and other Allied Aircrew left to fly their missions in Catalina and Sunderland Flying Boats of RAF Coastal Command (18 Group) during the period 1939 – 1945. Sadly, and with deep regret, some did not return to these friendly waters.

This memorial is dedicated to their memory and is in recognition of their supreme sacrifice. The memorial also remembers all of the other aircrew, ground and marine support personnel who also served at this station during the Second World War.

Throughout the Station's history, many hundreds of missions were flown to the limits of endurance by aircrews and their Catalina and Sunderland Flying Boats. Routine anti-submarine patrols were part of everyday Operations as "Constant Endeavours" were made to search, find and destroy enemy U-boats. Some operations were designated "Special Missions", and involved flying deep into occupied Norway, North to Spitsbergen, Russia and the Arctic Circle. At war's end RAF Sullom Voe could record with pride the award of a Victoria Cross and many other decorations to its aircrew for acts of outstanding bravery.

THEY SERVED AND FOUGHT AND DIED SO
THAT WE MIGHT BE SAFE AND FREE

Chapter Four

"Dinghy Drops And Top Gun"

Dinghy Drops A Gunner On Air–Sea Rescue

After 201 Squadron moved to Lough Erne from Sullom Voe, Tom also moved on in December 1941, fit once again, this time to 16 Group of Coastal Command with 279 Squadron, a newly formed Air-Sea Rescue Squadron, based in north-west Norfolk, England.

After Hitler flexed his muscles in Europe, prior to the outbreak of the Second World War, the Air Ministry produced an expansion of the RAF by developing new modern aircraft, in order to replace the obsolete biplanes; they also abolished the geographical groupings of the Air Defence of Great Britain and introduced the command structure based on functions; thus: Fighter Command, Bomber Command, Coastal and Training Command. Sir Arthur Harris (later Commander-in-Chief Bomber Command) looked across the Atlantic to the United States of America for replacements, and the outcome was 200 of the new maritime Lockheed Hudson reconnaissance aircraft. Eventually 2000 of these aircraft were delivered to the RAF during the war, and they became an enormous asset to Coastal Command, and were to play a major and distinguished part in Bircham Newton's wartime history.

An early development for dropping supplies to ditched aircrew was the "Thornaby Bag", named after RAF Thornaby in County Durham, where it was developed. It consisted of a container of food and first aid supplies. It was subsequently replaced by the "Bircham Barrel" which had been developed at RAF Bircham Newton in Norfolk, and proved more robust than its predecessor, being fashioned from the container of a 250lb bomb. Next came the Lindholme Dinghy, devised, not surprisingly, at RAF Lindholme, Yorkshire. This was even

279 Squadron Crest.

more successful and consisted of a well-equipped dinghy to which survivors could transfer, and four containers stocked with food, warm clothing and distress signals. The Lindholme device was so good that many years later it was still being carried by Hercules, Shackleton and Nimrod aircraft.

This brand new squadron was formed at Bircham Newton on the 16 November 1941 as an Air-Sea Rescue (ASR) Unit; following approval given in September that year for the formation of two long-range ASR Squadrons, 279 Squadron at Bircham Newton to cover the North Sea area, and 280 Squadron at Thorney Island on the south coast to cover the English Channel area. Both squadrons were meant to be equipped with Lockheed Hudson MK 1, 279 Squadron received seventeen of their allocation of twenty. It would be February 1942 before 280 Squadron received any aircraft and they were then moved to Detling, near Maidstone in Kent, to cover the east coast up to East Anglia. Here they received Avro Ansons, but were moved to Bircham Newton later in 1942.

No 279 Sqn was the first squadron to drop the "Lindholme Dinghy", and later, in 1943, the fully equipped MK1 Airborne Lifeboat for stricken RAF crews ditched in the sea. The fully canvassed lifeboat was carried under the wide belly of the portly Hudson. One of the first aircraft employed was nicknamed "The Pig". The squadron operated in detachments between Bircham Newton, north to the River Humber and south to the English Channel; between the English coastline of the North Sea and those of Holland, Belgium and France. Thorney Island on the south coast and St Eval in Cornwall became annexes of 279's Bircham Newton main base. From these two bases the squadron could cover the English Channel, the Celtic Sea, and the Atlantic to the Bay of Biscay. Bircham Newton by virtue of its location as being one of the nearest operational RAF Stations to the continent of Europe and Germany, became one of the most important Coastal Command Stations on the East Coast, with many varied squadrons operating from its busy airfield and hangers.

One of the first lectures for 279's Wop/AGs (wireless operator/air gunners) was not on Air-Sea Rescue, but on gunnery. This was to be fully justified, as on rescue missions they had to contend with attacks by enemy fighters, including Ju88s, Me109s and FW190s. It was significant, also, that they flew with side guns in addition to forward and rear guns. There was an awareness of the need to provide better survival equipment for those who had ditched far from Britain's shores.

The task of 279 Sqn was to fly patrols over its area of responsibility, searching for crews of the many RAF fighter and bomber aircraft shot down, out of fuel, or mechanical failure, who had crash landed in the North Sea, returning from missions over enemy held Europe. Later in the spring of 1942, when the United States of America heard the bugle call, this was extended to members of the USAF 8th Air Force. During the course of the war over 4000 RAF and over 1000 USAF lives would be saved by this squadron alone.

Tom joined 279 Squadron as a Flight Sergeant dorsal AG (Air Gunner) on the 14 December 1941, with Flying Officer Heywood's crew on Hudson E T9398, which consisted of Phil Heywood, pilot, Flight Sergeant "Slug" Slugoski, navigator, Flight Sergeant "Ginger" Orr, wireless operator/air Gunner and Flight Sergeant Tom "Nobby" Clark, Air Gunner in the rear facing "egg" dorsal turret. They formed one crew of twelve in "A" Flight and a similar number were in "B" Flight; the four crew mates would be together from the infancy of the squadron until the end of 1942.

Lockheed Hudson aircraft.

The procedure followed by the crews of the squadron would be to fly at no more than 1000 feet, and upon sighting a dinghy or ditched aircraft wreckage, would drop a smoke flare to mark the position and to determine wind direction and speed. The Lindholme Dinghy consisted of one large and four smaller containers which would be dropped from the bomb racks of the Hudson so that it would drift onto the survivors' position. The large container, upon impact with the water, would automatically inflate into a dinghy to provide a large and fully equipped emergency accommodation. The other four containers would contain food, water, hot drinks, warm clothing, flares and other survival equipment. In later trials a solid hulled lifeboat, designed by yachtsman Uffa Fox, would be carried slung below the belly of the aircraft.

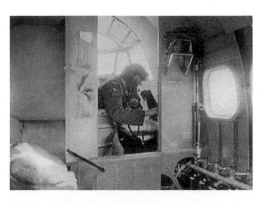

The interior of a Lockheed Hudson showing the Wireless Operator/Air Gunner at his post.

The Squadron celebrated its first Christmas by flying until

The Dorsal Gunner, Tom's position.

Internal view aft showing the dorsal cupola.

Phil
Heywood

Slug
Slugoski

Ginger

Nobby
Clark

mid-morning and then the senior NCOs (Non Commissioned Officers) were entertained in the Officers' Mess and then both Officers and NCOs made their way to the Sergeants' Mess, before going to the Airmens' Mess to serve them Christmas Dinner.

Dinner was at 1830 hours and consisted of:
Tomato Soup (followed by a choice from)

....

Dover Sole with melted butter

....

Roast Turkey

....

Roast Chicken

....

Roast Pork

....

(With stuffing and sauces)
Mashed and Roast Potatoes, Sprouts

....

Xmas Pudding with sauce

....

Mince Pies

. . . .

Trifle

. . . . . .

Coffee and Cigarettes

. . . .

Fruit

. . . . . .

Brandy and Spirits

The photograph portrays a group of young men happily celebrating Christmas together and without a care in the world; nothing could be further from the truth. Most were by this time battle hardened, combat service, seasoned campaigners, after serving over two years service in a raging World War; and several, including "Slug" would not live to see victory some three and a half years later. Others, including Tom, would have lucky escapes after brushes with death.

Bircham Newton Xmas 1941. In this photograph of Tom's, he is clearly shown in the centre of the group, in the third row and second from left and "Slug" is seated on the front row far right.

Poem Ode To The Wop/AG:

Dave Webster 38 Squadron

"It takes guts to be a Wop/AG
And sit out in the tail
When the Focke-Wulfs are coming in
And the slugs begin to hail.
The Pilot's just a chauffeur
As he only flies the plane,
We do all the fighting
And take all the blame.
We have all the shooting
At these Axis swine,
All the Pilot ever shoots
Is his horrible line.
The Pilot and Observer
Each has tons of room,
We're caged in a turret
And it's like a tomb.
When the flak gets sticky,
And things are looking hot,
The Pilot hopes his Wop/AG
Will save the festering lot.
Then if the kite should ditch itself
Into the raging sea,
Who throws the dinghy out?
The poor old Wop/AG.
And when we're on the ocean
With a hundred miles to go,
The Pilot yells at his Wop/AG
"Row you Bastard Row!"
Then when each trip is over
And the crew to the Mess all fly
You'll find the poor old Wop/AG
Still doing his D.I.
But when it's cleaning Browning guns,
The Observer's always late,
He does not seem to realize
That he's the Gunner's Mate.
But when this war is over,
And they add the final score,
They'll find it was the Wop/AG

Who won this bloody war.
So hail then to the Wop/AG
For he's the best of man.
If he can't bring the aircraft back,
No other bugger can!"

The Squadron continued to build its strength and carried on training. By New Year's Eve it had eighteen Lockheed Hudson aircraft on base and had flown one hundred and forty eight hours in its six week existence. The accommodation was satisfactory and equipment sufficient; American tools for the Hudsons being the only things in short supply. During January 1942, the Japanese advanced into Borneo and Celebes, and German U-boats continued to plague the North Atlantic, dramatically affecting the transportation of the urgently needed vital supplies from America.

During January nearly forty more ground crew were posted into Bircham Newton from 407 Squadron at North Coates, which was mainly manned by Canadians of The RCAF.

Tom's photograph of members of a crew of 407 Squadron.

There was no let up in the activity of a large RAF station like Bircham Newton in the early days of January 1942, as recalled by Hugh Wilkins of 279 Squadron: "On the 2 January a large draft of armourers and other trades arrived to report to the guard room in bleak weather. Of course as usual we were unexpected and we were left standing outside the guard room for some hours. Eventually we were detailed to collect beds and bedding and to find room where we could. I and the others found that the camp was already bursting at the seams and our beds had to be erected in spaces between beds already in use, so that we could only enter our beds over the foot of somebody else's." In the early part of the month the weather closed in and it was so cold that flying training was severely disrupted due to the oil coolant freezing up. Some six Hudsons left in mid January and moved to RAF Horsham St Faiths, just outside Norwich (now Norwich Civil Airport). A further four were scattered to other bases in Norfolk, Lincolnshire and Yorkshire; leaving eight on ASR at Bircham.

The ASR role at Bircham Newton was becoming more prominent as more fighters and bombers were ditching in the North Sea on return from operations, and the freezing cold at that time of year meant that ditched aircrew without a liferaft could not hope to survive for more than ten minutes in the open sea, hence the importance of speed in locating downed aircrew. It was not only the squadron aircrews who endured the conditions, life was hard for the ground crews in that grim start to 1942, as Donald Samson, Corporal-Fitter recalled: "I was detached from No. 30 Maintenance Unit at Sealand in North Wales for what was supposed to be five to seven days at Bircham Newton for a hush-hush job. 'Take your small kitbag and a change of underwear in your side–pack' I was told. We travelled by service lorry, all day, to RAF Grantham where we bedded down for the night, reaching Bircham Newton the next afternoon. It transpired that some Vickers Wellingtons had been recalled from Iceland to have their engines changed and prepared for dispatch to the Middle East. These aircraft were in the white camouflage of course. We had trouble!!! Temperatures in January 1942 were a good deal below zero centigrade and restricted the use of spanners etc to around five minutes, after which fingers and tools 'merged'. We were working outside of course. Being from another unit we were not on the strength of Bircham Newton so we had to make the best of off-duty hours, which we did in a Nissen hut full of tables and forms, all of which we burned in the single stove to raise the sleeping temperature to zero. We slept fully dressed and froze stiff. My boots wore out in the third week and I had to go on sick leave to replace these. They gave me a pair of service PT plimsolls, big deal! We left with no regrets and returned courtesy of LNER (London North Eastern Railway) train to London and LMS (London Midlands Scottish) train to Chester. Norfolk in winter was definitely no place to be."

Hugh Wilkins also recalled the grim winter weather of early 1942: "The airfield was snowed up for long periods and with only grass runways it was difficult to keep the aircraft flying. Early one morning, with a blizzard blowing, and with no chance of aircraft taking off, a duty gun armourer and I set off to a dispersal point on the other side of the perimeter. Spotting a wind-sock in the driving snow we thought that we had reached our destination, only to find that we had completed a circuit of the 'drome and had arrived back at the main hangar."

Poor weather continued into the middle of the month and further curtailed flying. The squadron's first operational flight was on 22 January on a search, followed by an announcement on 26 January that it was now fully operational; albeit with fewer aircraft. On 27 January, three Hudsons piloted by Flight Lieutenant Fitchew, Pilot Officer Phil Heywood and Pilot Officer Long, with "Slug", "Ginger", and Tom as crew ; all flew operational patrols and on that date, the Commanding Officer (CO), V.H.P Lynham, DSO was promoted from Squadron Leader to Wing Commander, and he flew his first operational patrol with 279 on 28 January. On 29 January, Sgt Jackman, flying Hudson 9024 N, and Flying Officer Tyrrell in T9414 V, flew an unsuccessful search. Three sorties were flown on 30 January during which Sergeant Garrard, on a buoy patrol, twice hit the sea in very bad visibility.

In February 1942, the Japanese bombed New Guinea and landed in Singapore, followed by the surrender of the British forces, many who were interned in the infamous "Changi Jail". They also invaded Sumatra and Bali, and by the third week of the month, were approaching Rangoon in Burma.

Air Marshall "Bomber" Harris was appointed Commander-in-Chief of Bomber Command, who were now in a bombing offensive over enemy occupied territory, and many would finish up ditched in the sea on their return and this made a busy time for 279 ASR Squadron. During this time the Hudsons were equipped with ASV radar equipment which was serviced by Canadian technicians.

Patrols continued into February, often hampered by poor weather and there was little improvement in the weather until the 7 February when other squadron operations at Bircham Newton resumed. The New Year brought yet another challenge for Coastal Command and squadrons based at Bircham Newton. Hitler had become convinced that Britain intended to invade Norway in order to repatriate it and therefore ordered major naval units to move into the sector of the North Sea, including the Battle Cruisers "Scharnhorst" and "Gneisenau", then sheltering at Brest.

Aerial photographs revealed increased German naval activity in the area and British Intelligence drew the conclusion that a break out of these naval units through the Channel and into the North Sea was imminent. At Brest a Coastal Command aircraft, diving out of low cloud, flew at 500 feet over the most heavily defended harbour on the Continent to take the photograph of a "Hipper" class cruiser in dock. The Bomber and Coastal Command units were placed on high alert and the main hope for offensive attacks lay with the torpedo-bomber Beauforts, centred on RAF North Coates, located near Grimsby, and the Royal Navy Swordfish torpedo-bombers.

Matters came to a head on the 12 February, when the German battleships "Scharnhorst" and "Gneisenau" broke out of Brest and a large enemy convoy was sighted. When the news leaked out, 279 Squadron felt sure that it would be called upon at any moment. Unfortunately the day turned out to be an anticlimax due to lack of coordination and preparation, combined with bad weather. Four Hudsons of 500 Squadron took off from Bircham Newton at 1335 hours ready to attack the ships, but the expected rendezvous with fighters and other aircraft over Manston did not materialize and the aircraft returned to base. Later in the afternoon a Beaufighter of 248 Squadron sighted the enemy convoy near the Dutch Coast, in visibility of only half a mile. They flew inside the destroyer screen to within 100 yards of the "*Scharnhorst*", having to take violent evasive action because of the flak. Beauforts from Thorney Island were unable to locate the convoy and landed at Docking after a sea search. A number of unsuccessful attacks were made on the ships by Beauforts, and an Avro Manchester from 83 Squadron landed at Bircham Newton after one such bombing sortie, having been damaged by flak.

The following day, Friday, 13 February, the Squadron carried out five unsuccessful search sorties during which Hudson V8993 J, flown by Sergeant Garrard, failed to return. Garrard, and Sergeants Redhead, Schulty and Logan were the squadron's first casualties. During the next day, Saturday, 14 February, Flight Lieutenant Tyrrell, known as "Happy" to his colleagues, was returning to Bircham Newton from Thorney Island when his Hudson collided with a tree. Tyrrell managed to keep it flying and landed safely at Woodley, near Reading. No one was hurt, but "Happy" Tyrrell had to suffer much leg pulling. During the first week of March, a film crew visited 279 Squadron to make a film on behalf of the Air Ministry. Several aircraft flew out over Hunstanton so the film crew could get shots of them departing on searches. Pilot Officer A.A. "Gus" Henderson was filmed in the cockpit for pilot closeups and the squadron diary noted that he "is now hoping to be re–mustered as a film star!" On 6 March 1942, Tom was made a Wireless Operator Grade 11 and the squadron was kept very busy through this period, and even more in the months ahead. Whilst the filming progressed, several real searches were flown with no success, though Henderson, whilst searching on the 10 March, found an oil patch, two wheels and other wreckage. The following day, the 11 March, Hudsons flown by Sergeant Marchand, Flight Sergeant Spencer, Pilot Officer Somerville and Pilot Officer "Phil" Heywood, and crew; all carried out searches and all found patches of oil and floating wreckage. "Phil" Heywood, "Slug", "Ginger", and Tom, came across the sad and lonely sight of an empty capsized dinghy.

The shortage of Hudsons in early 1942, and the need for training, meant that the squadron did not become fully operational for a number of months. During 1942 the dinghy was developed into the Mk 1 Airborne Lifeboat, designed for use with the Hudsons. Ernest Farrow was an LAC, who joined the squadron in 1942, and he recalls his life and operations there. "During the time that I was posted to 279 Squadron we were based at Bircham Newton in Norfolk, the nearest airfield to Germany proper in the British Isles. The squadron was engaged in Air-Sea Rescue work and was equipped with Lockheed Hudson aircraft, which were fitted with

Tom, Ginger, Slug and Phil. Bircham Newton early 1942.

the latest version of ASV radar equipment. This was serviced by the Canadian technicians seconded to 279 Squadron. The aircraft carried in the bomb bay two 'large life rafts', which were dropped by parachute to downed aircraft crews, who were found floating in their much lighter dinghies. I understood that these heavy-duty rafts were equipped with a signal device, which enabled Air-Sea Rescue vessels to quickly locate them. Several rescues were made using this equipment.

"Bircham Newton was a peacetime airfield, with permanent built hangars, barracks etc. It was a major overhaul facility, and, so as not to attract German night bombers, night flying was not permitted. All our night flying was done from our satellite airfield, Docking, about six miles from Bircham. When Bomber Command's airfields in Yorkshire were fogged in, their aircraft were diverted to Docking, where we were required to carry out the 'Between Flight Inspections', so that these aircraft could return to their bases as soon as the weather cleared. The biggest worry was that Docking and Bircham Newton were so close to Germany, that these bombers were serviced quickly and got out of harm's way. We were kept very busy, especially in the summer, when it did not get dark until 2200 hours."

Hugh Wilkins, a bomb armourer with No. 279 Squadron recalled: "Our main job as armourers was loading the Lindholme dinghies onto the bomb carriers. These dinghies were inflated after being dropped into the sea when a soluble plug activated an air bottle. On several occasions, doubtless by reason of a faulty plug, the dinghy became inflated whilst loading, so that one or two armourers were trapped in the bomb bay – quite a humorous situation. Later on, the squadron became more aggressive and we loaded anti-sub bombs. Gun armourers were always in trouble, usually after accidentally firing guns without unloading them when testing. On one occasion when the guns on a Hudson were being harmonized in the hangars, a burst was fired through the Squadron offices which had windows looking onto the hangar. It was reported that had the adjutant not been stooping at that moment to retrieve some papers from the floor, he would have had it. In fact it was a fairly regular sight to see gun armourers reporting to the Guardroom with full pack."

Inevitably, there were times when things went wrong, either through carelessness or inexperience, as Syd Roberts of No. 279 Squadron explained: "Every aircraft had its own Form 700 that is a daily record of its Daily Inspection (DI). There are two of these, one in the squadron office, and a 'travelling 700', which remains on the aircraft in case it should be grounded on an away field, and would still be required to undergo an inspection. This form had to be signed by each tradesman after his inspection. One evening whilst doing my checks I opened the bomb doors to find there was no equipment loaded.

"After I loaded the equipment I sought out the bloke who had signed the form the previous day in order to tick him off. One of my mates, on hearing me in action so to speak, remarked that the aircraft had been on an operation, but had been unable to find any sign of a downed aircraft or crew in the North Sea. Imagine if there had been, and the bomb-aimer had pressed the button, nothing would have happened." Equally serious was a further incident related by Syd Roberts: "In addition to checking that all the equipment and electrics were in working order, we also had to 'break' the Very pistol, to ensure that it wasn't loaded and the strikes were in order. On one occasion an armourer, whilst doing the daily inspection, instead of breaking the pistol pressed the trigger with the result that the Hudson went up in flames, thus losing an aircraft (valued today at £30,000) in a few moments."

Another armourer, Corporal Geoffrey Cardew, remembered squadron routine at the time: "I was posted to 279 Squadron from the station armoury, Felixstowe, shortly after Easter 1942, as a fitter armourer/gun…the armoury was in the hangar so it was no distance to go when an aircraft had a major service, but it was a bit of a drag to the dispersal… There must have been about half a dozen armourers, two corporals and a sergeant. Our job was to service the guns and Very pistols, and to load and check the Lindholme dinghies. These latter consisted of four containers, each about four feet long, made of cardboard, and painted yellow, one with an inflatable dinghy and the others with an assortment of rations, flares and fluorescent dye etc. They were linked together with ropes and had a drogue that kept them in line, making it easier for them to be grabbed in the water. At night the aircraft would be flown to the satellite aerodrome at nearby Docking".

Just a bunch of "Pussy Cats" left to right; Slug, Phil, Tom with binoculars and Ginger 1942.

Coastal Squadrons operating from Bircham Newton and Docking were often caught out by low cloud, or North Sea haze drifting inland. Consequently, to get back to base, the pilots would fly at low-level round the coast to Hunstanton and fly in over the pier, pick up the Docking road and follow it to the Docking airstrip. Bircham Newton, as with other east coast RAF Stations, was on the Luftwaffe's "calling cards" and Docking was used as a "safer" location for storing 279 Squadron aircraft when not on active duty; but even this was bombed in May, August and September of 1941 and again on 27 July 1942; when Dorniers destroyed a Wellington and damaged buildings and three cottages. The earliest incident occurred on the 16 May 1941 when a farmhouse at Docking was hit by German bombs and crew sleeping quarters were demolished, resulting in the deaths of three airmen and a further fifteen being wounded.

The nearby town of Kings Lynn, having a dock and industrial works, was also a regular target, and suffered its worst raid on Friday, 12 June 1942, when a lone Dornier Do17 dropped a stick of bombs, hitting the Eagle Hotel in Norfolk Street, with the loss of forty-two lives; the City of Norwich was another Luftwaffe target.

German Intelligence had been at work even before the war had broken out in mapping and photographing, from the air, large parts of the British Isles, as evidenced by the detailed photographic record captured after the war. Britain was particularly vulnerable to air attack, due to the concentrated nature of its population, especially in the industrial areas. So "Starfish" sites were set up to attempt to draw enemy bombers away from cities and towns, utilizing dummy buildings, fires, lights, and anything that would suggest a built-up area, albeit in the middle of agricultural land! Another prime target for the enemy was the airfields, especially in East Anglia with its extensive network of aerodromes, and its proximity to the enemy coastline in the Low Countries and Scandinavia. This was indeed a Home Front, and urgent measures were taken to ensure maximum protection, with airfield defences and decoys wherever possible. A "K" decoy site had a full range of dummy aircraft and buildings, mock bomb dumps, old vehicles, tents, and anything else that would assist in confusing the enemy by day; such a site was established at Sedgeford, to the west of RAF Docking and Bircham Newton. At night "Q" sites were established, sometimes on the same site as the daytime decoy, with lighting in place to simulate landing lights. One can only admire the courage of the men who manned these sites, and also the landowners and farmers who made the sites available from private land knowing they were meant to be in the front line of any attack.

Oblique, looking east, 31 March 1940. Dummy hedges have been painted on the airfield and the hangars have been camouflaged. (P.H.T. Green Collection)

During the month of April 1942, 279 Squadron's search patrols continued and on the 21 April, eight Hudsons were out on searches. Pilot Officer R.M. Lacey in T9414 V sighted an empty rowing boat with its oars shipped, and Sergeant Jackman flying V9031 P, came across an empty dinghy. The sight of so much wreckage and empty dinghies must have been extremely frustrating for the crews on these sorties. At the end of April, the squadron began detaching aircraft to other airfields, an occurrence which would become the norm over the remaining years of the war. Three aircraft and crews were detached to Sumburgh in the Shetlands, via Kinloss, arriving on the 28 April.

Although air-sea rescue was Bircham Newton's task, many ASR operations were flown from Docking, particularly those that were conducted during the hours of darkness. A typical night operation from Docking, conducted on 4 May 1942, illustrates the difficulty of locating and rescuing ditched aircrew at night. Aircraft T9414V/279, captained by Pilot Officer Lacey, took off from Docking at 0433 hours to carry out a search for a ditched Wellington, returning back at base at 0924 hours. The following extract is taken from an entry in the Operational Record Book (ORB): "V/279 took off from Docking to carry out a Sea Rescue Night Patrol. A last fix had previously been received from a Wellington a/c in distress at coordinate MBGM 2554. At 0516 this position was reached and flame floats were dropped, it being too dark to search. After circling the position for six minutes, a course was set for coordinate MBBR 5443, being the previous fix of the Wellington a/c, with intention of flying up and down that track until broad daylight. Two white flashing lights sighted at 0524 but no more recognizable. After circling for four minutes, it was concluded that the flashes were caused by the flare floats dying out. Then decided to resume original track.

"At 0528 hours turret gunner (Pilot Officer H.T. Calvert) saw a Signal Distress Marine two miles dead astern, and informed pilot who altered course by 180 degrees. A flare float was dropped after one minute the S.D.M having ceased. At 0530 hours a second S.D.M was observed about three miles from float. Flew over S.D.M and sighted dinghy in its glow. Dropped additional flame floats and made sighting reports. Lost sight of dinghy at 0609 hours from a height of 2000 feet. Sighted Wellington a/c floating with tail fin above water. Set course downwind and resighted dinghy at 0613 hours. Five or six occupants could be seen in dinghy, four of whom stood up and expressed great joy. Dropped Lindholme dinghy and Wellington dinghy, eventually drifted within reach of it. U/279 and A/279 arrived at 0715 hours. Rescue carried out by two MLS (Motor Launches) at 0839 hours."

The Wellington was from No. 305 (Polish) Squadron captained by Flying Officer Skarpetowski, and based at Lindholme (a strange coincidence). This aircraft had been one of two Wellingtons lost along with three Halifax's, from a force of aircraft despatched by Bomber Command to raid Hamburg that night; and they had been sighted by the 279 Hudson within an hour of them ditching. This had saved them from many desperate hours, or even days, clinging to life in their dinghy. Another report of this V/279 sortie, made by the Observer, mentioned also that they sighted a German Ju88 and took avoiding action.

A new face arrived in Britain in May 1942, The United States 8th Air Force; Hooray! With the first contingent arriving on the 12 May, many members of this new force would eventually find themselves at the mercy of the unforgiving sea and be grateful to 279 Squadron for their deliverance.

During 1942 several of the Hudson aircraft crashed after being shot down, through mechanical failure, or pilot error. Tom told my youngest sister of an experience he had when the aircraft he was in ditched in the sea; he was knocked unconscious and when he came to he found himself floating on a mattress, strapped to one of the aircraft's doors which had been blown off the aircraft. For a second time in two years the cold waters off the British coast had failed to claim yet another victim; otherwise I wouldn't be writing about it now!

The Squadron Gunnery Officer, Flight Lieutenant Barrett and seven others, including Tom, departed for a "cat's eye" course at Felixstowe on 17 May; 279 Squadron crews often encountered enemy aircraft during search and rescue operations and the dorsal gunners were the aircraft's "eyes". The squadron was able to take a well-earned rest on 19 May, when a party was held in the Sergeant's Mess. The guests included members of the four crews from 10, 35, 300 and 305 Squadrons, successfully rescued by 279 Squadron. An excellent dinner was provided and earlier in the day a BBC Recording Unit interviewed several of the squadron aircrew. Three days later, the squadron were back in the thick of it, in their ASR role.

On 29 May, Bomber Command carried out the first of the "thousand bomber" raids against Cologne, dropping 1,455 tons of bombs onto the city and its surroundings. Luckily, the services of the squadron, to search for downed crews, were not required on this occasion.

Following the second "thousand bomber" raid on Essen on the night of 1 June, the squadron was airborne before dawn on 2 June with Pilot Officer Lacey in V8979 W, and Flight Sergeant Spencer in T9405 U. Flying patrols and searches were carried out in two areas with a total of ten Hudsons, including Tom's. During one patrol Sergeant Scott in T9414 V, and Sergeant Werrin flying V9031 P, sighted a dinghy with six men on board miles off the Dutch coast. They then came under attack from two German Me 109's. Hudson P/279 sustained several hits during the attack, Pilot Officer Allan, the Observer, and Sergeant Parsons, the dorsal Air Gunner, were injured. Both men continued to man their guns, and Parsons claimed one of the Messerschmitts destroyed. Werrin evaded the German fighters skilfully, and, with the rudder unserviceable and over 100 holes in the Hudsons fuselage, managed to land safely at Eastchurch. Sergeant Scott and crew were more fortunate and escaped with no damage. Sergeant White loosed off some bursts at one of the German fighters at a range of 300yards. A further search by F/279 later failed to locate the drifting dinghy and the search continued the following day, the 3 June. Pilot Officer Whittaker and Squadron Leader Pye, both carried out night sorties from Docking; during which coloured pyrotechnics were sighted in the probable position of the dinghy.

The following morning, 4 June, Sergeant Marchand and his crew were off before dawn in Hudson F/279 to continue the search. Shortly afterwards, four more Hudsons, including T9399 R with Tom's crew, were airborne to search for another ditched crew. After reaching the search area they dispersed to widen the search and at 0650 hours Sergeant A.W. Campbell, the Observer on board N/279 flown by Sergeant Faux, spotted distress signals. Closing on them they soon discovered a dinghy with six men on board. N/279 was not carrying a Lindholme dinghy and could offer no assistance to the ditched fliers, other than to continue circling their position. Wireless Operator Sergeant Darwin got off a sighting report to base, which was intercepted by Sergeant Guthrie, flying T9405 U.

Arriving at the scene at 0735 hours, Guthrie dropped his Lindholme gear to the crew of Flying Officer Mandala, who had ditched their Hingham, Norfolk, based 300 (Polish) Squadron Wellington, thirty five miles east of Cromer, some two hours before their sighting by Sgt Faux. The Poles had scattered fluorescing marker dye and this showed up well from 3,000 feet, assisting in their location. The lucky crew was seen to transfer to the Lindholme dinghy, and two hours later they were successfully picked up by rescue launches. Madala's Wellington was one of four lost, along with seven other types, in a raid on Bremen by 170 aircraft of Bomber Command. 279 Squadron were kept extremely busy during this time searching for downed bomber crews on return from German offensives.

On the 9 June 1942, 279 Squadron were in action in the English Channel when the crew of a Handley Page Halifax, based at Linton-on-Ouse, were forced to ditch in the North Sea some forty-five miles east of Orfordness; after their aircraft incurred damage from enemy anti-aircraft fire while raiding Essen in Germany. The seven-man crew scrambled out of the doomed aircraft and settled down to await rescue. 279 Squadron dispatched six aircraft in two waves of three to commence the search. Squadron Leader Binks, in Hudson T9399 R, soon sighted them and very soon all six Hudsons arrived and circled their position. At 1022 hours two rescue launches arrived and the airmen and their dinghy were taken on board for their journey back to Gt Yarmouth. The photo below shows an aerial photograph taken from a Lockheed Hudson of 279 Squadron; in it is High Speed Launch HSL 130 from Yarmouth, rescuing the crew from their dinghy.

On 14 July, Tom's RAF Personnel Record is endorsed "Detached to Benbecula". Four crews returned on 15 July, whilst Sergeant Scott and Flight Lieutenant Tyrrell and their crews were detached to Leuchars. The Benbecula detachment continued throughout July and the squadron was further scattered when the Commanding Officer Squadron Leader Pye, and Pilot Officer Somerville and crews, detached to Iceland on the 26 July.

The early days of August 1942 saw immediate success when Pilot Officer Somerville, in H/279, operating from

High speed launch rescuing crew.

Reykjavik, sighted three ships' lifeboats sixty miles south-west of the Westmaan Islands on the 2 August. They contained twenty-three survivors from the SS *Flora*, which had been torpedoed and sunk. Somerville directed a trawler to the boats and the survivors were rescued. August also saw much movement, with Pilot Officer McKimm, Sergeant Faux and Sergeant Woolford, together with "Phil" Heywood's crew with Tom.

On 14 and 15 August 1942, Tom was photographed together with Phil Heywood, "Slug" Slugoski, "Ginger" Orr, "Titch", and others on detachment to Thorney Island, situated in Hampshire, between Chichester and Portsmouth; from where they covered the English Channel. Around this time Sergeant Stapleton, an Air Gunner, supplemented "Phil" Heywood's crew as a fifth member whilst he was being trained by Tom and awaiting Tom's eventual posting away from 279 Squadron; he was still on the "A" Flight aircrew list on 30 September 1942 and 1 January 1943.

The following day they were moved to Chivenor, located in North Devon near Barnstaple, where Zumar, Werrin and Scott, joined them. Success was not long in coming for the Chivenor detachment and two dinghies were sighted ten miles off Land's End on 16 August and they were rescued by high speed launches. The same day, two more dinghies were sighted sixty miles off Brest in France, and a Lindholme dinghy was dropped to the six survivors of a Wellington, and a sole surviving crew member of a Sunderland Flying Boat, the latter had attempted to rescue the Wellington crew and sank. The detachments returned to Bircham Newton on 16 and 19 August respectively.

Going back to 1941, as well as remembering Tom's narrow escape from death during August, in the Sunderland Flying Boat crash with 201 Squadron; there was another who would cheat death that year and eventually finish up on 279 Squadron. Owen Valentine Burns was a twenty-five year old Wop/AG with 235 Squadron during the Battle of Britain; flying Blenheims from Bircham Newton, or on detachment from St Eval, in Cornwall. On 14 February 1941 (St Valentine's Day) three Blenheims returning from a moon patrol over the North Sea were caught up in an enemy raid, one Blenheim was shot down, a second went down in flames just before landing at Bircham Newton, and the aircraft containing Burns crashed on landing, as the flare path at Bircham was extinguished during the raid. Owen Burns was thrown out onto the ice hard rutted field and suffered a broken collar bone, the Observer/Navigator was killed and the Pilot spent twelve months in hospital.

Owen Burns joined "A" Flight, 279 Squadron, during the summer of 1942, and was a dorsal Air Gunner on the crew of Flight Lieutenant Fitchew, the Pilot (later Squadron Leader, DFC), Pilot Officer Scott, the Observer/Navigator (later Flight Lieutenant), and Sgt Field, DFM as Wop/AG (later Flying Officer). Owen Burns was commissioned in February 1943, and the makeup of that crew remained the same until Burns left them in December 1943 for

Thorney Island. Phil Heywood, Slug Slugoski, Titch, u/k, u/k, Tom Clark, u/k, u/k.

279 Detachment at Thorney Island 15/16 August 1941, with Ginger Orr kneeling.

Flight Lieutenant O.V. Burns.

Gunnery Instructor duties, and later on during the war, he became part of a small team rewriting gunnery manuals for all aircrew. During January 1945 he became Gunnery Officer for 19 Group.

During the summer of 1942 there was a renewed German offensive against Britain's airfields, and Bircham Newton was that well camouflaged it was invisible from 2,000 feet up. Corporal Cardew, an armourer with 279 Squadron explains: "Black paint or some substance was used to camouflage the airfield, imitating hedges and ditches. There was no concrete runway so it was probably quite effective. There could not be one hundred per cent security against the threat of attack by Luftwaffe aircraft acting independently or in small formations, as the tragedy at Docking in May 1941 amply demonstrated. Every effort had to be made to disperse air and ground crew around the area in local villages and country houses, while at the same time guaranteeing the operational efficiency of the station. The pressure on accommodation in a busy station like Bircham Newton was another factor. Large country houses and halls in the nearby villages of Heacham, Ringstead, Docking, Stanhoe, Sedgeford, and Fring were ideal for the purpose. It would be the first, and possibly the last time that personnel of all ranks would experience a style of gracious living that had echoes of the nineteenth century."

Fring Hall, situated about six miles from Bircham Newton, was brought into use during the summer of 1942, as Syd Roberts of 279 Squadron recalled: "On another occasion a Polish squadron arrived at the camp, for which no accommodation had been arranged. What a panic! All of our section had to move out of our billet and take up sleeping quarters in various places, and others in the guardroom, stores, library etc! This was my first experience of the super-efficiency of the RAF administration, and the happy result was the fact that we were in the party that had to take up residence in Fring Hall, for sleeping only. This was a lovely country estate belonging to Lord Llewellyn. We were issued with new bicycles and were allowed half an hours grace for breakfast. Three of us, on a rota basis, were supposed to stay at the Hall, one to clean the baths and hand basins, one to clean and tidy the dormitories and the other to prepare the midday meal".

Hugh Wilkins, also of 279 Squadron, had a similar experience: "In the summer of 1942, with the idea of dispersing personnel as a precaution, a lot of us were issued with bicycles and billeted at Fring Hall. This was a pleasant diversion but it involved rising early to ride and report for breakfast at Bircham."

A summer 1942 photo of Tom, Slug and Ginger with a station cycle showing Monks Close RAF Quarters in the background.

The Squadron reportedly organized the best dances on Bircham Newton base, and at one of these Tom met Stella Stringer, a twenty-one year old local single woman who lived in nearby Stanhoe. She was the mother of a four year old illegitimate son and a nanny for (Major) Lord Thomas William Edward Coke, the 5th Earl of Leicester at Holkham Hall in north Norfolk; and his wife Lady Elizabeth Mary (nee Yorke). She looked after their two daughters, Lady Anne Veronica, age nine and Lady Carey Elizabeth, age seven. One of Stella's sister's, Marjorie, also worked at Holkham Hall as a maid, along with Marjorie's husband, Lovell Loose, who was the family chauffeur. Lady Anne was a train-bearer at HM Queen Elizabeth II's Coronation in 1953; in 1956 she married Colin Tenant, Third Baron Glenconner. She was extra Lady-In-Waiting to HRH

"Titch" and "Slug" with cycles.

Princess Margaret, Countess of Snowdon between 1971 and 2002 and lived at East End Farm, Burnham Thorpe, Norfolk, before moving to Mustique and St Lucia. Lady Carey married Bryan Basset in 1960 and lives at Quarles, Wells-next-the-Sea, Norfolk. I contacted Lady Carey Coke (Basset) at her home during early 2010, she couldn't remember Stella, but she did remember Marjorie, and recalled when the family were living in Surbiton, in Surrey, when her father was a Major and she was aged just two and a half years old. They were driving near the Crystal Palace, which had just burnt down the night before (30 November 1936), when Marjorie lifted Lady Carey up to look out of the car window and said, "You will remember this day for the rest of your life!" (And she has).

Tom dated Stella (to be his future wife and my mother) regularly, but due to her having given birth to an illegitimate child, Trevor Stringer, my half-brother, her parents, John (Jack) and Florence (Florrie), already bringing up two of their children's offspring, did not want to have to bring up another child on a farm labourer's wage; and she was made to stay in. However, Tom would find a ladder and place it under Stella's bedroom window, a bit like "Romeo and Juliet", and they would carry on their "tryst" in the local GPO phone box, bus shelter, or a meadow, with dad using his RAF greatcoat as a groundsheet. I remember when I was an adult, Mum telling me of one occasion after an evening of "merriment", they got up only to find that Dad had placed his coat over a fresh cowpat! Mum also said that Ted Beales, who was the Docking and Stanhoe rural policeman, would turf them out of the phone box and bus shelter when he was around.

I knew Ted for his last two years of service when I joined Norfolk Constabulary as a Constable during 1966 and later as a Special Constable. Locals referred to him as "Dixon of Docking" or "Beales on Wheels", the latter, as he always performed his duties on a bicycle.

Ted recalled in an interview with the *Lynn News* in 1992, that at the "Norfolk Hero" pub (previously known as the "The Nelson" and "The Hero") situated on the Bircham Road, Stanhoe, frequented by airmen from Bircham; the bar staff would sell the airmen beer by the pail. A group of them would club together and buy a pail of beer, which they would consume throughout the evening by dipping their glasses in the pail. It so happens that Stella's parents (my grandparents) would run this pub during the war, which I did not learn until recently and that this venue was very popular with all of the various squadrons based at Bircham Newton at that time.

Amongst them was Bill Davis, a Wop/AG on 521 "Met Office" Squadron, during 1942 and 1943, flying Blenheims and Hudsons, and it was one of his favourite drinking haunts, and an escape from the horrors of the war. He describes one party when the squadron

PC Ted Beales, one of Docking's wartime policemen.

Jack (John) and Florrie (Florence) Stringer taken in 1952.

Pilot	Navigator	WOp/AG	A/G	A/G
A Flight				
W/Cdr Lynham	F/Sgt Harrington	F/Sgt Singleton	F/Lt Creeggan	
S/Ldr Pye	Sgt Cave	Sgt Lees	P/O Puxley	P/O Knight
F/Lt Fitchew	Sgt Cheslyn	F/Sgt Field	P/O Webdell	F/Sgt Burns
P/O McKimm	Sgt Frost	Sgt Buller	Sgt John	F/Sgt Hollingworth
F/Sgt Marchand	P/O Stephenson	Sgt Preece		
Sgt Groom*	Sgt Evans	Sgt Gendron		
P/O Heywood	F/Sgt Slugoski	F/Sgt Orr	F/Sgt Clark ●	Sgt Stapleton*
P/O Zumar	Sgt Edgley	Sgt Adams FA	Sgt Wallis	Sgt McFadden
F/Sgt Faux	Sgt Bedale	Sgt Darwin		
	Sgt Campbell	F/Sgt Aslett		
Sgt Woolford	WO Lansdall			
Sgt Kitteringham*	Sgt Beard*	Sgt Barnes*	Sgt Bailey	

Tom still with his original crew, end of September 1942.

bought all of the beer available in the pub for a private party, hanging a "no beer" sign on the door to discourage anyone else from using the pub. Beer was served in buckets as usual, and twelve squadron members consumed approximately 144 pints of it. When they had consumed all of the beer, two of them were sent to the next pub in the village ("The Crown", now "The Duck"), to obtain two more pails full. Bill recalled that everyone finished up "very tight" and had a grand time singing to their heart's content. Their only regret was that they had to be up early for an operational trip. Ex-pilot, Frank Goff, who in 1941, was serving at Bircham on 206 Hudson Squadron, (and later in 1944 would serve on 279 Squadron) thought that the practice of serving beer in a pail had started during his first tour, whilst on 206 Squadron.

The Hero was a favourite drinking place for squadron personnel at that time. He recalled: "The beer was kept in wooden barrels in a kind of outdoor lean-to (a scullery), which would keep it nice and cool. However, it took an age for the landlord to pour each pint from the barrel, so the airmen borrowed a NAFFI pail, which they took to the pub for the landlord to fill while they were enjoying their first drinks. After

Frank Goff in 1941.

The Norfolk Hero Public House, Bircham Road, Stanhoe.

a time, they marked the pail with the squadron's number and left it at the pub for use on subsequent occasions."

I contacted Frank Goff by phone calls and letters, with regard to his time at Bircham Newton and his 279 Squadron times. This is what he wrote to me:

"I was with 279 for most of 1944 so did not meet Tom Clark; who was with them from late 1941 to early 1943. At that time in 1944 we had three Hudsons fitted with the airborne lifeboat. We had one incident where one of the gunners had his life saved through drinking and smoking! We were on a search of the Norfolk Coast when one of the aircraft plunged into the sea. The rear turret broke off and the gunner floated to the surface and was picked up by a salvage vessel. He had been on a heavy drinking party the night before and just changed to the turret so he could have a smoke! There's not many of us left as most are dead." Frank Goff, 23 September 2009.

This is a passage from a narrative from WAAF Cpl Eunice Ravell: "The local pub, the 'Norfolk Hero' was situated on Bircham Road, about a mile and a half from the Bircham Newton camp, and it was downhill to cycle there, and uphill to cycle back, which was the wrong way round for drunks! It was a spartan place, with a stone floor and benches all around, and a blazing fire in winter, where the bar staff got the poker red hot and plunged it into a bucket of slap ale, to mull it, and then ladled it all round into everyone's mugs. It was matey and warming, the air thick with Norfolk accents, and after a time, one of the locals would get up and do a clog dance on the stone floor, while others clapped to the rhythm."

Tom and Stella carried on their courtship throughout 1942, until it was rudely interrupted by Tom being posted in early 1943 to the Desert Air Force in Egypt, and then Italy, where he remained until 1945, and then brought me home!

During the autumn and into the winter of 1942, Tom had a spell on Squadron Leader Pye's team on "A" Flight of 279 Squadron; this consisted of Pye as Pilot, Pilot Officer Cave as Navigator, Flight Sergeant Lees as Wireless Operator/Air Gunner, Flying Officer Knight as Air Gunner, and Tom, Flight Sergeant Clark as Air Gunner.

He was shown as the fifth member of that crew as at 1 January 1943. His old crew were supplemented by Flight Sergeant Saunders and Sergeant Groome as Air Gunners.

On 27 September, Tom was on detachment with the squadron at St Eval in Cornwall; covering the southern approaches and the Bay of Biscay. On 6 October he was back at Bircham Newton, before a further stint at St Eval on the 31 October.

Leading Aircraftsman Ernest Farrow remembers the many detachments of 279 Squadron aircraft and personnel: "279 had permanent detachments at two airfields. Two aircraft were based at Benbecula, in the Outer Hebrides, covering the Western Approaches, a route used by Ferry Command flying aircraft from North America. The second deployment was at St Eval in Cornwall, where the squadron covered the Bay of Biscay. Several successful rescues were made in this area. One that was not successful involved a Canadian pilot, Flying Officer Zumar, whose brother was lost over the Bay of Biscay. Flying Officer Zumar flew three six-hour missions and was prepared to fly a fourth until ordered to stand down due to fatigue. The St Eval detachment was always reinforced from Bircham when dignitaries were flying back to, or away from, the UK. On one occasion Winston Churchill, who had been to a conference in North Africa, was well covered by at least five aircraft. I was also at St Eval when three German Generals, who had been captured in the Western Desert, were flown back to Britain for internment. Our squadron also had temporary detachments to Leuchars in Fife, covering Beaufighters equipped with torpedoes, which were attacking enemy shipping off the coast of Norway."

Gunnery Leader

On Monday, 11 November 1942, Tom was posted to a Gunnery Leaders Course, situated at the Central Gunnery School at Sutton Bridge, on the Lincolnshire/Norfolk border, close to The Wash.

The first weekend leave saw him back at Bircham Newton, as on Friday, 16 November 1942, 279 Squadron held a dance to celebrate the first year of its existence; this would be Tom's last one before exchanging Britain's winter for the heat of the Egyptian Desert. Tom did miss a successful search and

Gunnery Leaders Course, Sutton Bridge. Tom middle row second from left.

rescue on 13 November from St Eval, where his old crew were attached. Three Hudsons from St Eval were ordered to look for a missing Whitley crew from No. 10 OTU, it was unsuccessful initially, but on the following day Pilot Officer Stephenson worked out a new search area, which resulted in the sighting of six survivors in a dinghy 170 miles south-west of the Scillies. Pilot Officer J.P. "Phil" Heywood and his crew of "Slug" Slugoski, "Ginger" Orr and Sergeant Groome, in Tom's position, who were searching in company with McKimm and Marchand's crews, spotted the dinghy. A Lindholme dingy was accurately dropped to the survivors who were subsequently picked up by destroyer the following day.

The Sutton Bridge Camp had hutted accommodation, these included living/sleeping quarters, messes, a hospital and a NAFFI, where the men were fed and watered and could buy groceries. Gunnery training consisted of two main practices; air-to-ground and air–to-air. The ground targets were mainly located along the marsh and sand banked shore of The Wash, between Holbeach Marsh and Wainfleet, over which the RAF had rights to some seven and a half miles, and extending to about eight thousand yards out to sea. These targets consisted of old aeroplane fabric stretched over framework, each with a large Roman numeral indicating the target number.

Wellington Bombers (known as "Wimpies") were used and the course students were split into fours and allocated an aircraft; one in the Navigator's position, one at the Wireless, one in the crash position at the main spar of the wing, and one in the second pilot's position. To board a Wellington, the crew had to enter from underneath and climb into the aircraft through the second pilot's position. When everyone was in position, a piece of board was put down over the hole and that was the seat for the second pilot, with a couple of "stirrups" folded out from the sides for footrests. The air-to-air firing was at flags or drogues towed by one of the station aircraft, generally on a cable some 1000 feet long.

After the flag target had been fired at, the towing aircraft dropped it to the ground and then released a drogue type – without having to land – this target resembled a wind sock. In order to make the most use of the drogue, the bullets fired at it during different practices were smeared with different coloured paint. This left distinguishing marks around the holes caused during each practice, after various attacks, the drogue was also dropped to the ground for marking. Under normal conditions, firing was carried out between ranges of one hundred and three hundred yards.

The Station Commander at RAF Sutton Bridge from 5 September 1942, until 26 November 1943, was Captain J. Beamish, and the Officer Commanding Gunnery Leader (Bomber Wing) from June 1942 until June 1943, was Wing Commander J.J. Sutton.

On 1 December, Tom was made a Flight Sergeant Wireless Operator/Air Gunner Grade 1; and he completed the 49th Gunnery Leaders Course on Friday, 21 December 1942, attaining an 82.2 percent pass and his proficiency was graded as A, Superior and B Satisfactory and his character was described as Very Good. A Gunnery Leader was a specialized position devised and developed during the Second World War for Bomber Squadrons. The Gunnery Leader took charge of battle operations for the formation, and would command and control it as a "single leader" in the event of air-to-air combat when in flying formation.

This is what "Monty" Dean, a former Second World War member of 55 Squadron had to say with regard to Tom's Gunnery Leader qualification: "His original training, leading to his Air Gunner's badge would have been concerned with knowing the actual weapons inside out, and with handling, aiming and firing them. The Gunnery Leader Course would have added training on the tactical application of fire power and the Gunnery Leader would, under various circumstances, have advised the Commanding Officer on gunnery matters, taking responsibility for the efficiency of the unit, Air Gunners routine duties (cleaning guns etc), organized training to keep the unit gunners up to date and operationally, would have had an input into directing the fire of a formation."

Tom was able to get back to Bircham Newton in time for 279 Squadron's 1942 Christmas.

XMAS FARE 1942 Sergeants Mess RAF Station Bircham Newton Programme

Wednesday December 23rd 2015 hours Cinema Show Sgt York
Thursday Christmas Eve 1930 hours Dance
Friday Christmas Day 1145 hours Visiting Airmen's Mess
1200 hours A "Help Yourself" Running Buffet
1515 hours Will Be Open In The Servery
1520 hours Repeat Cinema Show
1800 hours Christmas Dinner +
1900 hours Mess Staff Dinner
2000 hours FUN & GAMES Including
Dancing To Radiogram, Mixed Partners
Indoor Games Competition
Grand Inter-Section "UCKERS" Championship
Saturday Boxing Day Dance at 1930 hours

Christmas Dinner Menu
Soup
. . . . . .
Roast Turkey & Stuffing
. . . .
Roast Chicken & Bread Sauce
. . . .
Roast Pork & Apple Sauce
. . . .
Brussels Sprouts
Mashed & Boiled Potatoes
. . . .
Christmas Pudding & Sauce
. . . .
*Mince Pies * Trifle*
. . . .
Cheese & Biscuits
. . . .
Fruit Coffee*Cigarettes Beer & Spirits*

On 31 December, Tom's personnel record had been endorsed as follows: Rank, T/Flight Sgt., Character Very Good, and Trade Wireless Operator/Air Gunner 1. Proficiency, A Superior, B Satisfactory (this classification would again be endorsed on the 13 May 1943, when he was at Gianaclis and on promotion to Flying Officer). His last duty with 279 Squadron was on the 11 January 1943 and on the 12 January he was at Service Personnel Despatch Centre at Uxbridge awaiting posting overseas.

During 279's first year, the squadron had found a total of fifteen dinghies containing seventy-four RAF aircrew and three lifeboats with twenty-three seamen, making a total of ninety-seven lives saved.

Just before Tom left 279 at Bircham Newton, and whilst on his Gunnery Leaders Course, his old crew of Heywood, Slugoski, and Orr, suffered a near fatal attack incident on 30 November 1942, when Flight Sergeant Groome had taken Tom's place as rear facing Air Gunner. Pilot Officer Heywood sighted two Fokke Wulf 190s which attacked his aircraft from beneath and astern, both scored hits on the Hudson. "Ginger" Orr had his gun turret put out of action and he was wounded in the head. Sergeant Groome was also injured and both he and Orr were hospitalized. Here is a copy of the preliminary combat report of the incident, which gives a graphic account of what it was like to be under enemy fire:

"Pilot Officer Heywood in aircraft 'L' (V8993) was flying on an easterly course one mile to port and slightly behind aircraft 'N' (V8999). Both enemy aircraft were sighted and identified at approximately 700 yards range. Aircraft 'L' opened up fully and headed for 'N', hoping to formulate, but both aircraft turned to starboard. Enemy aircraft on the port side started attack from the port quarter and port side; gunner of Hudson fired a burst at approximately 400 yards. Rear gunner instructed pilot to do a steep climb turning to port and own aircraft successfully evaded fire from this attack. Second enemy aircraft immediately came in from starboard quarter and carried out an attack from astern and below. At this time through haze, 'N' and 'L' lost contact. It also wounded rear gunner and through hits in the turrets put one gun u/s. Starboard side gun was also hit and jammed magazine. Hudson then climbed ahead without rudder control and entered cloud at 2,500 feet.

"During this time more attacks were carried out either three or four in number, and it was then found that the intercom had also been rendered u/s in this first attack. Pilot was only able to hear rear gunner very faintly and was in any case, unable to take evasive action. Those subsequent attacks were all carried out from below and astern and consequently rear gunner was unable to open fire, excepting on the last attack when enemy aircraft appeared to think that rear gunner must be out of action. On this attack he came in to thirty yards and enabled rear gunner to get a burst in at that range as he came up dead astern, instead of beneath. Although the rear gunner cannot definitely claim hits, the enemy aircraft then broke off his attack and allowed Hudson to gain cloud cover. The estimated time of combat was three to four minutes".

At a different place and time, Tom would have been that rear gunner, who knows how many close shaves he was involved in and how many enemy fighters he shot down or deterred whilst with 201 and 279 Squadrons.

A couple of worthy notes before we leave 279 Squadron. About the same time that Tom left; Phil Heywood and "Ginger" Orr also moved on, and the original crew was broken up. Flight Sergeant Saunders and Sergeant Groome moved onto a crew including Flying Officer Sherwood as Pilot, and Flying Officer Tidswell as Navigator. On the 4 February 1943, "Slug" Slugoski, Tom's friend and former colleague, not having a crew of his own, was the Navigator on board Hudson E (T9398), the original aircraft of his former crew, making a search for crashed aircraft personnel off the north Norfolk coast at Happisburgh (pronounced Hazeborough), near Cromer. Flight Sergeant Marchand was Pilot, Flying Officer Stephenson Navigator, and Flight Sergeant Adams Wireless Operator/Air Gunner. The plane developed difficulties and crashed into the North Sea, and despite a large search of the area, no trace was found of the aircraft, wreckage, or crew; the cold waters of the North Sea had claimed four more young victims, including Tom's friend.

Now that 279 Squadron had become fully operational, during April 1943, a ceremony was held at Bircham Newton at which the Squadron Crest was presented by the AOC No. 16 Group.

I have what I believe to be, an original plate drawn by the College of Arms in January 1943 and "Approved" by His Majesty King George V1. It has his endorsement on the front and on the rear it is dated April 2nd 1943.

Chapter Five

"Gianaclis End of the Desert War And Italy"

1943

We now set the scene of Tom's next Posting, 75 O.T.U. Gianaclis.

75 Operational Training Unit (O.T.U.) Gianaclis, Egypt.

No 75 O.T.U. RAF ME (Middle East) was originally set up from Britain during 1942 from the former 75 (GR) O.T.U. to provide seventeen crews per month for squadrons operating in the Middle East during 1943. The unit left England on 22 August 1942, and arrived in Durban, South Africa on 29 September. On the 13 November, they embarked for Aden, where they arrived on 30 November 1942. On 6 December they disembarked at Port Tewfik, where they were placed under the command of 201 Group.

An advance party comprising of three officers and sixty-five other ranks proceeded to Gianaclis for the purpose of erecting the additional tentage required, and to prepare the site for the remaining personnel. They left Aboukir, situated on the Mediterranean coast of Egypt, near to Alexandria, on 8 December and arrived at Gianaclis 75 O.T.U. in mid December 1942. Jack Farley was an RAF Wireless Operator/ Air Gunner who was at 75 OTU in December 1942.

Here he narrates the journey: "The journey from Avonmouth, Bristol, to South Africa took nearly six weeks. During that time I had to man an anti-aircraft gun position on board the troopship with an airman as ammunition loader. At Clarewood Transit Camp near Durban, we slept under canvas for six weeks, before boarding a former enemy liner which took us to Egypt. During our time in the camp we were offered great hospitality by the local civilian population who invited many of us to their homes for meals and loaned us their cars. We arrived at Port Tewfik in Egypt, in early December 1942. We then travelled north to Suez, and on to an RAF base in the desert called Gianaclis, some forty miles south-west of Alexandria, where we established 75 OTU."

Tom would join him the following February and both would be there for the rest of 1943; Jack Farley first flew as an instructor on 2 March 1943, with Flying Officer A.W. Proctor as pilot, in Anson DJ569. I have continued Jack Farley's narrative where it overlaps Flight Sergeant Tom Clark joining the Training Unit.

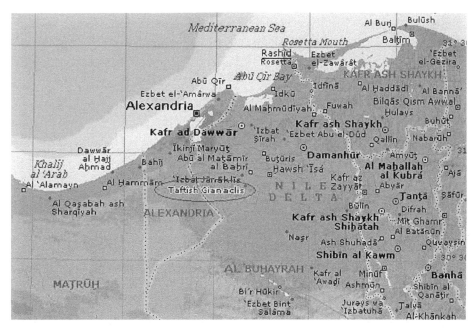

Location of Gianaclis encircled.

The following personnel embarked on the posting to the unit:

Group Captain E.A. Hodgson, Station Commander
Acting Wing Commander G.H. Wherry, DFC, Chief Flying Instructor
Acting Squadron Leader R.J. Peacock, DFC, Chief Ground Instructor
Acting Squadron Leader J.B. Levien, Navigational Instructor
Acting Squadron Leader E.N. Ventham, Senior Engineering Officer
Flight Lieutenant E.A. Townsend, Accountant Officer
Acting Flight Lieutenant J.K. Owens, Signals
Acting Flight Lieutenant T.A. Warren, Observer/Instructor
Acting Flight Lieutenant N.F. Waters–Webb, Flying Instructor
Acting Flight Lieutenant J.B. Wall, Signals (Radio)
Flying Officer L.A.M. Buckingham, Admin Duties Maintenance HQ
Pilot Officer G.B. Blackman, Code & Cypher
Pilot Officer W.A. Schrier, Link Trainer Instructor
Pilot Officer S.J. Clayton, Observer Instructor
Pilot Officer J.O. Knight, Observer Instructor
Pilot Officer T.H. Williams, Engineer Duties
Pilot Officer G. Davies, Physical Fitness & Welfare
Two Warrant Officers
Forty-four Senior NCO's
361 Corporals/Aircraftsmen

Here are some excerpts from the Operations Record Book of No 75 O.T.U. M.E,
narrated by the C.O., Group Captain E.A. Hodgson, whose shorthand typist was
LAC 1213534 Colin Pye:

1942.
8th Dec. Flt Lt T. Campbell–Davis, Equipment Officer; Acting Flt Lt T.G.M.
Young, Armament Officer; Acting F/O E. Smith Intelligence Officer, all posted
to unit 14th Dec. First aircraft three Ansons arrived but not equipped to meet
training purposes.

17th Dec. Further three Anson.
22nd Dec. All remaining personnel arrived from 24 PTC.
25th Dec. One Anson.
31st Dec. Six Anson.

1943.
1st Jan. One Anson.
2nd Jan. One Anson, one Bisley.
3rd Jan. One Bisley. Extremely heavy sandstorm experienced. This gave a very
large majority of the personnel of the unit their first idea of a storm of this nature.
Further three Anson arrive.

Warrant Officer Vic Brown, who was an Air Gunner with 55 Squadron in the
Desert Air Force mentions this storm in his War Diary: "Sunday January 3rd:
Rose 0700 and left Derna at 1030, had a rough trip back to LG86, it took two
and a half hours. I had gone to bed when the sand began to blow, and the tent
rocked until eventually the middle pole snapped, and we had to sit up until
0300 hours.We had to go out and put on the ropes, blinded by the dirt and
the tent was covered in it inches thick; I lay down exhausted and slept until
0800.

"Monday January 4th: The storm continued all day and it was impossible to
see, we just sat in the tent smothered in dirt; it continued until 1600 and I was
then able to have a wash and removed a lot of the dirt."

Back to 75 O.T.U. ORB:
8th Jan. Three Anson despatched to 132 MU for wiring and fitting of WT and
electrical equipment.
9th Jan. One Anson three Baltimore arrives.
On 12 January 1943, Tom was at the Service Personnel Despatch Centre, en
route to the Middle East and 75 O.T.U. (Operational Training Unit).

16th Jan. Wing Commander H.G. Wisher, and Pilot Officer G.F. Croaker arrived, posted to 75 O.T.U. Engineer and Code Cypher Duties respectively. Air Marshal Sir Hugh Lloyd, KBE, CB, MO, DFO, visits station.

Between 23 and 28 January further personnel were posted to 75 O.T.U. including Flight Lieutenant J.M. Welshman, Armament Instructor.

Vic Brown's Diary continues: "Monday January 20th: Today I went to a lecture on the Glen Martin turret, it is very small and it has many switches.

"Tuesday January 21st: Heard that we may be getting .50 guns in turrets. Took 'N' on an airtest, this involved forty minutes of low flying and messing about; we then flew in formation for one hour, weather very rough. The Germans are retreating in Tripolitania."

Barney Watkins was ground crew on 55 Squadron, he also kept a diary. "Coming out of the desert into Tunisia was so lovely! The soil was red and instead of miles and miles of sand, we started to chase 'Jerry' through miles and miles of mountains. Though we still had them on the run, Rommel was more used to this country. We heard also that Hitler had released 50,000 troops, guns, planes and tanks from the Russian Front. As most of the fighting was being done along the ten mile stretch of the coast road, Rommel also had to fight a rear guard action, so our hopes of reaching Tunis in double quick time went out of the window. We knew of course that our supplies were never interrupted and replacements were coming all the time. It was a matter of time that 'Jerry' would be pushed from one line of defence to another by the shell fire of the 8th Army, and our planes bombing round the clock.

"Rommel attempted to hold us up with lots of tanks and guns but after the heavy rain everything got bogged down. At this time the squadron was given a 'stand-down' which was very nice for me because, being a driver, I got extra duties going to the army dumps, collecting rations of meat, and fresh vegetables, and also being able to see more of the country. If I took Sgt Bond with me he made sure what was worth drinking! Our camp was right next to the sea, so there was plenty of swimming, and our tent was pitched beneath a grape vine, so it was a peaceful time. But not for long; 'Jerries' supplies were getting such a bashing he had to withdraw."

On 23 February 1943, Tom arrived at LG226 (Landing Ground 226) 75 O.T.U. (Operational Training Unit), Gianaclis, as a Qualified Gunnery Leader. There he was involved as a Gunnery Instructor, teaching Air Gunners their trade before they moved onto Western Desert Squadrons such as 55 and 223 Squadrons. 75 O.T.U. was reclassified Gianaclis on 24 March 1943 on Tom's Personnel Record.

Also, on 4 March 1943, Tom's brother, James Wares Clark (known as Wares), who was just under three years younger than Tom, joined the Royal Corps of Signals, from the Scottish Post Office, and trained at Prestatyn in North Wales. His stay was short-lived, as in that December he transferred to the Royal Navy

(Signals), and during 1944 served in the Middle East (strange how they both became Signallers by trade and were in the same area of theatre of war).

By the 11 March, Rommel had had enough of the British and his Afrika Corp slipped out of North Africa and across the Mediterranean to the Island of Sicily, the ball at the toe of Italy's boot.

In the extract from 75 O.T.U. Group Captain Hodgson has a conference on the 22 March 1943, with Wing Commander Mason from HQ ME, and Squadron Leader Horner of 201 Group, as to the future policy. This being to provide thirty-eight trained crews monthly. Group Captain Hodgson pointed out that an intake and output of thirty-eight crews monthly, on the basis of nineteen new crews every fortnight, would require approximately 120 aircraft. He also pointed out that the present aircraft provided were most unsatisfactory to train the current eleven crews on course. On 27 March, a further 112 airmen arrived on posting from the UK.

Sgt Tom Clark Gianaclis 1943 in desert uniform.

During May 1943, some trained elements of No 1 Course at 75 O.T.U. were posted to 459 Hudson Squadron, based at LG40 Burg-el-Arab, some forty miles west of Alexandria.

With reference to the submarine spotting exercise of 4 May, an instructor at 75 O.T.U. with Tom, Jack Farley, recalled: "It was while I was with 75 O.T.U. I had a narrow escape from a serious accident. On one training exercise our Avro Anson aircraft was due to stage a mock attack on a Royal Naval submarine just off the coast of Egypt. While I was in the process of instructing a trainee how to send a sighting report, the aircraft suddenly filled with smoke! The pilot, who had recently joined the O.T.U. from a Beaufighter Squadron, had to fire the colours of the day so the submarine could identify us. However, instead of opening his port window to fire the pistol, he fired it through the floor of the aircraft! The exercise was immediately aborted and we returned to base to discover a square

R.A.F. Form 540

*See Instructions for use of this form in K.R. and A.C.I.,
para. 2349, and War Manual, Pt. II., Chapter XX. and
note in R.A.F. Pocket Book.*

OPERATIONS RECORD BOOK

901.
14 APR 1943

of (Unit or formation)   NO.75 O.T.U. R.A.F. M.E.

Place	Date	Time	Summary of Events
Gianaclis	1943 March. 1st.		First course assembled and lectures commenced.
	1st.		Following officers arrived on the dates stated against their names, for Instructor Duties.
			Flying Officer C.BUTTERFIELD (129225) - 28.2.43 - Pilot
			" " C.A.COLLINS. (113923) - 28.2.43 - Navigator
			Pilot Officer B.E.T.ROSTRON. (158906) - 28.2.43 - Pilot
			F/O.(A/F/Lt.) M.J.GRIFFITHS. (109959) - 28.2.43 - Navigator
			Flying Officer A.W.PROCTOR, R.A.A.F. (A403073) - 28.2.43 - Pilot
			Flying Officer G.E. FERGUSON, R.A.A.F. (A404338) - 28.2.43 - Pilot
			F/O. (A/F/Lt.) H.D. FOOT. R.A.A.F. (A404095) - 1.3.43 - Pilot - For duty as Officer i/c C, & R. Flight.
			Pilot Officer I.D. DOCHERTY. (130715) - 1.3.43 - WOP/AG.
	2nd		Flying Officer G.K. CROWTHER. (106887) - Arrived for C.&C. Duties.
			Flight Lieutenant (A/S/L) A.H.BAYNES (77446) - Arrived for duty as Senior Medical Officer.
	3rd		2 Blenheim I's transferred from No.1 M.E.T.S. for use of Conversion and Refresher Flight.
			1 Blenheim IV " " " " " " " " " "
			2 Blenheim V's " " " " " " " " " "
	3rd		F/O. (A/S/Ldr) E.N. VENTHAM posted to No.71 O.T.U.
	4th		F/O. K.R.W. EAGER (63858) arrived for duty as Instructor (Pilot).
			Detachments of 459 Squadron (2 Hudsons) and 454 Squadron (2 Wellingtons) operated from here.
			Instructors completed 2 hours each night flying.
	5th		Detachment of 459 Squadron continued to operate from this aerodrome.
			F/Lt. H.F. HUDSPITH arrived on posting for Engineer Duties.
	6th		Instructors completed 3 hours night flying.

Page No. 2

Place	Date	Time	Summary of Events	References to Appendices
Gianaclis.	March 8th		Orders received from 201 Group to lay flare-path for operational aircraft. No operations carried out.	
	10th		Flying Officer B.J. HUGHES (107912) posted for Navigation Duties.	
	10th		Air Commodore J.R. SCARLETT-STREATFIELD, C.B.E., A.O.C. No.201 Group, and Group Captain N.H. O'Aeth visited the Station.	
	10th		First flying accident occurred. This was caused by the port tyre of Blenheim V, B.A.533 blowing out on landing, the aircraft being tipped on its nose. Category II assessment.	
	12th		A terrific windstorm occurred in the evening with gusts of approximately 60 to 70 miles per hour. The roofs of several of the newbrick buildings were blown off and the walls of certain buildings which were partly erected, were blown down. Fortunately no damage was sustained by any aircraft.	
	13th		Eight aircraft serviceable this morning.	
	15th		Night Flying by Instructors and Pupils.	
	16th		First Navigation exercises. Crews briefed at 06.00 hours but owing to unserviceability of aircraft allotted, were not airborne until 07.30 hours.	
	19th		Owing to extremely adverse weather conditions six aircraft on navigation flights were recalled with instructions to land at EDKU. Four of the aircraft landed here and two at EDKU.	
	20th		Yesterday's sandstorm continues and a signal despatched at 14.30 hours stating that aerodrome visibility was from 10 to 50 yards. All flying was cancelled at 12.00 hrs.	
	20th		Wing Commander H.G. WISHER posted from Station and Flight Lieutenant C.W.TEBB., M.B.E. assumed the duty of Chief Technical Officer.	
	21st.		Once again bad weather caused the cancellation of navigation flights. Of the six aircraft which took part in these flights, five landed here and one at EDKU. Flying for pupils subsequently cancelled for the day due to the continuation of the sand-storm which died down between 18-1900 hrs. The roof on the Photographic Section was lifted badly due to the storm.	
	22nd		Conference today with W/Cdr Mason. D.F.C. (H.Q.M.E.) and Squadron Leader HORNER, D.F.C. (No.201 Group) as to future policy, this being to provide 38 trained crews monthly. Pointed out that an intake and output of 38 crews monthly, on a basis of 19 crews every fortnight, would require approximately 120 aircraft. It was also pointed out that the present aircraft provided, was most unsatisfactory to train eleven crews and unless additional aircraft were received by 28th March, 1943, the operational training due to commence on 29th March 1943, would have to be postponed.	

Extract from 75 O.T.U. ORB.

Tented accommodation Gianaclis 1943.

Tom's Tent Mates ready for de-bugging Gianaclis 1943.

metre of the port wing where it joined the fuselage had burned away, just inches from the fuel line. If that line had been hit, the aircraft would have blown up and we would have all been killed."

With reference to the entry of 8 May; on the 12 May a body was washed up, on the beach at Idku and was identified as that of 1128675 Sergeant Bateman, Wireless Operator/Air Gunner. Jack Farley goes on: "There was one fatal accident while I was at 75 O.T.U.; one of the training crew crashed into the sea

Place	Date	Time	Summary of Events	References to Appendices
				Page No. 2
Gianaclis	6/5		through successfully. Three Blenheim I's L.1386, K.7161, and L.6815 arrived from 72 O.T.U. ferried by O.T.U. Staff and Pupil pilots. These are reported to be for Drogue Towing, but we have not been instructed as regards this.	
	7/5		S/Ldr. J.M. Milburn joined H.M. Destroyer -- to observe methods employed by the Navy. This practice will be followed, and as much of the Senior Instructor Staff as possible will be given these opportunities.	
			S/Ldr. Dunning, Command Gunnery Officer and F/Lt. Burns, Group Gunnery Officer visited this Station today. Flying was carried on by Anson and Conversion Flights, by the Baltimore Conversion Flight, and by the Blenheim Operational Flight, throughout the day. The remaining four Blenheim IV's, V.6157, Z9480, V.5949 and Z9805 were ferried by our own Staff Pilots from 135 M.U.	
			F/O. L.A.M. Buckingham, (A.&.S.D.) proceeded to 3. M.E.T.S. on a Junior Officers Adminstrative Course.	
	8/5		Anson No 34, pilot - Sgt. Barry and crew did not return from "Navigation 10" and were reported lost, ten miles out to sea from Aboukir.	
	9/5		F/O. Eager, airborne by 04.00 hours with F/Lt. Trigger as Observer, failed to locate aircraft or dinghy and returned to base at limited endurance. F/Lt. Shankland took over and has been assisted by one Bisley aircraft of 15 S.A.A.F. Five Anson aircraft with Staff Crews were briefed, and took off at 16.15 hours to carry out further extensive search. It is hoped that the wind may fall before evening and that small objects at sea will become easier to detect. No aircraft of Air Sea Rescue Flight were available.	
			Three Baltimores were ferried by Staff Pilots from No.135 M.U.	
			One Blenheim I, advised as being available at B.A.R.U., Helio by No.201 Group yesterday and confirmed today by telephone, was not available when the pilot called to collect it.	
			Postings for all pupils of No.1 Course, w,e,f, 12th May 1943, arrived today.	

R.A.F. Form 540

OPERATIONS RECORD BOOK

of (Unit or formation)   No.75 O.T.U. M.E.

Page No. 3.

No. of pages used for day

Place	Date	Time	Summary of Events	References to Appendices
Gianaclis	9/5		Squadrons 203, 244, and 459. F/O. F.L. Barcroft, Photography Officer, arrived on posting from No.22 P.T.C.	
	10/5		Two Hudson crews posted to this unit for Instructor duties from No. 459 Squadron arrived today. Visit by Wing Commander Revell, Command Navigation Officer.	
			F/O. L. Davies arrived on posting for Instructor duties.	
			F/O. F.W. Madsen arrived on posting for Instructor duties.	
			Blenheim aircraft L.8517 arrived from No.70 O.T.U.	
	11/5		Five aircraft briefed with crews of No.2 Course and Staff Pilots and Wireless Operators, for anti-submarine exercise. Take-off 13.30 hours - return to base 18.00 hours.	
			Arrangements made today for C. & R. Flight to move to South West corner of aerodrome. Anson Flight will move tomorrow if convenient.	
	12/5		Baltimore "H" crashed on landing. This aircraft belongs to C. & R. Flight. Cat.II Station was visited by Air Commodore M.L. Taylor, C.B.E. A.F.C., A.O.C. Training and Group Captain Mermagen, S.A.S.O.	
			It was reported to the Controller that a body had been picked up on the beach at Idku, which was identified as that of 1138875 Sgt. Bateman, Wireless Operator, Air Gunner.	
			Night Flying programme carried through successfully.	
			F/Lt. R.M. Lemonius arrived on posting from M.A.P.O. for duty as Equipment Officer.	
	13/5		Arrangements made by 201 Group for the funeral of Sgt. Batemanon Friday 14th May 1943 at 14.00 hours. Bearer party of Wireless Operator, Air Gunners provided by this Station.	
			W/Cdr. G.H. Wherry, D.F.C. proceeded to Shallufa for Court of Enquiry on the Flying accident.	

Extract from 75 O.T.U. ORB relating to the finding of a body.

Avro Anson at the Imperial war museum Duxford showing the rear gunner dorsal position.

on a night flying exercise. The bodies were recovered later and given a military funeral in Alexandria and the instructors, including myself, carried the remains."

On Thursday, 13 May 1943, Tom's NCO personnel record was endorsed, "Discharged on his appointment to Commission"; he had served 3 years and 335 days as other ranks. On Friday, 14 May 1943, he received an Emergency Commission Flying Officer rank on probation, General Duties Branch RAF, when he was recommended for appointment to Commission Rank from the incoming (10 May 1943) AOC of No. 203 Group, Air Vice-Marshal Malcolm Lincoln Taylor.

On 14 May 1943, Tom was still at 75 O.T.U. Middle East, at Gianaclis, in Egypt, now as a commissioned officer, a Flying Officer Gunnery Leader Instructor. Gianaclis had been formed on 8 December 1942, formerly Landing Ground 226, as a General Reconnaissance Training Unit to convert crews to local flying conditions. The trained crews then went on to Middle East Air Force (MEAF) Squadrons to replace those killed or injured in action, or time expired crews. On the 10 May 1943, 75 O.T.U had joined 203 Group, and the group was under the leadership of Air Vice-Marshal M.L. Taylor. 75 O.T.U. was at that time equipped with twenty-eight Hudson Mk III. Later other aircraft complimented its fleet, including Anson MkI, Blenheim Mk I, IV and V, Baltimore MkI-V,

Beaufort Mk I & II, Ventura Mk V and Wellington Mk XIV with support aircraft consisting of Oxford, Argus, Beaufighter, Defiant and Hurricane.

Two other aircraft crashes which occurred whilst Tom was at 75 O.T.U. Gianaclis, were 1 May 1943, Bristol Blenheim Mk I L8383, and 19 June 1943, Bristol Blenheim Mk I L1098.

One anonymous crew member narrated the following: "We had all been sent to the Middle East instead of Bomber Command in the UK and that is where we first met each other, in the mess. A nucleus of the crew was formed by the three of us and we awaited a Navigator/Bomb Aimer. A few days later, the four of us found ourselves in a road convoy on our way across the Sinai Desert to Egypt, pausing for the night at the lousy flea ridden transit camp of Port Tewfik opposite Suez. There was no sleep that night as the ferocious fleas

Photograph of Tom taken on promotion to Flying Officer Emergency Commission "Cometh the hour cometh the man".

fed on us poor mortals. Next day we were on our way to 75 O.T.U. in the desert west of Cairo, at a place called Gianaclis, which I remember as a place of hard clay pans and sand. It was to be our home until we became familiar with the Baltimore light bomber. Our 'sprog' crew did not see much of each other for the first couple of weeks as our Pilot converted to this twin engine aircraft. Our Navigator/Bomb Aimer learned to fit himself into and work in the confined space of his 'office' in the almost fully Perspex nose. The Wop/AG and I myself, the Air Gunner, found out all we could about the radio; the gun turret with its .50 cal twin guns, the .30 cal loose mounted bottom gun; and the rest of the bits and pieces in our domain. Eventually we came together as a crew and finished the O.T.U. course with pretty decent results."

At 75 O.T.U. Gianaclis, other crews were being put through their paces in order to join the ever expanding need for fresh crews. Flight Lieutenant Peter Henry Lambert, a South African, was one of these "fresh men". He converted onto Blenheim Mk I, 4 and 5 on the 6 July 1943, and then onto Baltimores between 17 and 22 July; before transferring and going on operations with 15 Squadron, SAAF.

At Gianaclis, Group Captain A.P.R. Revington, OBE, AFC, had taken over from Group Captain Hodgson as Commanding Officer on 16 July 1943.

AUTHORISED ESTABLISHMENT		RANK AND NAME OF OFFICER OR AIRMAN PILOT FILLING VACANCY	BRANCH OF SERVICE	DATE POSTED	IDENTITY DISC. No.	REMARKS
Rank	Duties	Name				

FIVE TRAINING FLIGHTS (Cont).

		Sgt Ferrand R.	WOP/AG	22.9.43	1059382	
Sgt	A/G(W/Op)	F/S Gregg H.L.	WOP/AG	8.7.43	1187226	
Sgt	A/G(W/Op)	F/S Harrison W.C.	WOP/AG	25.8.43	1101056	
Sgt	A/G(W/Op)	F/S Ladbrook S.G.W.	WOP/AG	2.10.43	952781	Det
Sgt	A/G(W/Op)	Sgt Burrell J.C.	WOP/AG	25.8.42	NZ411062	Det
		Sgt Trump R.S.	WOP/AG	7.4.43	1360455	
tSgt	A/G(W/Op)	Sgt Ward V.J.	WOP/AG	19.7.43	915488	Det
Sgt	A/G(W/Op)	Sgt Carruthers C.L.	WOP/AG	27.11.43	1190734	
Sgt	A/G(W/Op)	F/S Gillard B.I.	WOP/AG	9.7.43	A405807	
Sgt	A/G(W/Op)					

MAINTENANCE WING HEADQUARTERS.

F/O	Admin(G)	F/O L.A.M. BUCKINGHAM	A&SD(Ad)	25.8.42	110109	A/R/C
W/Cdr	Eng.	S/Ldr(A/W/C) L.T. WRIGHT	T(E)	11.11.43	35326	
F/Lt	Eng.	P/O A.C.P. Campodonic	T(E)	14.8.43	51813	
F/O	Eng(Elct)	F/O G.P.Bugden	T(E)Elec	28.6.43	114721	

MAINTENANCE SQUADRON.

F/Lt	Eng(G)	F/O(A/F/L) F.J.Gibney	T(E)	20.10.43	118086	A/F/L

SERVICING SQUADRON.

F/Lt	Eng(G)	F/O(A/F/L) R.B.Griffiths	T(E)	11.10.43	46049	A/F/L

'B' OFFICERS AND AIRMEN PILOTS, AIR OBSERVERS AND AIR GUNNERS ON THE
STRENGTH OF THE UNIT NOT FILLING VACANCIES IN THE ESTABLISHMENT.

(i) NON FLYING PERSONNEL.

F/Lt J. Ireland	Dental	8.8.43	102281	
S/Ldr (Rev) T.R. Owen	Chaplin	18.10.43	88379	
Capt Z.Popovic	T(E)	8.7.43	Y.490	R.Y.S.
P/O F. Wells	Education	19.10.43	156725	

(ii) INSTRUCTOR PERSONNEL.

F/Lt(A/S/L) J.P. Balfour DFM	Pilot	22.4.43	44872	A/S/L Det HQ RAF ME 20.9.43
F/Lt D.I. Brown	Pilot	4.4.43	108985	
F/Lt N.Evans	Pilot	27.11.43	A403671	
F/O J.K. Norwell	Pilot	29.6.43	129717	
F/Lt A.R. Tubbenhauer	Pilot	28.11.43	A402895	
F/O W.I. Chapman	Nav(W)	14.5.43	142921	
F/O R.G. Hampton	Nav.B	28.11.43	A406077	
P/O S.W. Taylor	Nav.B.	28.11.43	A405087	
F/O J.B. Westgate	Nav.B.	25.11.43	136055	
P/O A.G. Wintle	Nav.B.	16.9.43	156016	
W/O Duce E.B.	Nav.B.	27.11.43	A406229	
F/S Evans W.D.	Nav.B.	25.10.43	1252556	
W/O Hughes D.A.	Nav.B.	18.11.43	1380450	
Sgt Noble K.C.H.	Nav.B.	7.10.43	1515035	
F/S Scott R.W.E.	Nav.B.	27.11.43	1055961	
F/S Watkins T.M.	Nav.B.	28.2.43	616571	
F/O D. Baird	WOP/AG	27.11.43	A405704	
F/O R.P. Clancey	WOP/AG	10.5.43	A405146	
F/O A.V. Cliffe	WOP/AG	14.5.43	NZ405075	
F/O T.B. Clark	WOP/AG		52222	
2/Lt S. Fourie	WOP/AG	2.10.43	118497	
F/O E.V. Gayer	WOP/AG	14.8.43	A400704	
F/O W.J. Greer	WOP/AG	27.11.43	d.8601	
Lt. L. Havemann	WOP/AG	2.10.43	209357	

List of trained personnel for August 1943.

Opposite is the list of some of the instructors, including Tom, who were based at the unit at that time.

At 75 O.T.U. Gianaclis, No. 10 Course had completed its flying, and on the 19 December its former Commanding Officer, Group Captain E.A. Hodgson, now CO of Cairo West, visited the station by air.

On 22 December 1943, Tom's brother, James "Wares" Clark, transferred to the Royal Navy (Signals) and did his training at HMS Mercury, a shore establishment situated at Leydene House, East Meon, near Petersfield in Hampshire, and at the wireless telegraphy school at St Bede's Prep School, in Eastbourne.

At Gianaclis on Christmas Day 1943, a full programme was embarked upon, dry sunny weather making outdoor activities possible. Church services, a special football match, and a donkey gymkhana were held during the morning. Christmas Dinner for the airmen was held in one sitting, with six E.P.I.P's having been erected specifically for the overflow from the dining halls.

On the 27 December, the AOC of No 203 Group, Air Commodore M.L. Taylor, CBE, AFC, arrived by air and visited most sections of the station. Tom celebrated the old year and looked forward to the new one, which was to bring probably the most exciting and dangerous period of his Second World War service; this time in Bomber Command and in the front line.

1944

A notable advance in the system of cooperation with the ground forces was initiated during the first winter in Italy. Previously targets on the battlefield had been described and their attacks requested by army officers stationed at Wing and Group HQ, whereupon, after due consultation, the appropriate squadrons were detailed and pilots briefed for the attack. But now mobile observation posts were established, with the forward troops at Brigade HQ and in direct communication, via radio-telephone, with a squadron or squadrons already airborne. The pilots carried a photographic map with a grid superimposed upon it, and by using the same map, controllers gave them their targets. The area of operation would be settled on the evening preceding each day of battle, at a conference attended by representatives of the Army and Air Force.

In operation the plan was simple and direct; a squadron of fighters or fighter-bombers would patrol overhead, in line astern; on receiving a request from the Army for attack on a specific target, the controller would call up his pilots and give them its position, along with a short description of its nature. A few seconds later, one or more aircraft from the formation, or "cab rank" as it was soon known, would dive upon it and drop bombs or open fire with cannon. The scheme proved an instant success, for now fixed or moving targets could be bombed, or subjected to cannon or machine-gun fire very swiftly; often within a matter of minutes after they had been chosen. At first operations were controlled from armoured cars fitted with very high-frequency radio transmitters, but soon the equipment included a lorry, a jeep and a trailer manned by an Army and an RAF officer with a mechanic. The absence of the Luftwaffe over the battlefields had made this scheme possible.

On 16 January 1944, General Clark conferred together with Generals Eisenhower and Alexander, the supreme Allied Commanders, on a new Monte Cassino offensive, which, if won, would take the "Gustav Line". The diversion of the amphibious operation at Anzio would divert German resources and cut the supply route to their Tenth Army and force a withdrawal from the "Gustav Line". First, Clark had to take the town of Cassino, the anchor of the German defence. This was dominated by a 900 feet high hill which commanded a view of the valley; atop of the rise was Monte Cassino; a Benedictine Monastery, which the Allies knew that the Germans would use as a safe vantage point from which to aim their artillery fire into the valley below. Reaching the German defences would be no easy task as they were fronted by the Garigliano and Rapido Rivers. The following day, the 17 January, three divisions of allies crossed the Rapido River and they secured a beachhead, and more ground was secured during the ensuing days. This attack resulted in the German reserves moving to the "Gustav Line" and on 22 January, troops led by General John Lucas, landed at Anzio; but he decided not to push ahead straight away to the Alban Hills as ordered. This enabled General Vietinghoff to order the German Fourteenth Army to return to the area and contain the Allied Sixth Corps on the Anzio bridgehead.

The dorsal guns on the early models of the Baltimore soon proved to be troublesome, and were blamed, perhaps unfairly, for heavy losses suffered in an early mission on 23 May 1942, in which four unescorted Baltimores were all shot down by Messerschmitt Bf 109s. The existing aircraft all had their American Brownings replaced by British equivalents on a different mounting, and unescorted missions came to an end. So when Tom eventually joined 55 Squadron as a rear facing Air Gunner, the technical problems with the weaponry had been sorted out. Unlike the Sunderland

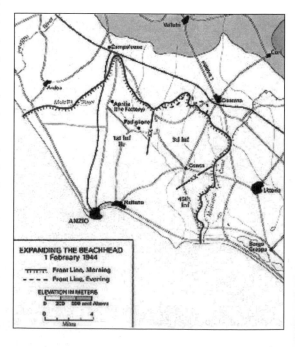

EXPANDING THE BEACHHEAD
1 February 1944

and Hudson that were twin finned, the Baltimore had a single central fin which could get in the way of sighting enemy aircraft coming up behind. The RAF eventually placed three orders for the Baltimore. The first, for four hundred aircraft and placed in May 1940 resulted in the delivery of fifty Baltimore Is and 250 Baltimore IIIs. The second order, for 575 aircraft, was placed in June 1941 and produced 281 Baltimore IIIAs and 294 Baltimore IVs. The final order, for 600 aircraft, was placed in July 1942. All 600 aircraft were delivered as Baltimore Vs.

The Baltimore had the same wingspan as the Maryland, and was only slightly longer, but had a wider and deeper fuselage, giving the four-strong crew a limited ability to move between the three crew positions; the fuselage was still too narrow for easy movements, as Tom would find out to his cost on 26 June 1944. The Baltimore I carried four more guns than the Maryland, with four fixed Browning machine guns in the wings, one each in the dorsal (Tom's position) and ventral positions and four fixed guns to fire downwards and to the rear. The Baltimore was powered by 1,660hp Wright GT-2600 engines, which more than made up for the increase in weight, and gave a top speed of just over 300mph and the capability to carry 2000lbs of bombs. The Baltimore was the second most numerous Martin aircraft, after only the B-26 Marauder. It was given the American designation A-30, but never entered USAF service.

Bomber Command Crest.

Number 55 Squadron Motto "Nil Nos Tremefacit" "Nothing Shakes Us".

Poem Bird Life–The Lesser Half–Brevet

By an unknown New Zealand Air Gunner

Come all ye men of tongue and pen
Who spend your nights and days,
By press or mike– just as you like,
The pilot's deeds to praise.
Publicity – it seems to me,
Should still find time to sing,
A song of love – in favour of–
The Bird of the single wing.
Who mans the guns to keep the huns
Off the back of the pilot's neck?
Who will twist and turn till his eyeballs burn
As he searches the sky for a speck?
Who will first expose his unfortunate nose
To the Fokke-Wulf's murderous sting?
Ask the pilot he'll tell you to see
The Bird of the single wing.
And who must know all his radio
From "A" to the bitter "Z"?
Able to read what some clot has keyed
In a fit of insanity?
Who's got to crawl in a space so small
That a cat you could never swing?
This contortionist I present to you
Is the Bird on the single wing.
Who gets the girls with the heavenly curls
And the lips like a cupid's bow?
And sings out "Ooh! You wonderful you,
How high do you really go?"
On whose manly chest does her little head rest,
As his nose gets set for the ring?
On the pilot's of course–she'd have to use force
On the Bird of the single wing"

During January 1944, Wing Commander Joel left 55 Squadron with a further Bar to his DFC (Distinguished Flying Cross) and on 17 January his place was taken by Wing Commander "Cookie" Leon. The write-up to Joel's Bar reads: "Joel, now on his third tour of operations over East Africa, Western Desert, Sicily and Italy. An excellent Squadron Commander, he has always evinced outstanding qualities of leadership and determination, attacking at low-level in adverse weather to ensure accuracy of aim. During the evacuation of Sicily he led his squadron against the beaches of Messina, setting a fine example of courage and devotion to duty."

Wing Commander Lionel Edward "Cookie" Leon, DSO, DFC, born in Johannesburg, South Africa.

"Cookie" Leon was another of the Royal Air Force's leading bomber pilots and another colonial; he served in the Desert Air Force in the early days of the war with 223 Squadron, flying Blenheims, and later converted to Baltimores and flew with 13 Squadron as Squadron Leader.

"Cookie" Leon assumed control of 55 Baltimore Squadron on 17 January 1944, and had Tom as his Gunnery Leader in the formation when he joined the squadron on the 29 January; Leon remained Commanding Officer of 55 Squadron until August 1945. Throughout this long time he was in command, an unprecedented period for an Operational Squadron Commander; the squadron had many successes over the retreating German Forces, their motor and rail transport, communications, and supply lines.

Air Gunners of 223 Squadron being briefed by their Gunnery Leader at Celone in Italy during 1944 before taking off on a raid on enemy targets in the Popoli area. Tom would hold a similar function with 55 Squadron.

Also joining 55 Squadron on 17 January were former 13 Squadron personnel; Flight Lieutenant A.G. Robinson, Navigator; Warrant Officer K.L. Nattrass, Wireless Operator; and Warrant Officer R.P. McMillan, Air Gunner. These three formed, with Wing Commander Leon, the Commanding Officer's crew.

From Gianaclis with Tom came two other Wireless/Air gunners, Flying Officers C.H. Crowley and A.B.C. Nunn.

APPENDIX A TO FORM 540 FOR MONTH OF JANUARY, 1944. NO. 55 SQUADRON, R.A.F.			
ARRIVALS		Trade or Branch	Posted from	Date
88409	S/Ldr. A/W/Cdr. L. E. Leon, D.F.C.	Pilot	13 Squadron	17th
106916	F/O C. L. M. Haigh	Int.	HQ.RAF.ME.	19th
SA.807184	Lt. B. J. Marais	Pilot	22 P.T.C.	14th
139108	P/O R. A. Pitts	Nav.B.	22 P.T.C.	14th
52221	F/O T. B. Clark	W/AG.	Gianaclis	29th
52316	F/O C. H. Crowley	W/AG.	Do.	29th
48051	F/O A. B. C. Nunn	W/AG.	Do.	29th
89315	F/Lt. A. G. Robinson	Nav.B.	13 Squadron	17th
A.407989	W/O Nattrass, K. L.	W/AG.	13 Squadron	17th
A.406220	W/O McMillan, R. P.	W/AG.	13 Squadron	17th
1317446	Sgt. Stogdale, C. W.	W/AG.	22 P.T.C.	14th
924625	Sgt. Ives, R. E.	A.G.	22 P.T.C.	14th

55 Squadron frequently changed stations between January 1944 and January 1945; from January to March 1944 they were at Kabrit, March to May at Biferno, May to June San Severo, June to July Tarquinia, July to October Cecina, in October at Perugia, and October to January 1945 at Marcianise.

One crew consisted of J. A. C. Russell, pilot; E.A. Brown, Wireless Operator; Cyril Mort, Bomb Aimer; and G.J. O'Neil, an Australian Air Gunner.

On 29 January 1944, Tom was posted to 55 Squadron, who were at Foggia and then still part of MEAF (Middle East Air Force), but the command had changed on 10 December 1943 to MAAF (Mediterranean Allied Air Force). He was flying in the Martin Baltimore of 55 Squadron, the Desert Air Force, again as a rear facing dorsal Air Gunner, but this time as a Gunnery Leader who would lead the formation, fly with, and advise the Commanding Officer "Cookie" Leon, on gunnery tactics. He was crewed with Flying Officer Campbell (Pilot), Flying Officer Hulme (Navigator/Bomb Aimer) and Warrant Officer Evans (Wireless Operator).

On 12 February, the exhausted US Army at Cassino was replaced by the New Zealand Corps, and General Alexander now decided to use these fresh troops in another attempt to capture Cassino.

General Bernard Fryberg, who was in charge of the infantry attack, asked for the monastery to be bombed, despite claims from front line troops that no enemy fire had come from the ancient monument. General Alexander reluctantly agreed and the monastery was destroyed by the US Air Force on 15 February, dropping some 450 tons of bombs, but the fortified building held. Again on 15 March, Cassino was attacked by Allied Air Forces, this time dropping some 1,100 tons of bombs. Once the monastery was in ruins, the Germans moved in and used the rubble as an excellent cover and vantage point from which to launch defensive artillery mortar and machine-gun fire.

On 17 February 1944, "A" Flight Commander Squadron Leader J.L. Griffiths went sick with a broken wrist; his replacement was Flight Lieutenant Leslie Leethall 'Les' Harland, later Wing Commander Harland, (previously with 223 Squadron during the El Alamein and Tunisian battles and amassing sixty sorties). He was eighteen months older than Tom. Harland led numerous sorties of eighteen Baltimores against German communication and supply targets, together with Tom as Gunnery Leader, over the next eight months. By the time Harland was rested during October 1944, he had flown 109 sorties and had been awarded a well-earned DFC (Distinguished Flying Cross) whose citation particularly noted the success of his leadership "For leading his Flight with brilliant success".

On 4 March the squadron moved briefly to Tarranto before a further move to Biferno, close to Campobasso on the south eastern side of Italy, where they stayed until May.

On 19 March 1944, "Operation Strangle", the rail interdiction programmes in Italy began, and continued until 11 May 1944; thus began an all out campaign against the German supply lines.

On 31 March 1944, the squadron, led by their C/O Wing Commander Leon, DFC, began their first raid of a new series by attacking road and rail bridges south of Roscto Degli Abruzzi, on the east coast of Northern Italy. Direct hits were scored on the north and south approaches and some light flak was met. Meanwhile, Tom's crew of Campbell, Evans, and Hulme in Baltimore FW 441 "S", were flying No 3 in a flight of twelve Baltimores led by Squadron Leader F. Brierley, attacking rolling stock in San Benedretto Station. Tom's later friend and 55 Association Secretary, Ivor Calverley, was rear gunner in Baltimore FW 291 "X", with crew of Flight Sergeant Smith, Sergeant F. Hughes and Flight Sergeant G. Day.

Flight Lieutenant Ivor Calverley, MBE, RAFVR, a Former Air Gunner 55 Squadron wrote this short account:

"Dear Chris, thank you for the copy of your book which I enjoyed; especially the period that Tom was on 55 Squadron. Tom was a regular supporter of the Annual 55/223 Squadron Reunions and as Hon. Secretary for over forty years I got to know him very well. We often had long chats about our time together on 55 Squadron during the Italian Campaign. His help and advice will never be forgotten to a very young twenty year old Air Gunner."

Ivor Calverley, 5 November 2010.

Wing Commander Hampton was also involved in Operation Strangle with 223 Squadron. Here he recalls:

"In March, as a Flight Lieutenant, I was given details to carry out a raid on railway buildings and sidings in the north-west of Rome. The mission involved dangerous flying due to cloud, during daylight hours leading twenty-four aircraft. Twelve of the aircraft were from 223 Squadron and the remaining twelve were from the South African Air Force. We were met by strong enemy defences."

A newspaper article at that time reported the great success of the mission being "entirely due to the ability, initiative and determination of the leader. He has completed numerous other missions and invariably proved himself a very able pilot." The aim of the attack was to stop the Germans from reinforcing. Hampton was awarded the DFC for his valiant efforts on this crucial mission. He later left

A Baltimore bombing road and railway bridges over the Vomano River at Molino San Antino Italy on the 31 March 1944.

Baltimore 1V, FA463 "U" of 223 Squadron logged at least 102 operational sorties, seen at Foggia (232 Wing) in early 1944.

223 Squadron and became a Forward Bomber Controller, this was a new position which involved tying in the bomber raids with the fighter escorts, and briefing bomber crews on their targets.

On 2 April 1944, twelve Baltimores of 55 Squadron led by the CO Wing Commander Leon, and Flight Commander Flight Lieutenant Les Harland, were airborne to attack road and rail depots north of Sulmona. The other twelve from the squadron, led by Flight Lieutenant Gooch attacked the railway bridge and aqueduct south of Terni. Russian forces also entered Romania on the same day.

On 3 April a further sortie of twelve Baltimores led by Leon attacked the railway bridge at Pedaso. Tom and his crew of Campbell, Evans and Hulme were in FA 623 "O", flying third to the leader.

On April 5 1944, the first of a series of day and night attacks by American and British aircraft from the Mediterranean started on the oil refineries at Placati; and on the 8 to 10 April, RAF bombers flew the first mine-laying mission to the Danube, and mines were laid near Belgrade.

On 7 April, Tom and his crew in FW 441 "S", flew tenth to the leader in a formation of twelve when they attacked hydroelectric works at Papigno near Terni. Baltimore FA 623 "A", crewed by Flight Sergeant Cowley, Flying Officer Hetherton, Flight Sergeant Caldecott, and Flight Sergeant Turner, was attacked by a German Messerschmitt Me109e and blew up, killing all aboard.

Also during the month of April 1944, Air Vice-Marshal (later Sir) William Forster Dickson, DSO, AFC, (later included GCB, KBE) took command of the Western Desert Air Force in Italy, and he visited 55 Squadron on 8 April; he remained in that post until December 1944 when Air Vice-Marshal R.M. Foster succeeded him, until Air Commodore C.L. Falconer took over at the end of August 1945.

On 8 April, Tom and crew flew at No 2 to the CO, when the twelve Baltimores attacked Rigti Aerodrome. The attack commenced at 0900 hours from 9,500 feet and bombs fell across the hangars and other buildings resulting in fire explosions.

On 11 April, Tom and crew in FW 355 "R"were flying at No 3 to Squadron Leader Brierley; this time the target was Fabriano and two direct hits were observed. On 12 April the target was Silvano when they flew with Wing Commander Leon at No 10. This was part of the opening attacks against the Gustav Line by Allied aircraft in northern Italy on 11 and 12 April. Further attacks against the "Gustav Line" continued during the month and the squadron, including Tom and his crew, were kept very busy on daylight attacks against the German line.

On 20 April 1944 it was announced that Acting Squadron Leader H.R. Harrison; Flight Lieutenant J.F.C. Melrose; and Flight Lieutenant E.G. Shears, all RAF (VR) of 55 Squadron, had all been awarded the DFC (Distinguished Flying Cross). During May the squadron moved again, this time to San Severolo, an Italian Island in the Venetian Lagoon and to the south-east of San Giorgio Maggiore.

April 1944, a vertical aerial photograph taken from a Baltimore of the Desert Air Force during an attack by Baltimores and Curtiss Kittyhawks on an airfield at Rieti, north of Rome, showing bombs exploding on the hangars and landing areas.

During the month of May 1944, 55 Squadron began a campaign of night flying bombing and overnight the 2nd/3rd six Baltimores, with Tom's crew in FW 441 "S" flying at No 5, and with Ivor Calverley's crew flying at No 6, took off in moonlight and good weather to attack ports between Pescara and Ancona and did a night raid at Coshlianova which was bombed for the second time that night. On 5 May Tom was appointed Gas Officer for the squadron.

On 14/15 May 1944, twelve Baltimores of 55 Squadron led by Wing Commander Leon (on the squadron's fiftieth operation since taking Command),

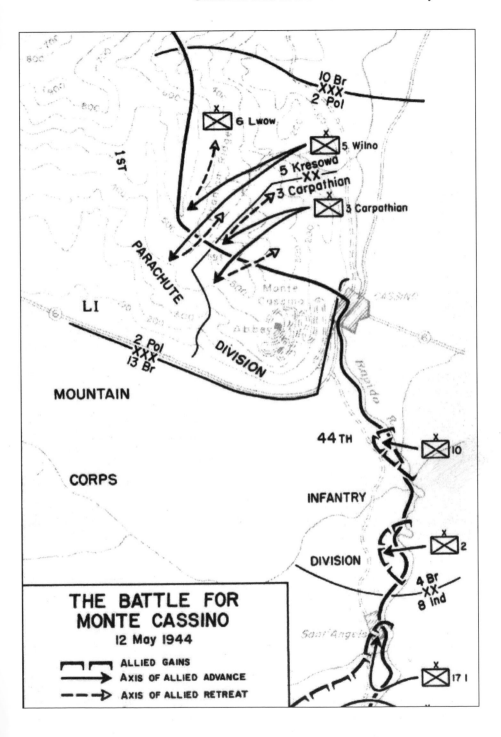

THE BATTLE FOR MONTE CASSINO

12 May 1944

ALLIED GAINS

AXIS OF ALLIED ADVANCE

AXIS OF ALLIED RETREAT

This is an extract from 55 Squadron ORB for 29 April 1944. It shows Tom's crew flying at No 4 to the CO Wing Commander Leon, in Baltimore FW 441 "S", and Ivor Calverley's crew at No 3 in Baltimore FW 391 "X".

with Tom's crew flying at No 2, were on a night sortie to cause a roadblock and hinder motor transport on roads leading south from Rome, which was en route to reinforce the beleaguered Monte Cassino. This was repeated on 17/18 May, when they attacked motor transport and caused roadblocks between Valmontone and Frosinone.

It took until 18 May for Allied Troops, led by General Anders of the Polish Corps, and General Juin of the French Corps, to capture Monte Cassino. This then opened the corridor for the Allies, and they reached and met up with the Sixth Corp at Anzio on 24 May.

On the night of 21 May, Tom was again busy when the squadron were detailed to do a road recce north of Rome and the central sector. This time the crew were flying at No 4 and they dropped their load of bombs on four different motor transport targets. 55 Squadron continued night flying operations during the remainder of the month of May.

At this point I will return to, *One Man's War in The Desert Air Force* by Fred Henderson 223 Squadron:

"Certain actions stand out, such as the maelstrom of aircraft and flak over the monastery at Cassino, the dawn attack on Anzio on 23 May 1944 against German gun positions as the Allied forces prepared to break out of the beachhead, and a disastrous raid near Chieti when the leading aircraft in the formation received a direct hit in its bomb bay just as it started its run onto target – the sky was filled with flaming lumps of aircraft, a complete engine whipping past our starboard wing–tip and striking the machine next to us, setting it on fire; while the aircraft abreast of the one that exploded had almost the full length of its fuselage dented in by the blast. Almost miraculously, all except the machine which had been hit returned to base, albeit some of them in very sorry states and with casualties aboard.

"As the spring and summer of 1944 progressed and the better weather at least removed some of the natural hazards of flying, operations continued on similar lines, but now included some diversions to Yugoslavia to co-operate with Tito's partisans. An extraordinary feature of these raids was that after crossing the Adriatic Sea we would rendezvous with Spitfires which were operating from the small island of Vis, within sight of the enemy-occupied Dalmatian coast! Our base had, with the advance of ground forces, moved first to Termoli (Biferno) and then to Pescara. A further move to Ancona was imminent, but the days of 223 Squadron were numbered, and thus my long spell with the Desert Air Force ended."

On the 24 May 1944, the squadron did a night sortie to cause a road block at Subiaco, Tom's crew flying at No 7 to Wing Commander Leon, and their bombs were dropped at 2336 hours.

On 26 May 1944, Tom's crew flew at No 1 on an armed recce of the east coast roads to Ancona.

Overnight 31 May to 1 June, Tom's crew flew in FW 441 "S" at No 8 to Wing Commander Leon on an armed recce on the roads of Pescara, Popoli, Aquila, Celano, Avergano and Sulmona.

On the night of 1 June 1944, eleven of 55 Squadron Baltimores operated in the Central Sector of Northern Italy attacking German motor transport in the Avezzano-Sora area. Bostons illuminated the target area, whilst other aircraft attacked railway yards at Fano. The other thirteen of the squadron's strength went to Montefiascone to create roadblocks and seemed to perform their task successfully. Further roadblocks were created during 2 June at Avezzano by twelve of the squadron aircraft, flying between 2105 hours and 0515 hours.

On 1 June 1944, the formation of the RAF Balkan Air Force came into being; and the German defence then started to disintegrate, and General Alexander ordered General Clark to trap and destroy the retreating German Tenth Army. This order was ignored, and Clark, wanting the glory, instead marched for the capital of Italy, Rome, and liberated the beleaguered city on 4 June 1944, on the

...ation Overlord began; but the planned date of the landing was ...eptionally bad weather.

...to 3 June, Tom's crew flew at No 3 to Lieutenant Morum and ...ls east of Fabriano to bomb motor transport and create a road block. ... on 4 June they flew No 4 to Lieutenant Dietrich and attacked the northern approaches of Viterbo at 0104 hours from 9,000feet. The station and square were bombed as well as the south end of town.

Unusually severe weather occurred during early June 1944, turning the Atlantic Ocean, English Channel, and Normandy coastal areas into a boiling cauldron. On 4 June, Allied troops began climbing aboard their ships and went on standby; a twenty-four hour "window of opportunity" in the weather was made, and on 6 June 1944, the Invasion and the Normandy Landings got underway. Thus the Longest Day began, and what followed was indelibly imprinted on the minds of the British, French and American people.

During June the squadron moved on to Tarquinia, situated on the west coast of Italy above Rome, some three miles inland of the Tyrrhenian Sea, and some twelve miles north of Civitavecchia, where they stayed until July.

Also in June 1944, Tom's brother, James "Wares" Clark was posted to the Middle East, and served on the shore bases at HMS *Nile*, situated at Ras El Tin Point, Alexandria, and the Greek Port of Piraeus during the German withdrawal and the establishment of Civil Law. He also, during this time, served in Malta and Israel and on board the Cruiser HMS *Sirius*, which in August 1944 returned from duty in Normandy for the landings in the south of France, Operation Dragoon. She then served again in the Aegean, where in October 1944, she was present during the reoccupation of Athens. She then remained with the Mediterranean Fleet.

He also served with the Minesweeper HMS *Brixham*, which in July 1944, together with four other ships, helped to clear a passage between Anzio and Leghorn. During August 1944 it sailed from Naples as part of an escort for a convoy and was then involved in clearing a beach south of St Tropez before going to Malta and then being involved in minesweeping duties off the Greek coast in September 1944.

Photo of James Wares Clark, 1944.

"Wares" was also stationed aboard the Frigate HMS *Byron* which earned battle honours for service in the English Channel, the Arctic, and the Atlantic in 1944, and in the North Sea in 1944 and 1945. In the course of these operations, she participated in the destruction of two German U-boats; U-722 on 27 March 1945, off the Hebrides, by depth charges in company with HMS *Fitzroy* and HMS *Redmill*. The second U-boat, U-1001 on 8 April 1945, south-west of Land's End, was again destroyed by depth charges.

Wing Commander Leon, with 55 Squadron, and Tom as Gunnery Leader led many large formations of bombers against the rail and road networks of occupied Italy as the German forces retreated northwards to various lines of defence. During June 1944, his squadron switched to night intruder attacks (the time that Tom's Baltimore was shot down) to harass the enemy and to attack supply lines, marshalling yards and harbours.

Overnight of 6 June, eleven of the squadron's aircraft carried out an armed recce of the Sora-Aquila-Rifti area; the results of the bombing were mostly unobserved due to cloud over the target. From this operation one aircraft failed to return. On the 7 June 1944, 55 Squadron lost a Royal Yugoslavian Air Force crew, when Captain Djonlic, Lieutenant Popovic, Flight Sergeant Simitch, and Sergeant Cernigoj failed to return from a sortie.

55 Sqn ORB entry for 13 June 1944.

During the night of 8 June, fourteen aircraft of the squadron attacked a concentration of sixty motor transport in the Avezzano area with bombs falling on the targets.

Overnight of 10 June, nine aircraft operated in the Rieti area, finding further MT movement. Tom's crew flew at No 5 to Flight Lieutenant Gooch and they attacked Fano, creating a direct hit on the railway track and buildings, setting them on fire.

On the 11 June, Air Officer Commanding, Air Vice-Marshal Dickson, sent a message of congratulations for the excellent work carried out by the Air Force since the push started on18 May.

Overnight of 13 June, five aircraft carried out armed recces in the Central Sector, whilst another five attacked the harbour installations at Civitanova and San Benedetti on the east coast. Tom's crew flew in Baltimore FW 387 "T" at No 1.

They did a further sortie later the same night, flying Baltimore FW 364 "W" at No 4 to Flying Officer Warren, and attacked motor transport at Foliona, Canerino, Fabriano and Ancona, bombing from 9,000 feet.

After the capture of Rome, the German puppet Italian Government there resigned, and a new one was formed. The Allied Armies then pursued the fleeing German Tenth Army and took Grosseto on 16 June, Assisi on 18 June and Perugia on 20 June.

On 21 June, the Allied soldiers found themselves facing the "Albert Line", yet another German defensive line, whilst world focus was on the gains being made in

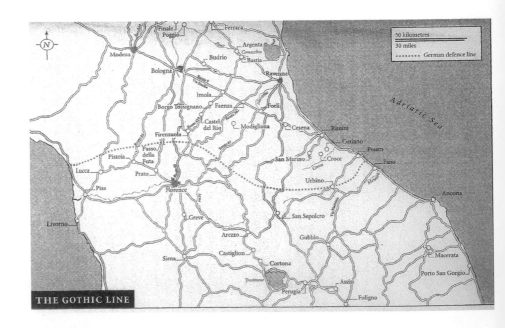

THE GOTHIC LINE

France since the Invasion and Normandy Landings. During the week it would take to penetrate the "Albert Line", many of the Allied seasoned troops were taken off in preparation for Operation Lagoon, the amphibious assault on the South of France. Immediately after conceding the "Albert Line", the Germans set up the "Gothic Line" further north of Florence to run across the summits of the Appellations.

Poem: Lest We Forget

Bunny Austin Ex 99 and 40 Squadrons

"One day a breed of men were born
from every walk of life,
they came from near and far to fight,
for a certain way of life.
Some were tall and some were short,
And some were dark and lean,
And some spoke different languages,
But all were young and keen.
They all trained hard, and then one day,
A Wing Commander came
And pinned upon their breast, a badge,
Air-Gunners they became.
A squadron was their final goal,
To join an aircrew,
On Wimpys, Lancs and Stirlings,
And some on Blenheims and Baltimores too.
They fought at night and in the day,
Their op's increased in number,
Some returned — and some did not,
For "thirty" was the number.
Some survived to reach this mark,
And some continued flying,
Some spent years behind the bars,
With many of them dying.
At last the victory came in sight,
The runways now are silent,
The echoes of the past remain,
A conflict, long and violent.
This breed of men are now but few
But they remember others,
Who flew with them so long ago,
Their Royal Air Force brothers"

During these various Allied gains, 55 Squadron still continued to give air support to the ground forces. So more or less as soon as the "Gothic Line" was set up, the resulting German ground defences would have a profound effect on the near future of Tom and his Baltimore crew.

The rear gun turret of a medium bomber on a night sortie could be the loneliest place in the sky. Encased in a metal and Perspex cupola at the end of the fuselage, the rear facing gunner was almost literally on his own, with the occasional crackle of muted voices bouncing into his earphones to reassure him that three of his crew of four were nearby. Most of his airborne hours were suffered in silence, except for the soft hiss of his own oxygen tube when flying high and the spasmodic creak and groan from his metal surroundings and immediate impediments of his trade. At times it took a conscious mental effort to remember that he was not the sole occupant of the aircraft. Every second inside the turret was spent in constant vigilance, searching the surrounding inky blackness methodically, quarter by quarter, for the telltale grey shadows which might at any moment solidify into an oncoming German night fighter. At night, the majority of Luftwaffe interceptors favoured initial attacks from the rear or from under the belly of an Allied Bomber, thereby placing every rear gunner first in line for elimination.

Between 22 and 24 June, 55 Squadron moved en masse to Tarquinia and overnight of 24 June three aircraft operated, the remaining sorties being cancelled due to unsuitable weather. Bostons of 114 and 18 Squadrons also arrived at Tarquinia and for the first time one wing operated at night from the same airfield. Five of the squadron aircraft carried out a recce between Florence and the bomb line, and large numbers of motor transport were attacked near Arrezzo.

Overnight of 26 June, twelve aircraft went in search of heavy motor transport movement which had been reported by the Mustangs on dusk patrol, on the Pistoia-Bologna roads. Heavy and accurate fire was encountered and much transport was bombed. From this operation two aircraft were reported missing, one with Campbell, Evans, Hulme and Clark; the other with the Yugoslav crew of Pilot Captain Zarkov, Navigator Lieutenant Zlatanovic, Wireless Operator Flight Sergeant Grozdanic, and Air Gunner Sergeant Starc.

The following I received during early 2010 via The Air Historical Branch, and the MOD at RAF Cranwell, from 55 Squadron record entries:

"On 26 June 1944, Flying Officer 52221 T. B. Clark, was one of the crew of four aboard a Baltimore MK V, serial number FW441 that was tasked to bomb enemy motor transport on the Pistoia – Bologna Road (map reference Q.5383 – L.8948) named the 'Gothic Line'.

"The crew, consisting of Flying Officer I.C. Campbell, Pilot; Flying Officer S.F. Hulme, Navigator/ Bomb Aimer; Warrant Officer E.H. Evans, Wireless Operator/Air Gunner; and Flying Officer T. Clark, Dorsal Air Gunner; took off from Tarquinia airfield situated in the Lazio Region of Central Italy at 2118 hours. At about 2230 hours, after completing the bombing run, the aircraft was flying south between Bologna and Pistoia at 8,000 feet. The aircraft was badly hit by flak;

very rapidly the starboard engine 'revs' went to maximum and the oil pressure fell to zero. After a few minutes the aircraft began to shake violently and, believing it to be breaking up, Flying Officer Campbell ordered his crew to abandon the aircraft. They all acknowledged and the Pilot called several times on the intercom and was sure everybody had baled out successfully. At about 2235 hours the starboard engine finally responded and the terrific vibration consequently stopped, however the aircraft was not maintaining height and the Pilot then abandoned the aircraft some few minutes later. Officially, as Flying Officers Clark and Hulme failed to make contact with their unit, 55 Squadron, and the Air Ministry, it was thought that they had been killed in action or taken Prisoners of War and it was not until some eight weeks had elapsed that the Air Ministry knew different."

In the meantime, Tom, upon landing and spending the night in a maize field, was taken in by Italian peasants and he and Flying Officer Hulme met up in a barn near the village of Campi Bisenzio. They were given civilian clothes and remained for four days, hiding in a disused shooting box. On 1 July they were taken into Florence by a member of the Partisan forces and hidden in a bombed house belonging to another member of the movement. They were fed by the owner of the house and his friends. The Germans closed all the roads and it became impossible to leave the town. On 12 August they heard that the Allies had reached the southern bank of the River Arno, and they decided to try and get in touch with them. They crossed to the southern outskirts of the town and hid in the house of another member of the Partisan movement. About 14 August the first units of the advancing British troops crossed the river and both Tom and Flying Officer Hulme got in touch with an officer of the Intelligence Corps. On 18 August both men were sent back to Naples; Tom remained in Italy and Flying Officer Hulme returned to the UK.

Here is Tom's first-hand account of being attacked and having to bale out, compiled ready for inclusion in a 55 Squadron Association Newsletter, an Association he last attended during October 2004; but sadly, Tom died before the article was typed from his original work and before this account could be published. (I contacted 55/223 Squadron Association Secretary and an excerpt of Tom's narrative was published in the Annual, Issue No 83, October 2009, newsletter, and the full transcript was published in the 2011/12 edition; thus I have carried out his wishes.)

Narrative of the Experiences of 52221 Flying Officer Thomas B. Clark Behind Enemy Line June–September 1944

Originally typed by the narrator on the 7 September 1944 from his diary entries made at the time:

"On the evening of Monday, 26 June 1944, we were briefed to attack transport on the Pistoia-Bologna roads. (Map references Q.5383 – L.8948 named the

'Gothic Line'.) Our take-off time 2118 hours from Tarquinia airfield and our crew comprised of Flying Officer I.C. Campbell, Pilot; Flying Officer S.F, "Stan" Hulme, Navigator; Warrant Officer E.H. Evans, Wireless/Air and Myself, Air Gunner. We took off at time stated, in the Baltimore MkV FW.441 (S), and duly set course for the target. Flying at 8,500 feet, we crossed the bomb–line at approx 2150 hours and the IEP was switched off. Arriving over Pistoia we set course on 031 degrees, to take us along the road to Bologna, and saw some light flak ahead, as well as some bursts of heavy, silhouetted against the last light. We concluded that the Hun was shooting at one of our aircraft, as there were reputed to be forty Allies operating over the area at the same time.

"The flak gunners soon obtained our range, and soon we were the target for several batteries of heavy and light guns. We made a turn to bomb some lights on the road, with flak bursting very close all the time. After bombing, we turned up the road again and saw more lights, which we bombed, and when we dropped a flare, more guns opened up on us. Our work being finished for the night, we turned on a wide circuit, all the time weaving side to side, in order to try and miss the 'hot spots' previously passed. Eventually we set course for home; on 216 degrees, but in spite of our efforts, there was no respite from the flak, and it continued to burst uncomfortably close, in boxes of four or five. The W/CP, at the bottom hatch, reported seeing an aircraft below us to starboard and no sooner had he spoken, and there were two or three very brilliant flashes, one not far away on the port beam, accompanied by audible explosions, and the smell of cordite. I remember being amazed that none of us were hit, although the pilot reported

Baltimore 1V's approach their target in Northern Italy, Michael Turner 1979.

that a piece of shrapnel flew past his head through the cockpit. The aircraft began to vibrate, the pilot told us that the starboard engine was out of action, and the airscrew would not feather. He told us to prepare to abandon aircraft as we were losing height, but said that if he could stop the starboard engine, there might still be a chance. At this time I would like to put it on record that the pilot Flying Officer Campbell flew the aircraft with the utmost skill and coolness, and his calm observations and reports were an inspiration to us all.

"Eventually came the order to 'Bale-Out!' and I left the turret to clip on my pack, which was lying ready by the flare chute. The W/Op went first, and I attempted to leave in a similar fashion, immediately after, but my long legs (Tom was 6'3" tall) stuck in the metalwork on the other side of the bottom hatch. I then knelt down, and tucking my head in as far as possible, rolled forward and out, successfully clearing the aircraft. I waited until I thought I was dropping vertically and pulled the ring. There was a considerable jerk, and I was soon swinging slowly to and fro below the canopy. The moon was shining, in the first quarter, and I remember thinking that I might be shot at from the ground if the white parachute showed up. I eventually landed beside a tree in the middle of a farm track, and immediately dived into a ditch on the other side dragging my chute in after me. I lay 'doggo' for twenty minutes or so, until I was sure that no one was looking for me in the immediate neighbourhood. I lost my helmet on the way down, and cursed myself for not leaving it in the aircraft, as it might be found, to my disadvantage. I landed at approx 2230 hours. Cautiously, I climbed out of the ditch, and released my harness, taking great care that the metal parts did not clink together. I made a fairly compact bundle of the canopy and harness, and enclosed it in my Mae West, for easy portage."

(Author: Mae West was a popular well-endowed sex symbol, US Vaudeville and Hollywood Actress of the 1930s and 1940s, renowned for her many bawdy one line double entendres: "you only live once, but if you do it right, once is enough".)

Here I include the report of Flying Officer Campbell, the Pilot of Baltimore FW441 "S", who, after being the last of the crew to bale out, was behind enemy lines for a fortnight; and who was also helped by the Italians to evade capture by the Germans:

From:-   116906. F/O. I.G. Campbell.

To:-   Officer Commanding, No. 55. Squadron.

Subject:- Report on absence from 26th June, to 11th July, 1944.

Date:-   12th July, 1944.

Sir.,

        I have the honour to submit the following report on circumstances leading to my absence from the Squadron. I took off in Baltimore F.W. 441 at 21.15 on 26th June with the road from PISTOIA to BOLOGNA as the target. On setting course up the road we encountered severe heavy flak and only saw one light, on which we dropped one five hundred and a container of 40 lbs. We turned south down the road again and after a few minutes saw another light on which we released our remaining bombs and flare. We were flying at 8.000 feet and I had been taking evasive action since the flak was very accurate, Flying Officer HULME my navigator, gave me a course to steer for base and we set course. About three minutes later the wireless/operator who was at the bottom guns reported a machine beneath and slightly behind us and I made a sharp turn to starboard. At the same time he reported four bursts of flak under the tail and four more burst at our height and slightly ahead. A piece of shrapnel came in the top of my hood, but apart from that the machine appeared undamaged. A few minutes later the oil pressure in the starboard engine dropped to zero, and the revs went up to maximum. I attempted to feather the airscrew, but was unsuccessful so I put the mixture control to "cut out" and switched off. At the same time I instructed the wireless operator, W/O EVANS, to send off that we were returning on one engine and to put the I.F.F. on to the emergency stud. I do not know how much of the message he had sent when the machine began to vibrate and I called the rest of the crew to stand by to abandon the aircraft. I am under the impression that a portion of the rudder had been shot away since I was unable to keep the aircraft straight without putting down the left wing. This naturally increased the drag, and we were losing height at 200 - 300 feet per minute. The vibration increased until the instruments were a bluish blur, and thinking the aircraft was breaking up, I gave the order to jump. The wireless operator went first and was closely followed by the gunner and the navigator. A few seconds later the starboard engine siezed, and the propeller stopped in the fully fine position. Unfortunately the others had all left, for I had no reply to my shout not to jump. I was still losing height slowly and was at 7.000 feet when they left. I turned on to 325 o intending to hit the coast, and thus be able to come down to 2.000 feet, where I reckoned the aircraft would maintain height, and I would be able to fly back to base. After about five minutes on this course, during which I called up twice on the intercom to make sure the crew had all gone, the port engine failed and caught fire. I had already undone my straps in order to be able to exert more pressure on the rudder, so all that was left for me to do was to take off my helmet and jettison the hood. In my haste to get out I did not take off the rudder bias, with the result that, as soon as I took my feet off the rudder bar, the machine yawed to the left and the port wing started to go down. My parachute caught on something in the cockpit and until the machine was inverted I could not get out. I saw the tail coming towards me and shut my eyes, opening them a few seconds later, to find rather to my surprise that I had missed it and was clear of the machine. I pulled the rip cord and started to swing slowly down.

        I was under the impression, a short while before I touched down, that I was being fired on, because I saw lights blinking

beneath me, but then realised that they were fireflies. I came
down about twenty yards from a road but down in a little valley.
A truck, with Germans shouting, passed while I was gathering
my parachute, but they were intent on getting to the machine which
was burning about ½ mile away and did not see me. I bundled my
parachute, mae-west and dinghy under a hedge and went through my
pockets to check I had not left anything of value to the Germans.
There was considerable high ground to the east and I set off towards this, skirting a village en route. The general run of this high
ground was N.W. -S.E. and so I walked along the top. It was hard
going, for apart from the undergrowth being extremely thick, the
range was crossed at right angles by numerous valleys, some of which
had almost vertical sides. After about three hours I began to feel
rather tired and began to look around for somewhere to lie up. I had
had plenty to drink for there were streams at the bottom of most of
the valleys. I found a fairly flat piece of ground, covered by the
branches and leaves of a large bush, and crawled in there. I then
opened my escape packet and emergency ration tin and took stock of
what "aids" I had.

     I stayed in that place until the next evening, by which
time I was extremely thirsty. A collapsible rubber or canvas bag
which I could have filled at nights and drunk when lying up in the
day, would have been invaluable. It was hard to plan the next nights
travelling, for I could never tell what the country was like beyond
the next hill. I set off at dusk once again, and found the country
very similar to that of the night before, and once again by three
o'clock was feeling very weary and decided to lie up. I rationed
myself to two tablets every three hours and an occasional barley
sugar sweet.

     I had to leave the hills on the next night for the general
trend was becoming too much eastwards. I started out as usual at
dusk, and came down the hills into a fairly wide valley. I gave all
houses and fields a wide berth and kept to the hedges. By midnight
I was across and in hills once again, and heading south. Just before
dawn, I went down into a little valley where I expected a stream, in
order to drink as much as I possibly could to last me through the
following day, only to find it dry. It was getting pretty light by
the time I got up the other side, and I found a hiding place and
went off to sleep. I woke at eleven with a tremendous thirst, and
feeling very hungry, and seeing a lonely farm house on the next
hill, decided to take a chance and go there. Apart from considerable
surprise, they showed no hostility whatsoever, and in fact appeared
keen to do anything to help. I explained I was English and they
provided me with bread and two eggs and gave me lunch.

     Meanwhile it began to rain and I intended staying
in the house until dark, but just after lunch one of the men came
rushing in and began talking to me excitedly. The only word I could
make out was "German", and from his gestures I reckoned he wanted
me to leave. I left and hid for the rest of the afternoon at the
bottom of the hill. The country was now becoming rather less hilly
and I walked very carefully that night. Just before dawn I climbed
a small hill with very thick undergrowth on the sides and decided
to wait on top during the following day. I was coming fairly near
to the line, then, for the gunfire was very distinct. I was absolutely soaked and when the sun came up I stripped and laid out my
clothes to dry. I had a few nasty moments when a 3 foot snake came
up and investigated my presence. We held a staring match for what
seemed hours, I not daring to move, and then he wriggled away.

     Just before dark I came down from the hill and
seeing an old woodcutter, approached him for water and food. He
gave me water and food while I was drinking it, a man walked up
the path towards us. The old man pulled me behind a bush and we
hid there while the German, as he turned out to be, came up to the
hut and then walked away again. From what I could make out from
his manner of speaking, there appeared to be a considerable number
of huns around, and I decided to stay up on the hill for that night
and the next day, in order to spy out the lie of the land
and make plans as to the best way to leave. The next evening I
went down again intending to get as much information as to the
position of the enemy around the hill from the woodcutter, in

order to facilitate my departure. He wouldn't let me go,
however, and kept me there, talking, until a man and his
wife came up the path. I thought then that he must have
denounced me, and began to run, but he followed shouting
amongst other things "Inglesi". I stopped and realising that
I couldn't get away, anyway, waited until the man and his wife
came up to me. It turned out to be the Count andCountess
ULMANI. He was an Italian Naval Commander and spoke fluent
English. He was extremely anti-Fascist and anti-German. He told
me that the Germans had moved back two of their batteries to
the bottom of the hill and that Divisional Headquarters was
in his house about half a mile away. He didn't know which
division it was but he thought it was a Panzer Division, and
the General, he had a long name which he had forgotten, was
an Austrain and a Roman Catholic. He advised me to remain on
the hill for he thought I would have little chance of getting
through.

I found from him that the district was ULINAGUO, just
N.E. of VOLTERRA. From then until the 10th July I remained on
this hill and the Count supplied me with food which the
woodcutter, Baragati Francesco, brought up. I lost track of the
days while I was on the hill, but as the line moved up so the
shelling came nearer. When it came to the hill, one night, the
Count, his wife and little boy, and Italian army Lieutenant
and wife and baby, and a young girl Julian moved into a cave on
the top of the hill for safety, complete with mattresses,
food, wine, cutlery, table cloths and serviettes. I wasn't
very happy about this, for they talked incessantly, and the
baby cried and I wanted as little attention drawn to the hill
as possible. I had lunch the next day with them and it was
with relief that they told me they were moving back down again,
since the cave faced VOLTERRA, and it was from that direction
that the shelling was coming. From then on the shelling was
fairly regular and my hill seemed to attract a great many of
the shells, much to my discomfort. Francesco used to give a
little whistle each time he came up, in order that I would know
it was him, and I would come out of hiding to find he had
brought somebody else with him usually. I think I had become one
of the local sights and I didn't feel very happy that my presence
was known to so many people.

The shelling gradually drew away to the north of me,
but the Germans remained round the hill. There was a horsedrawn
battery to the south and a mechanised one to the north. I watched
the latter drawing out towards the end of my stay. A ten ton
truck took each gun out individually, and then came back for the
next. They withdrew to a hill not far away and opened fire on
a single farm house, continuing to fire until it was destroyed.

On the night of the 9th Francesco came up on to the
hill and collecting all my kit motioned me to follow him. He
led me down to the Priest's house, where I was given a great
welcome by the owner and all the people who had been upnto see
me during the previous 10 days. A room had been prepared for me
with a mattress on the floor and a hot supper was waiting. The
Count then told me that VOLTERRA had fallen and that although
there were still a few of the enemy round there, the majority
had pulled out, and that Francesco had volunteered to lead me
by a wooded path to VOLTERRA the next morning. I left the house
just before daybreak and hid in the hill until the woodcutter
came along, and we set off at 6.30. He went ahead with the
arrangement that if he ran into Germans, he would signal and I
could hide. In this manner we walked without any trouble into
VOLTERRA where I went to the 88th American, Divisional Headquarters. Francesco would take no money, but as he left I put a
500 Lire (B.M.A.) note into his pocket and wrote his name down.

I should like to express my appreciation of the
way in which he helped me. He knew the penalty was death if he
were caught, but even went to the extent of coming up the hill
one night to waken me and tell me the Germans were coming up
and that I must go down the side. He, or rather the Count
provided me with bread and cheese on all except two days at the

Contd/4

expense of running themselves short. When the Germans retired
they took everything they could lay their hands on, or what
they couldn't take, they destroyed. Consequently the peasants
were very short of food and it was with sincere regret that he
couldn't give me anything on those two days.

The loneliness was the most trying part of the
whole experience and after anybody had been to see me. I would
lie for hours going through just what had been said. One night
the Americans shelled the valley east of VOLTERRA very heavily,
and I thought that they were coming pretty near. The next day,
however, all was silent and I was certain that they had had
to retreat. I was so depressed that I decided to make a break for
our lines that night. I intended to leave the hill at 22.00 hours
before the moon was up in order to have complete darkness to get
through the Germans in the immediate vicinity, and then have the
moon to help me later. I dressed and at 1900 hours lay down to
wait. Unfortunately, or as it happened fortunately, I fell asleep
and did not waken until 2.0A.M., when the moon was well up and
it was useless to attempt a break through. The next afternoon
the shelling started again and I knew that we were still
advancing.

It was very cold at nights but I wore a polo necked
sweater as wollen drawers under my flying overall and apart from
a cold due to getting wet before arriving on the hill, I suffered
no ill effects. My feet were very sore after the first five days,
and I had a large blister on my right heel, but while I was on the
hill they recovered. For food I had five raw eggs and bread and
cheese. The money which I had in my escape packet was in 500 lire
notes which to the peasants as a small fortune, and because they
would have a hard job explaining how they came to get a note of
such large denomination should they be asked, theywould not
accept it. At the farm house where I had lunch, I gave them a
note to give to the British authorities to the effect that they
had fed me, but unfortunately, I have forgotten the name of the
family. The Italian Army Lieutenant, lent me his pipe and matches,
and I was never short of smoking material, for the ground was
littered with dry leaves. The ants were a constant source of worry,
for although I had the bread covered by my silk maps, they would
eat right through. Moreover at night when I was asleep they would
get into my hair, and I had to have a "delousing" session every
morning. Slugs and scorpions were also troublesome.

From 88th Divisional Headquarters, I went to IV Corps
where I was looked after by Captain WEBSTER, the only Englishman
I could contact. He took me to Intelligence, but owing to the
fact that I had spent all my time avoiding the Germans, I could
give them little news. He then arranged for a truck to bring me
to GROSSETO, where I hoped to get air transport, but owing to the
fact that a thunderstorm had swollen the rivers, Highway one was
unserviceable between PIAMBINO and GROSSETO and it necessitated
a detour inland. I decided therefore to go to the airstrip at
PIAMBINO in the hope of getting by air, or failing that, to signal
the Squadron to collect me. Unfortunately the landing strip was bogged, and so I sent off a signal to say I was safe and spent the
night with 93. Squadron. The next day 324 Wing were sending a
truck to NAPLES, and I came to TARQUINIA on that.

I have the honour to be, Sir.,
Your Obedient servant.,

(Signed). I.C. CAMPBELL. F/O.

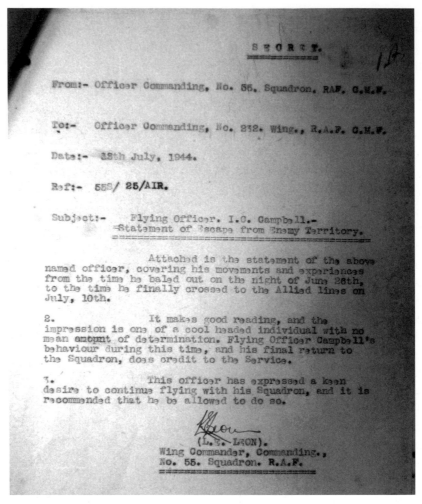

Wing Commander Leon's commendation for Flying Officer Campbell.

Back to Tom's story:

"I was reconnoitring for about two hours before I found a hiding place which suited me. Even then, I was in two minds whether or not to start walking south immediately. Eventually, the fact that we had no sleep the night before, decided me, and I lay down in the middle of the maize field where I had decided to hide. The plants were about six feet high and would conceal me in daylight, I thought, while the heavy dew was refreshing, and could actually be licked off the broad leaves. Mosquitos were numerous, so I rolled up in the parachute canopy, shutting them out effectively.

"My mental state at this time is worth recording, I think. Just after I had landed, my thoughts were in considerable turmoil, and if cornered I think I would have done something rash, being rather desperate at the time. After a while I grew calmer and smoked a Camel in the ditch, carefully concealing the glow with my hands and overall. Just then a few aircraft passed overhead, one after the other, and I realized that it was probably the rest of the Baltimores and Bostons returning from the raid. All of a sudden I felt lonely, and I fell to pitying myself in my predicament. However, I realized that I had to do something about it, and as I set about looking for somewhere to hide, my spirits gradually rose again, there being something Boy Scoutish about the whole episode. I slept well in my maize field, and did not awake until the sun was well up, and the sound of church bells disturbed me. I lay looking at the sky thinking for some time, and then I smoked another cigarette, whilst exploring my resources. I had an escape packet containing maps, compasses, hacksaw blade, and both French and Italian money. Also, I had a tin of Flying Emergency Rations, which yielded me a frugal breakfast. Then I took stock of my position. From my map, I worked out roughly the course we had flown, and with the times, I pinpointed myself approximately north of Florence, and about twenty miles distant. At this point I would recommend that the maps, although accurate, and in considerable detail, be provided also with land contours; which would often facilitate one in orientating oneself, when all other ideas are hazy.

"Shortly after this, I heard the noise of farm carts and voices on the farm track where I landed the night before, and thanked my stars that I hadn't stayed in the ditch. A few minutes later, I heard someone whistling very close, and as they gradually came nearer and nearer, I prepared to make a dash for it. At length, I could make out the source, an Italian farm worker or peasant. I lay still, and he passed within a couple of yards of me still whistling. I breathed again, but he came back a moment later and this time he saw me. I think the white 'chute must have caught his eye, even though I was lying on it, and had tucked it under me as much as I could; I just lay still watching him; and he stood still watching me. I had a hand operated Very cartridge ready to fire at him if he acted wrongly, even if only to scare him and make it easier for me to get away. He said 'Buon giorno' (Good morning), and I said the same, deciding that he was of reasonable disposition. I pulled out my box of cigarettes and offered him one, and soon we were smoking together, and attempted to find out, each one, about the other. I said I was 'Inglesi' (English), and he on his part, made me understand that I was alright as far as he was concerned. My Italian amounted to no more than a word or two, but the use of gestures made up for this lack, and soon we understood each other perfectly. I was to remain in the maize field while he went off to bring me some civilian clothes, and some food. He was not more than half an hour, and returned with two others, a large sandwich of liver, and the required clothes. I changed immediately, and all my kit, parachute etc, was put into a big sack and taken away by one of them. I then fell onto the food, and while I finished it off, they made me understand that they wanted to take me to see another aviator, whom they said had a broken arm. I thought at first they meant the pilot, but when they said 'bionde' (blonde) I knew that this was not the case.

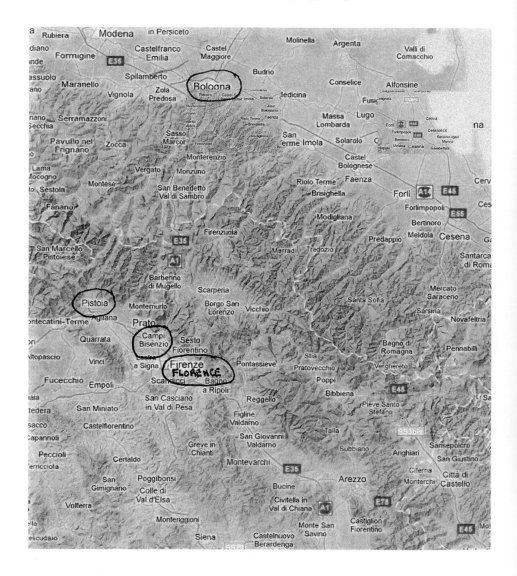

"We walked about two kilometres, and came at length to a two–storied house, which resembled a stable. Upstairs were quite a number of people, all–smiling as I came up amongst them. In a corner was a rough straw mattress, and on it was Flying Officer Hulme, our Navigator. He looked very pale and strained and told me a few minutes before, the village doctor, who was then bandaging him, had reset his dislocated left shoulder and generally treated him for shock and exposure. Flying Officer Hulme said that he had lain in the field where he had landed for fifteen hours, unable to move, when he was found by two Italians, of the same type as the one who found me. I was very glad to see him, and after helping him downstairs, we sat in the sun outside, with some of our new found friends acting as sentries. We discussed our position, and eventually decided, on the recommendation of the doctor, to hide in a nearby blockhouse for a few days, until Flying Officer Hulme should be able to move. We were provided with mattresses, and food, cigarettes, cognac etc, and were left alone for the rest of the day, until the doctor came just before sundown. He had another look at Flying Officer Hulme's arm and shoulder, and seemed satisfied. He was of a very cheery disposition, and we soon brightened up under his good spirits. He told us that his village was called Campi Bisenzio, and that Florence was only about ten kilometres away to the south-east. This was very helpful, and we thought there might be a reasonable chance of hiding up in Florence, as it was an open city or 'City Bianca', and would not be overfull of Germans".

Author's note: Campi Bisenzio was the place where the first combustion engine was built by Felice Matteucci and Eugenio Barsanti. It is also the birthplace (1942) of artist Marco Sassone. In the meantime, 55 Squadron reported the aircraft missing, lost in action, and it was assumed that the crew had been captured and were reported as being taken PoW (Prisoner of War).

Back to Tom: "After keeping fairly well, we woke up to a bright morning, and the sound of aircraft running up. Looking out through one of the gun slots, I saw a cloud of dust a few kilometres to the south-east, in the direction of Florence, and took it to be an aerodrome. Just then, two aircraft took off and circled in our direction, still fairly low. They were M.E. 109's G/s, and we could clearly see the markings and other details. I stood watching the aerodrome in case any more aircraft took off, but there were none (We found out later that the aerodrome was called Peretola and that there were only these Messerschmitts operating from it). Later in the day we were visited by three officials of the Italian Committee of Liberation, and they said we would be taken to Florence in a few days. By this time, we had the utmost confidence in these people and thought we were lucky to have contacted such patriotic and brave types; there was a considerable German garrison in the village, and the risks these people ran were considerable, although they never seemed to worry much about it. We were looked after in that locality, and on 1 July, were informed that we were going to Florence in a 'carrozzi' or horse drawn gharry. Soon after, we were led from our hiding place, and there was the gharry, complete with driver waiting for us. With hurried goodbyes to the Doctor, Conte Alfredo, and Tesi Silvano and Rolando Beogiotti, we climbed in and were off. The first Germans we saw were two bleary eyed soldiers sitting on a wall. They never even gave us a look, and we concluded that they were suffering from a hangover, as we had been told of habitual heavy drinking on the part of the Germans in the village.

"Further along, we passed more soldiers, some marching and some on bicycles, but we might not have existed as far as they were concerned. We saw a very carefully camouflaged double-bowser, parked at the side of the road under some trees, and this was an unspoken comment on the shortage of German vehicles in Italy. Next we saw a herd of sound looking horses, which our escort said, were bound for Germany. He further elaborated on this statement by saying that the Germans were systematically cleaning out the country, and in his opinion, that was the only reason they were holding out in Italy at all. His name was Frossini, and he came from Florence. Approaching the outskirts of the city, we turned off the main road, or 'autostrada', in order to avoid the interrogation posts ahead. We took a narrow side road, and were soon surrounded by houses in the district known as Peretola, near the aerodrome. There were quite a few S.S. troopers around, and a few Grenadiers and Fascist Military Police. We were about to pass a garage, when out drove a German medium tank, with five German soldiers sitting on top – one straddling the gun – and we were obliged to stop while it manoeuvred in the narrow street. When it turned, the gun was pointing straight at us, and for an unforgettable minute, we were the subjects of what seemed careful scrutiny. However, the Sergeant waved us past, with a leer on his face, and a mocking bow as we drew level. Later the humour of the situation caused us considerable amusement, but just then, we did not feel much like laughing.

"Eventually we arrived in the district of Florence known as Campo Di Marte, and waited for the owner, who came up on a bicycle. The house looked uninhabited, as it had been shaken by a bomb blast, and it suited our purpose down to the ground. The owner's name was Guido Targioni, and he had moved out when the marshalling yards were bombed (by Allied aircraft) on 1 and 2 May, damaging the building. The back room was practically intact, except for the ceiling, and had been cleaned up prior to our arrival. There was a double bed with feather mattress, and the usual bedroom furnishings. We said 'molto buono' and our host went off for some food while we inspected the rest of the house, which was not in such good condition. We had a good meal, and Targioni left us, with a warning about looking out of the front windows, as the Germans often came walking in the evenings past the house. We were in this house for seven weeks, and until 11 August, we never even went outside the front door. Most days were uneventful and to cut a long story short, I will merely comment on the happenings of importance during this time".

Author: At this point we will break from Tom's story, to fill in what was going on just to the south of his "safe house".

From late June, the Allied Army slowly made its way north, and by mid July it had secured further towns and cities. The Germans withdrew towards the Arno River and the defensive line called the "Gothic Line", whilst Tom was ensconced in his hideout. On 17 July the Eighth Army crossed the Arno River further north. Between 12 and 16 July, twenty bridges across the Po River were put out of use by 55 Squadron and others.

Back to Tom's narrative: "We had daily news of the fighting from Targioni, who brought our food twice a day during all that time and at considerable risk to himself. Often the news he brought us was over–optimistic, as we found later, to our dismay, but for the most part, it was a fairly concise and accurate report of the situation. His source was the bulletins of the National Committee of Liberation, who were responsible for us he said, and we decided it safer and better to stay there for some time to give Flying Officer Hulme's shoulder a chance to mend. At the rate the Allies were advancing, we expected that Florence would be liberated in a couple of weeks or so. We had been about seventy miles behind the lines when we baled out, but now were only about fifty or fifty-five, due to further advances, and to our coming south into Florence.

"On 5 July a representative of the Committee of Liberation, arrived escorted by Targioni, and took our numbers, ranks, names and trades, in order to have them transmitted across the lines to the Allies. We never found out whether the message got through or not, but thought it a pretty good idea at the time. That same day, a teapot complete with some tea, sugar and milk, arrived via Targioni from an English lady who was being held prisoner (under 'house arrest') in a Florence Hotel, by the Germans. They wanted to put her in a Concentration Camp, but thanks to the efforts of her lawyer, Marini, she was allowed to stay in the comparative comfort of her hotel. We thanked her for the tea and the kind thoughts. On the 7 July we had a visit from an official of the Socialist Party, who brought cognac and wine. Around this time we became alarmed at the number of people who knew of our existence, and said as much to Targioni; however, he replied all was well, and we trusted him. We first heard the gunfire from the front line on these nights, and our spirits rose as the sounds grew nearer, even though they seemed to move extremely slowly. After the tenth day, our food mainly consisted of 'minostra' a kind of thick soup made with rice (later referred to as 'Minestrone'). Quite sustaining, but rather monotonous after a while, although we did not complain, as food was short all round. The main thing was we did have something, thanks to the committee and Targioni. They even brought German emergency rations and gave them to us to conserve, in case no one was able to get to us with food. We were often given books to read, which had been left around in days gone by, when many English and American people used to visit Florence. We had a 1937 *Daily Telegraph*, and two *New Yorkers* of the same year. I also read the *Seven Pillars of Wisdom* and *Hatter's Castle*, and a few more of the R.M. Ballantyne variety. I also did some sketching to pass the time away, as it was very tedious being cooped up, with the weather glorious outside.

"We often heard aircraft during the night, and concluded that they were from our wing. I even saw a Baltimore against the moon on one occasion, and one night a Boston roared over the house at fifty feet. During the days, our fighter-bombers were continually harassing the retreating German columns, although we heard the latter best at night, when all was fairly quiet. There were a considerable number of light and heavy A.A. (Anti-Aircraft) defences in our area, and we often watched the Kitt bombers and Mustangs running the gauntlet through the hail of white and black smoke-puffs, as the flak-gunners went into action. As far as we know, they never shot down one, and a lone Spitfire was the only 'kill' made near Florence, with the pilot landing behind Allied Lines.

"At night, we often heard the Germans moving heavy guns by horse-power, and on two occasions, we actually saw them. They would stop whenever an aircraft came overhead and carry on when it had passed. It seemed that they were desperately short of mechanized transport, and they pressed all the local civilian cars into service, telling the outraged owners, to walk; many able-bodied men were pressed into service for the German Labour Camps in the North. There they were worked to exhaustion, and more often than not, died from lack of food. The favourite method adopted by the Germans in Florence, for seizing these men, was to stop the streetcars in the main thoroughfares, and press-gang all the men inside. Both entrances were guarded, so those inside were trapped.

"Whilst staying in the house, we made it a rule for people who came to visit us to use a special knock on the door – three taps spaced well, and not too loud. More than once the bell rang, and different knocks came on the door, but we never answered, and kept as quiet as mice until it was clear again. Among our visitors were a middle aged lawyer, Francesco Marini, who spoke English perfectly, and his wife, who made excellent doughnuts. He was responsible for the high state of morale always with us, and his sober, well-thought observations were steady rock, after the continual shifting sands of rumour we had been used to."

Again we will briefly leave Tom's narrative to keep the context in chronological order. During the month of July the squadron moved to Cecina, which is further north up the west coast of Italy and to the north of Livorno, where they stayed until October 1944. On 16 July an RAF Hurricane roared across the Italian countryside looking for targets of opportunity and came across a German staff car, which the pilot realized was carrying Field Marshall Erwin Rommel. The Hurricane strafed the vehicle and Rommel was severely wounded but survived the attack; the RAF had succeeded where Montgomery had failed; to tame "The Desert Rat". On 18 July the Allies took Caen, after saturation bombing by the RAF who dropped seven thousand tons of bombs, and Montgomery's Army went in and mopped up the town.

Back to Tom's narrative: "On 20 July, the Germans began to blow up the remaining railway system in the city, and we naturally thought they would be leaving any time at all. Very heavy explosions echoed for miles around all day, and we could see the columns of dust and smoke rising in several different places. By this time the Front had advanced considerably, and every night we were treated to long barrages from both sides. The Germans were reported to be leaving the city, and only leaving a garrison of S.S. troops and paratroopers to delay the inevitable advance. By 25 July, the Allies had advanced to within twenty kilometres of

Florence, in three directions. That evening, we had a visit from a certain Doctor Gesini, who had been sentenced to be shot by the Fascists, for being instrumental in effecting the escape of Air Vice-Marshal Boyd, and eight other Generals, from Florence over a year previously. He informed us that the Germans were saying that Florence was no longer an 'open city', and thus we thought that we might have fighting to do. We were expecting a 'State of Emergency' to be declared any day. On 29 July, the Germans began evacuating the people from the riverside area in Florence, and these homeless people invaded our district. We were a little afraid that some of them would attempt to enter our supposedly empty house, for want of something better, but Targioni did sentry duty outside, and we were not disturbed. That evacuation was a sign of the times, and the Germans began to guard the bridges with rifles and machine guns, allowing no one to cross the river from either side.

"We heard that, if the Germans fought it out in Florence, the Allies would bomb Dresden, the corresponding city in Germany, but that did not seem to make much difference to anyone."

Leaving once again briefly to "outside matters":

On 1 August, the RAF pummelled the "Gothic Line", following prolonged artillery fire. The Germans fought tenaciously, and with everything they had; but ran out of ammunition. The Allies climbed the hills and could see Florence some ten miles away. On 3 August, the city of Alromala was taken by the Allies and declared an "Open City". The Germans decided not to stay and fight at Florence and offered no resistance. The Arno River was spanned by several bridges which bisected the city and the Germans blew these, as well as buildings some one hundred yards on each side; this to hamper and slow down the Allied advance.

Back to Tom. Here I will incorporate parts of his diary written day-to-day, which he later incorporated into this Narrative. Each part prefixed D for Diary and N for Narrative. "D: Wednesday 2 August thirty-seventh day. Slept well and woke to a cup of tea – Stan's (Flying Officer Hulme) making. We were caught on the hop by the three girls and had to slip smartly into proper dress before letting them in. At once they commenced to clean the place and ushered us away from under their feet. Yesterday Pontassieve and Signa were occupied. General Alexander had delivered an ultimatum that if the Germans had not left the town by midnight tonight he will attack them in it. Things are coming to a head all right. Girls came again in the afternoon and we all mucked in to clean the other rooms, which were full of broken glass and powdered mortar. Quite a busy day. At night B. Aldo and his brother came with smokes, heard lots of horse-drawn vehicles moving around after dark and German voices shouting. No unusual barrage apparent after midnight.

"Thursday, 3 August thirty-eighth day. The professor came again at midday with a formal note from Smilya. 'Stato di emergenca exists from today'. More or less confines everyone to the house. Yesterday someone killed an S.S. Trooper...

The 'avocatto' lived just a few yards from there! Bartoli and our little armico came this afternoon to bring us a last minute supply of water. Don't expect G.T. for a while, much firing around us today. Think they are long-range, more heavy local explosions all night.

"N: The long expected 'State of Emergency' was declared from 3 August, and the Germans issued a proclamation, saying that any man seen on the streets after that day would be shot out of hand. One day before, an S.S. Trooper was killed as he was seizing wristwatches and jewellery from people in the street quite close to us. As a reprisal, the Germans blew up the whole street on both sides, and everyone was simmering with rage and waiting for the day to come when they could fall on the Germans as they retreated out of the city. The water and electric light was now cut off, and the installations blown up by the Germans. They also took away the streetcars and some of the overhead cables. The next day of the 'State of Emergency', we saw an Auster flying high over the city to the west, and thought we were in for a barrage, as General Alexander had issued an ultimatum to the Germans the day before, to be out of the city by midnight, or else. However, it did not materialize. On the afternoon of the 7 August, a Mitchell and Marauder came over low and everyone ran for it. No shots were fired on either side, however, and they even came round a second time. I think they were probably dropping leaflets. At night we could now see the tracer of our heavy machine guns crossing the river on the outskirts of the city, and the staccato reply of the lighter German arms; it was all very interesting and we could not sleep for all the excitement and nerves, as the heavy barrages were uncomfortably close – or so it seemed. Also, there were about a dozen heavy German batteries close behind our house, on the high ground, and they made the most ear piercing blast I have ever heard.

"D: Monday, 7 August, forty-second day. Six weeks tonight since we parachuted into this new way of living. Could almost be six months wondering wanderers – the three girls managed to come again and brightened our morning for us considerably. Sesto is the latest point reached by the Allies and is well to the north of Florence. A Mitchell and Marauder came shooting up the city this afternoon. Everybody ran for it but no shots were fired. Much activity at night, with a better view from the flat upstairs.

"N: As we were short of water, when it rained heavily on the night of 9 August, we put out pots and pans to catch some of the drippings. All this was changed abruptly, however, as on the morning of 11 August, fighting broke out in Florence, after the Partisan Forces had descended from the mountains, and the air was full of shots and explosions. The Germans actually left the city in the morning, although elements returned in the late afternoon. However, there was enough to do with Fascist and German snipers, who were taking a heavy toll on civilians.

"Two girls, whom we knew previously, came for us about 0900 hours and out we went for the first time in seven weeks. Between us, we had four hand grenades, a revolver (Barrette) and a long hunting knife. We were hailed by lots of people, and many drinks were forced on us before we set out with the two Partisans to cross the city, we dodged from doorway to doorway, always hugging the walls, and often heard bullets whine overhead, although they were probably not aimed at us. We picked up a couple of bicycles and, two on each, sped up the streets, and down the alleys, trying to miss the worst of the fighting. My hand grenades were well in evidence, and I resolved to sell myself dearly if we were stopped, as I had a recurrence of that old exhilarating and desperate feeling. A few shells fell around us, and mines began to go off to the north, so we added power into our pedalling, and got out of the area as soon as we could. We were obliged to stop more than once, as a bunch of Partisans were surrounding a house wherein was a Fascist or German sniper. They usually got them in the end. Soon it was a common sight to see dead bodies lying out of windows as well as in the streets. I never saw dead Germans, however, and think that was due to their superior craft and experience, as they were all S.S. troops and Paratroops.

"As yet, there were no Allies north of the Arno, but it was a Front Line war all right, and how those Partisans hated the Germans and Fascists; if anything, they went for the Fascists more than anyone else, and their hatred seemed more a personal one. They obtained good results at considerable cost to themselves, considering their inexperience and shortage of ammunition and weapons. The bridges over the Arno had all been blown up, except the Ponte Vecchio, at the order of Colonel Fuchs, the German town Commander, and this hindered the allies in their advance, as even the entrance roads to the Ponte Vecchio, had been considerably mined. This was in defiance of Field Marshall Kesselring's promise to leave the bridges intact, he was having trouble through not announcing his allegiance to Hitler at the time. We continued through the streets, and eventually arrived at our destination, a house near the Central Station, more or less out of breath, but all in one piece anyway. This was a sort of headquarters for the Partisans, and many conferences were held there. Many new faces were seen, and we held considerable status among them as English Officers, even though we did not resemble such in the least, at the time. In the afternoon, we were out with an armed guard to fetch water, and saw the bodies of dozens of Fascists lying where they had been executed. Quite a gory business. After our long period of inaction, we felt very fit and well in a couple of days of feverish activity and experience. I saw the first allied soldiers – six Ghurkhas – who had waded across the Arno at the ford, and were advancing cautiously through the streets to the scene of the fighting. It did my heart good to see them and I shouted to them in English. They took no notice of me however, and passed with eyes intent, on the houses on either side of the street.

"On 12 August, Flying Officer Hulme and myself went with a guide, to the Palazzo Vecchio, to see the advance field security officer there. After much elbowing and pushing, we managed to get near him, as he was being plagued by everyone, all claiming that they had vital information to impart. After shouting to him above the din, he looked at us, and then away again, and then we realized, that being in civilian clothes, he merely thought we were two Italians. After we told him that we were RAF Officers, he gave us all his attention, and apologized for not noticing us. We took this as a compliment to our disguise, and asked him what we should do. He said that he was mainly after military information, and we told him all we knew. Then, at our own request he allowed us to go back to the house, as he had no facilities for taking us out, having crossed the Arno on foot; his name was Major McIntosh, and he was the first Allied Officer in the city (Later awarded the DDO). We returned to the house, passing fresh evidence of fighting and delayed action mines. More bodies were being carted away, by the special black-cowled death squads, who had access anywhere in the city with safety. The reason we did not cross the river immediately, was that we had so many things to do before leaving, and we proceeded to clear up our effects right away. Fresh 'gen' (information) was forthcoming from some of the Partisans from the north, concerning the defences of the Gothic Wing, and we directed them to the aforesaid Major McIntosh. In the afternoon we went to the hospital, which was crammed full of battle casualties, and at length found Mario Ciccarelli; who aided us considerably in the days of our forced hiding, and who had been shot through the shoulder in the fighting. We also heard that Frossini, who had brought us into Florence in the first place, had been shot in the head, but was not on the danger list. That day the German Paratroops reoccupied Campo di-Marte, the district in which we had been hiding, and all the houses in our street had been taken over as strong points by snipers and grenadiers. It was just as well that we had left when we did, and we could not help thinking that someone had inside information on the whole situation. That evening, we met some soldiers of the 4th Canadian Tank Division, and they said that they would be across the Arno the next day with their tanks, when the Bailey bridge was completed across the piers of the demolished Ponte Santa Trinita. We had another disturbed night with shooting going on in the street below, but we were used to it by then, and knew from experience that we would be alright, as long as we stayed indoors.

"D: Sunday, 13 August, forty-eighth day. Went out early to get some food; managed to cross the river but had to come back empty handed, except for English cigarettes and tea; managed to get Minestra from the Convent near home, fairly quiet but shelling at night.

"N: Next day, the 13 August, we crossed the Arno for the first time, by the ford, in order to obtain some food for the people in the house and ourselves. However, we had to return empty handed, as there was none available, and had to fall back on the Convent which had provided for us before. We scrounged some English cigarettes from the soldiers we met, after they got over their surprise at hearing us, apparently Italians, speaking perfect English! In the morning (14

August) we went to see the Town Governor, (Captain Lampon) about getting through the mass of M.P's (Military Police) now guarding all exits to the south.

"D: Tuesday, 15 August, fiftieth day. Crossed the river again after seeing Captain Lampon; went to 7th Garrison, but had to go back to the Excelsior Hotel. Smilya was thrilled with her ride in the Jeep. Saw some people we knew and gave our information to Captain Cottrill (I), saw Targioni again, good old scout. Good job 'Jerry' didn't catch us as he is shooting RAF types now; slept Sullarno.

"N: (Captain Lampon) He gave us a pass and we crossed the Arno again, in search of the Allied PoW Repatriation Unit, to whom we had been instructed to give ourselves up. When we arrived at the address, we found that 'the bird had flown', to the north side of the river, of all places. Accordingly, we went back to the north side again, to the Excelsior Hotel, which had been taken over by the Field Security Service, and resembled the League of Nations, on account of the widely differing uniforms there, and the different languages spoken. The officer we were looking for, one Australian, Captain Stiedge, was tracing some other soldiers, back home we went having left a note for him to say that we would return at 1800 hours. We eventually met him in the evening, and he took us back to the south side of the Arno, to a villa, which had been set up as an escaped PoW rest camp. That night we were in the middle of a German-Allied artillery duel; as the Allied guns were emplaced on the hill just behind the villa. We could hear the 88mm and 210mm shells screaming and moaning over, and fall, with a vicious rush, a few hundred yards away. The explosions shook the house quite violently, and in the morning there were pieces of shrapnel on the balcony outside, as the nearest shell had fallen less than 100 yards away.

"D: Wednesday, 16 August, fifty-first day. After a perilous night on the south bank of the Arno, when shells fell within 100 yards of the house, we went back north again to finish up our affairs as far as possible. Introduced Capt Stiedge (Aussie), to Dottore Gencinis and Andre. Would have liked to have contacted L' Avocatto but he was still in German part of town. After lunch and much persuasion, Captain Stiedge allowed us to sleep at Eileen's house. She brought Bob with her in the evening and we all had a little party to the tune of machine guns and rifle fire. Bob slept at our house, as it was too dangerous to go out.

"N: The day before, we had an interrogation by Captain Cottrill, an advanced Area Intelligence Officer, and thought that we had finished with such things, but Captain Stiedge, who was our guardian, gave us another, and at first I must admit we did not take to him as much as we might have. However, we soon realized our mistake, and helped him in various matters, the most important of which was bringing through the lines his sister and niece, from San Domenico, just north of Florence. On 16 August we went home again, and had a bit of a party, as we expected to leave for the south the next day. It was too dangerous to go out after dark, so many of our guests stayed the night with us, and we drank toasts to the tune of machine gun and rifle fire. Next day, the Captain relented further, and

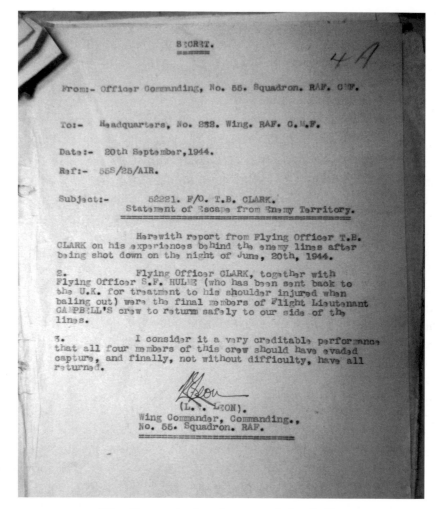

Wing Commander Leon's commendation for Tom.

gave us another day in which to say goodbye to our many friends and benefactors. This was really decent of him and we made the most of it, seeing scores of people, and getting quite sunburnt and tired in the sun.

"D: Friday, 18 August, fifty-third day. Left by three-tonner for the south; arrived at camp near Sienna for lunch. On again afterwards to No 1 C.R.U; where we spent the night.

"N: On Friday, 18 August, we left Florence, by three-tonner, having been provided with soldier's boots, berets and uniforms, and after various meanderings arrived at a camp near Arrezzo, where we spent the night on the ground.

"D: Saturday, 19 August. On to Rome via many of the places we had bombed previously.   Arreno-Magiore-Spoleto-Fermi-Castel-Vecchia-Roma;   slept at transit camp, utterly fed up!

"N: We made Rome the day after, and saw many places of interest on the way. The 20 August saw us on our way to Naples, and more interrogations at the No 1 Allied PoW Repatriation Camp. After a few days, I went to No3 S.P.D. Naples, while he, Navigator Flying Officer Hulme, went to No1 RAF General Hospital for treatment to his injured arm. After I had undergone a medical inspection at the B.P.D., I met Flying Officer I.C. Campbell, our Pilot, and Warrant Officer E.H. Evans, the W/Op, and was never more surprised and pleased in my life, as I thought they were still in enemy occupied territory. This meant that all the crew had returned safely, and was a comfort to Flying Officer Hulme and myself. After about a week at the B.P.D; I was able to return to the squadron (then stationed at Cecina) none the worse after my experiences, while Flying Officer Hulme was flown home for special treatment".

Signed: Flying Officer, Clark.

A signal was received by the Air Ministry in London on 24 August 1944 from the Base Personnel Office, North African Air Force, advising that Tom, and Flying Officer Hulme, had been located at the Allied Prisoner of War Repatriation Unit, Central Mediterranean Forces.

On 1 and 2 September, eleven Baltimores of 55 Squadron flew a sortie in the Adriatic Sector, attacking small barges along the coast. They were met with searchlights and heavy and light flak. Sadly, during the early hours of 2 September 1944, the same day as the Allies had broken through the "Gothic Line" at the southernmost part, Baltimore FW 482 "U" was hit and the crew consisting of Sergeant H.F.L. David, (Pilot), Second Lieutenant D.M. Cameron, (Navigator), Sergeant 1801228, James Walter Thomas Hudson, (Wireless Operator), and Sergeant W.B. Walker, (Air Gunner), died in a sortie over Malta. Hudson was a 21 year old from Putney, London, and the crew's memory is commemorated at the Commonwealth Air Forces Memorial on the island.

In the meantime, Flying Officer Campbell had walked back through the lines, and after rest and recuperation, restarted flying with 55 Squadron during the first week in August 1944; Warrant Officer Evans would rejoin his crew during the third week of August 1944. Their other crew members being Flying Officer R.A. Petchey, and Flight Sergeant D. Lea, Air Gunner, then later, Lieutenant L.W. Douglas. Tom would take Lea's place from 23 September 1944, making the original crew of three, less Flying Officer Stan Hulme.

On 7 September 1944, "Flight" magazine carried further awards of the DFC (Distinguished Flying Cross) and three members of 55 Squadron were included: Acting Flight Lieutenant E. Gooch, Flying Officer T.A. Newman, and Flying Officer V.B. White; all being RAFVR (Royal Air Force Voluntary Reserve).

During September 1944 the Baltimore Squadrons, including No. 55, came under the scrutiny of "Flight" magazine and a short article was published on 14 September entitled "RAF Owls". It said that the Baltimore Squadrons were the eyes of the Army after dark and had been on armed reconnaissance for the Fifth and Eighth Army over many fronts and were currently in the South of

France in the Rivera Region. The two commanders were Wing Commander James Wallace, 223 Squadron, and Wing Commander Lionel Edward "Cookie" Leon, DFC, a South African from Johannesburg who commanded 55 Squadron in Italy from January 1944 until August 1945. He was quoted as saying "Our prey is anything we can see on the roads. At the same time we are collating all the information possible about the German movements." So from this article we know what Tom and the squadron were up to at that time. Over a three week period during September 1944, Leon and his squadron flew thirty-one of these hazardous operations, before his squadron was taken out of the front line to convert to Boston light bombers. In September 1944 he was awarded a bar to his DFC. (Around the same time Tom was nominated by Leon for a gallantry medal; and was later, during June 1945, awarded a "Mentioned in Despatches".)

DATE	AIRCRAFT TYPE & NUMBER	CREW	DUTY	Time Up	Time Down	DETAILS OF SORTIE OR FLIGHT
23/24 Sept	Baltimore V FW 705	Capt. H.D. Seric / Lt. P. Katerinic / W/O R.M. Brown / 2/Lt. M. Milosavljevic	Armed recce / Savignano - / Bologna-Ferrara - / Ravenna	2151	0058	16x40 on 3+ MT 3 miles west of Bologna. 2+500 at one light on Forli landing ground. Bombs fell across Taxi-strip. Bombing from 4000' and 4500' at 2320 and 2355 respectively.
"	Baltimore V FW 354	Sgt L.C. Baker / Sgt T. Whatley / Sgt E.A. Pyewell / Sgt T. Nicholls	"	2155	0100	2x500 and 16x40 on 7 MT stationary 6 miles N/W of Forli. NRO. Bomb fell from 4000' at 0004.
"	Baltimore V FW 702	F/S F.W. Dalzell / W/O L.P. Griffiths / W/O H.W. Reynolds / F/S F.O. Matthews	"	2200	0045	16x40 on 1 MT on road West of Lugo. RNO. 2x500 on 4+ MT 4 miles s/w of Ferrara. RNO except for 1 direct hit on road.
"	Baltimore V FW 505	F/S G. Smele / F/O A.D. MacVe / F/S J. Tilley / F/S J.C. Bickle	"	2202	0055	16x40 on light N/W of Forli. RNO. 1x500 on light on Highway 9 4 miles N/W of Forli from 4000' at 2334. 1x500
23/24 Sept	Baltimore V FW 313	F/S S. Delow / Sgt H. Moncaster / Sgt W.A. Salmons / Sgt J.W. Francis	Armed recce / Cesinatico / Cesena-Ravenna / Porto-Garibaldi	2205	0120	light 3 miles east of Bologna from 4500' at 2331. One fire started. 2x500 and 16x40 from 3700' at 0120 on fire and lights on road 10 miles N/E of Portomaggiore. NRO.
"	Baltimore V FW 469	F/L I.C. Campbell / Lt L.W. Douglas / W/O W.F. Evans / F/O T.B. Clarke	"	2146	0035	1x500 and 8x40 at 2315 on 1 light on Highway 9 2 miles s/E of Imola. 1x500 and 8x40 on 1 light on rew road at 2335 north of Faenza. Both bombing from 4000' NRO.
"	Baltimore V FW 440	S/L J.F.W. Elliott / P/O H. Bailey / Sgt R. Thompson / Sgt J. Brooking	"	2137	0017	1x500 and 1x SBC on 2 MT north of Modigliano from 5000' at 2245. 1x500 and 1x SBC on 4 MT 2 miles s/E of Forli from 5000' at 2258. NRO.

Tom's Return: 23/24 September 1944, flying with Campbell, Douglas and Evans at No 6 in Baltimore FW 469.

The Allies moved on and took Rimini on 21 September, Lorenzo on 11 October; and were then held up by the "Gothic Line" further up in the North Appellations.

Overnight of 30 September/1 October 1944, 55 Squadron sent out twelve Baltimores in six pairs on a roving armed reconnaissance patrol of Northern and Eastern Italy. Now a Squadron Leader, Les Harland and crew, flew in FW 839 on an armed recce over Cesinatico, Ferrara, Porto Corsini, Ravenna, and Cesena. They were paired with a crew piloted by Sergeant Crowe in FW 512. Tom and his crew, consisting of Flying Officer Campbell, now a DFC, Douglas and Evans, were in FW 469 and took off at 0108 hours paired with FW 440 flown by Flight Lieutenant Boyle. They carried out an armed recce over Savignano, Bologna, Ferrara and Faenza, they found no motor transport movement, so at 0248 hours they dropped their entire load on the alternative target at Imola Marshalling Yards from a height of 4,000 feet, which was straddled, and black smoke emitted from it, they landed at 0345 hours. The target was further bombed by Boyle's craft at 0335 hours. A similar operation using thirteen Baltimores was carried out overnight of the 1 and 2 October.

During a four day period from 3 to 6 October 1944, torrential rain began to pour on the camp at Cecina. The tents of the Officers, Sergeants and Airmens Messes of 55 and 13 Squadrons became waterlogged and the Baltimores waiting to be replaced with Bostons were bogged down and unable to fly out. Drainage ditches were dug across the airfield using bulldozers and tractors and it wasn't until the seventeenth of the month that the Baltimores were taken to Pisa and on to Perugia. The main party of fifty–five personnel, including Tom, left on 21 October for Ancona and billeted in an excellent disused factory at Porto Potenezo–Picenzo; still more rain fell during the third week of the month.

At Perugia all of the Baltimores were handed over and the squadron strength was now two Bostons and one Pilot. On the twenty-eighth, Flying Officer Campbell, Tom's former crewmate and Pilot, was given a rapid conversion course by the CO, Wing Commander Leon; and on the twenty-ninth, Leon and Campbell flew the two Bostons down to Marcianise and seven more pilots left with Flight Lieutenant Lee, whilst a small servicing party went by road. Flying Officer Campbell held the unique distinction of being one of the first pilots in training and conversion to a succession of aircraft, from Blenheim to Baltimore to Boston; and being involved in the succession of campaigns, North Africa, Sicily and Italy.

The arrival of the Italian winter meant that a renewed offensive on the rest of German occupied northern Italy didn't begin until 9 April 1945. During October 1944, 55 Squadron remained in Italy, stationed at Perugia, situated halfway between Rome and Bologna and to the east of Castiglione Del L'ago, in the centre of northern Italy.

The squadron then withdrew from the front line to re-equip and train with Douglas Bostons; returning once again to the theatre of war in Northern Italy until the end of hostilities, but without Tom, who had gone to pastures new.

World War II Medal Summary

Eight Stars were awarded for the campaigns of the Second World War. The Stars are six-pointed, in bronze, with the cipher of King George VI in the centre. The title of each star appears around the cipher and also a different ribbon denotes each separate Star. The colours of the ribbon have symbolic significance and are believed to have been designed personally by King George VI. Two medals, the Defence Medal and the War Medal, were issued in recognition of General Service in the Second World War. These are circular medals made in cupro-nickel. The criteria for the award of medals to those who had fought in the Second World War were finalized in 1948. In accordance with the criteria, the medals were issued un-named. No more than five Stars may be awarded to one person (Tom received four, and wasn't in Europe, Burma or the Pacific Campaign). Regulations relating to the award of the Pacific, Burma, Atlantic, Air Crew Europe, and France and Germany Stars, prevented this from happening. Those who would qualify for more are awarded a clasp with the title of one of the Stars to which they qualify. This clasp is then attached to the ribbon of one of the other Stars, as laid out in the regulations.

Medal Entitlement 52221 Flt Lt Thomas Buchanan Clark

1939/45 Star For Operational Service between 3 September 1939 & 2 September 1945.

Atlantic Star For Operations in the "Battle of the Atlantic" between 3 September 1939 & May 1945.

Africa Star For one or more day's service in North Africa between 10 June 1940 & 12 May 1943.

Italy Star For Operational Service in Italy or Sicily between 11 June 1943 and May 1945.

Defence Medal For a minimum of three years non-combatant home service or one year in certain overseas areas.

1939/45 War Medal For a Minimum of twenty-eight days service in the Second World War.

"Mention in Despatches" An Oak Leaf Clasp, this was issued for Gallantry or Bravery which fell just short of a Gallantry Medal. (E.g. CGM, DFC, DFM, DSO) The Clasp was to be worn on the 1939/45, War Medal. This award was made on 14 June 1945 for specific acts during his service with 55 Squadron in 1944.

A Brief History of Mention In despatches

The practice of mentioning in despatches by military commanders has been around for a very long time, although it was Sir Charles Napier who, in his despatch of 2 March 1843 (*London Gazette 9 May 1843*), was the first to mention those below commissioned rank. The actual form of mention varied from a list of names to a description of the individual services performed. In 1902 it was decided that publication in the *London Gazette* was essential to constitute a mention. A very large amount of mentions were made in the First World War, and for this reason the vast majority of military despatches merely provided a list of names, and over 141,000 names were gazetted between 1914 and 1920.

Tom's Medals.

King's Crown Cap Badge.

Tom 1945 with his "King's Crown" cap, 6 medal ribbons and "MiD.

No official distinction was given for mention in despatches until 1919, when King George V approved of a special certificate to be awarded for all persons mentioned in the First World War despatches. To most this did not satisfy the need to recognize the mention in despatches, so in 1920, for the Army and Navy, it was decided that a multiple-leafed bronze oak leaf should be worn on the ribbon of the Victory Medal. Only one oak leaf per individual to be worn, irrespective of the number of times he had been mentioned. A smaller version was worn on the ribbon bar. The design of the emblem then changed to a single oak leaf emblem for the Second World War and subsequent wars and campaigns.

Arctic Star and Bomber Command Clasp to the 1939–45 Star Awards
There has been an ongoing campaign for some time for two awards to be made in recognition of the great bravery of those in the Royal Air Force and the other Services who contributed to two very significant campaigns of the Second World War.

Her Majesty the Queen has approved designs for the new awards, and it was announced on 26 February 2013, by the Ministry of Defence, that all the details have been confirmed for the issue of the Arctic Star and the Bomber Command Clasp.

With regard to the award of the Bomber Command Clasp, the criteria for eligibility is for any aircrew of Bomber Command who served at least sixty days, or completed a tour of operations, on a Bomber Command operational unit and flew at least one operational sortie from 3 September 1939 to 8 May 1945, inclusive.

The Arctic Star is granted for operational service of any length north of the Arctic Circle (66 degrees, 32'N) from 3 September 1939 to 8 May 1945. Eligibility is partially defined as follows: Air Force – Aircrew of the Royal Air Force will be eligible if they landed north of the Arctic Circle or served in the air over this area.

As a result of this announcement, I have applied on Tom's behalf for his issue of these two awards.

Bomber Command Clasp: For his service on 55 Squadron 1944.

Arctic Star: For his service on 201 Squadron North Atlantic/Arctic Patrol and North Atlantic Ferry Organization 1941.

Chapter Six

"A Family Man; The Cold War; Bus Service to India; Flying The Royal Family; Korea And Malaya"

Flying Training Command was an organization within the Royal Air force which controlled units responsible for delivering flying training. The Command's Headquarters were at Shinfield Park, Reading, in Berkshire. Flying Training Command was formed from the elements of Reserve Command which were responsible for flying training from 1939. The remainder of Training Command became Technical Training Command on the same date and No 21 Group was transferred to Flying Training Command on the 27 May 1940.

On 12 March 1945, Tom was at Central Aircrew Allocation Training as a Wireless Operator Air and on 30 April he was with 109 (Transport) Operational Training Unit (OTU) on a training and recrewing course. This had been formed at Crosby-on-Eden, north-east of Carlisle, in Cumbria, on 1 August 1944, under the control of 44 Group, to train transport crews from an element of No 9 OTU. Some Horsas were used at some time to carry out airborne forces training.

Technical Training Command.

Flying Training Command.

Transport Command.

It took until 27 April 1945, for the German Forces left in Italy to surrender. In the meantime, by the end of 1944, France and Belgium were more or less totally liberated; but the final push into Germany itself was meeting tenacious resistance. In December 1944, Hitler secretly assembled sufficient forces in the Ardennes region of Belgium to mount one last desperate counter attack and the Allied Armies were driven back. The "Battle of The Bulge" was the last despairing efforts of a doomed regime; by the end of January 1945, the Germans were driven completely out of France, and during March the Allies crossed the Rhine. Whilst the British and Americans advanced from the west, the Russians advanced in from the east.

Bombing in Dresden in February and Cologne in March, finally broke the will of the German people to fight on. On 30 April, Adolph Hitler committed suicide in his bunker in Berlin; his body was found together with that of his mistress Eva Braun. On 4 May 1945, Germany surrendered, and on Sunday, 2 September 1945, Japan surrendered after the Americans dropped "Atomic Bombs" on Hiroshima and Nagasaki.

After the cessation of hostilities in Europe, 55 Squadron was engaged in mail carrying duties (its pre Second World War role) before moving to Hassani in Greece, during the Greek Civil War, where it re-equipped with Mosquitoes, before disbanding in November 1946.

Tom was promoted to Flight Lieutenant (W) on 14 May 1945 and recategorized as a Gunner.

On 1 May 1940, No 1680 Flight at Doncaster was redesignated 271 Squadron for transport duties, and within a short time it was engaged in evacuation of units from France in the face of German Invasion. Then, from the end of June it was engaged in a lengthy period of transporting ground crews and equipment for squadrons moving base. It was re-equipped with the Douglas Dakotas in January 1944, and it became an airborne forces unit. They were involved in D-Day, operating casualty evacuation missions from the beachhead. They also supplied aircraft for the Arnhem landings in September 1944, and the Rhine Crossing in March 1945.

With the end of war, the squadron began transport flights to Germany, Italy, and Greece; this continued until civil airlines were able to operate on European

Motto "Death and Life" 271 Squadron.

routes. On 2 April 1945, a detachment of 271 Squadron arrived at Croydon Airport with Dakotas, but they moved out after a few days.

On 6 August 1945, the USAF dropped the first Atomic Bomb on the Japanese city of Hiroshima, this was followed three days later by a second Atomic Bomb on the city of Nagasaki. The same day Tom joined 271 Squadron as a Wireless Operator on the Douglas Dakota IV. The newly promoted Commanding Officer at that time was Wing Commander Paul Peters, DFC. The squadron was stationed at RAF Odiham, situated between Basingstoke and Aldershot, and were transporting fresh troops out to India, and on the return journey bringing back, repatriated Prisoners of War, and, time expired personnel from the Far East. For this purpose, several staging posts were set up from the UK to India and Japan; including locations in Italy, Malta, Aden, Rangoon, The Maldives, Pakistan, India, Ceylon, Singapore, Hong Kong, and the Philippines. For the next twelve months Dakotas brought back hundreds of thousands of time-expired personnel and former Prisoners of War.

When these long-haul flights came to an end, the squadron concentrated on transport duties throughout Europe, chiefly to Gibraltar, Malta and Naples; this was the theme for the remainder of 1946.

Signals Half Brevet.

The Douglas Dakota was powered by Pratt & Whitney R–1830–90C Twin Wasp Engines each giving 1,200hp, the wingspan was 95ft 6in and the length of the aircraft was 63ft 9in. Its empty weight was 18,135lbs and it could fly at a maximum load of 31,000lbs at a maximum speed of 224mph at 10,000ft (cruising speed of 160mph) with a maximum range of 3,600 miles.

On 9 August 1945, Tom joined Transport Command and 271 Squadron as a Wireless Operator and on 13 August

Dakota 111- 271 Squadron 1944–1946.

Another photo of Tom in 1945.

1945, he married Stella Stringer at Fakenham Register Office. I think that he knew that this would be the last available time to do it before I arrived, with his postings and travel overseas; and the fact that Stella (Mum) had a noticeable five month bump! At the time they had a rented house at Redman's Yard, Market Place, Burnham Market; but whilst he was away, Stella would stay with her parents at their tithe cottage on Burnham Road, Stanhoe.

On 2 September 1945 came the Japanese surrender, and "VJ" day as it was known.

On 5 October 1945, 271 Dakota Squadron had moved from RAF Odiham to RAF Broadwell, near Burford in Oxfordshire, not far from Brize Norton, and continued scheduled services within Transport Command's Continental Passenger and Casualty schedules. At the end of October 1946, Bicester was chosen, and then cancelled, as Broadwell had more to offer by way of accommodation and it had concrete runways. To ease administration, Broadwell was switched from 46 to 47 Group on 9 October 1945, and by December, 271 Squadron found itself flying along the busy trunk route to India. The Dakotas normally took four days to reach India on this long haul flight, with staging posts and stopovers en route.

This is why Tom (Dad) missed my coming into the world at 0300 hours on Christmas Day 1945; and I was born at my grandparents home, John (Jack) and Florence Stringer, at Burnham Road, Stanhoe; in a tithe cottage belonging to Major Riley of Church Farm. My birth was registered on 17 January 1946 at a cost of two shillings and six pence (about twelve and a half pence now). From then on, Tom brought "presents" home from various far flung places with increasing regularity, until I eventually had six more siblings.

THE DESERTED AIRFIELD

Once more I stand on these broad sweeping acres
Where once the stripling Lords of the Air held sway.
Now, peaceful blow the gentle evening breezes:
A distant church bell marks the passing day.

No more the mighty monsters of destruction
With loads of mass oblivion hugely stand.
Now, time transmuted, ply the wheeling ploughshares,
And men of harvest tend the fertile land.

Where once the hawks of war with raucous callings
The peaceful fields of air were menacing,
The songs of earth and sky are softly sounding
And smaller, gentler creatures now take wing.

And here's the spot where once-pulsating crew-rooms,
Now crumble into dust beside the trees.
I seem to see the forms of old companions;
Their laughing voices echo in the breeze.

Now heaps of rubble show the lively mess-halls
Where laughed and sang the fair young men of yore;
Who lived and loved with such a gay abandon;
Who lived with death and so loved life the more.

No more I see the watchful-eyed control tower,
Gone too the waving wind-sock; dead the lights.
Alone I walk the corridors of memory
And hear again the sound of other nights.

But over there still stands the spreading village
Whose fair young maidens once we held so dear,
Alas! Those tender lips and sweet caresses,
Are now but golden dreams of yesteryear.

Here, once, I walked with footstep firm and eager,
Here, once, I laughed and sang with vigour strong.
But nearly two score years have passed; and sadly,
Now come the days of my September song.

On 15 January 1946, one flight to India didn't make it, as one of the new model Dakotas crashed in bad weather near Marseilles in France, killing all twenty-five people on board. RAF Broadwell was returned to 46 Group on 5 April 1946, and throughout that year 271 Squadron concentrated on passenger and freight services, mainly to Europe, and particularly to areas where British Forces were stationed. Closure of Broadwell was discussed towards the end of 1946, likewise a new siting of 271 Squadron. On 1 December 1946, 271 Squadron was renumbered 77 Squadron, but Tom had already left them in July for V.I.P. work with The Royal Family.

The Development of Radio and Airborne Radar

During 1939, Marconi Wireless Telegraph Company (MWTC), and EKCO Domestic Products, jointly started development work on "Airborne Radar" in two forms. EKCO, because of their outstanding reputation for quality and innovation, were asked by the Air Ministry to participate in the research and development of Air Interception (AI) and anti–surface vessel (ASV) radars so as to bring the equipment up to a production standard – then to manufacture it. Needless to say, this work was done in absolute "top secret" conditions – on a strictly "need to know" basis. At the outbreak of war in September 1939 all work on domestic radios and televisions stopped, and following a plan laid out by government, production was switched to "war work", which for EKCO. meant manufacturing the W.S.19 (Wireless set) for the Army, with the "bakelite" presses turned over to munitions work (plastic practice bombs being one such item) and the lamp division returned to valve manufacture.

In 1940, at the time of Dunkirk, and with the invasion (seemingly) imminent, the order was given to disperse manufacture away from Southend, which was seen as being in the front line. Radar work went to a secret factory hidden inside a country house called Cowbridge House just outside Malmesbury in Wiltshire, and radio production went to Aylesbury, Buckinghamshire and Woking, Surrey. A site was also opened in Rutherglen in Scotland for component manufacture, especially transformers.

In 1941, AI Mark IV and ASV Mark VIII radars were being made at Malmesbury, while at Aylesbury work started on the TR–1154/1155 transmitter/receiver set, which was to become the standard set for Bomber Command for the duration of the war. Marconi worked on the T1154/R1155 at the Marconi Aeronautical Laboratory at Writtle near Chelmsford, and 1942 saw "centrimetric" AI Mark VII and Mark VIII radars being manufactured at Malmesbury; by 1944 over 8,000 people were working for the firm. EKCO eventually gave way to Pye and Philips during mid-1960.

Transmitter type T1154 and Receiver type R1155 were originally designed to provide long-range, high-frequency (HF) radio communications and navigation facilities for British Bomber aircraft in the Second World War. The equipment was also installed in Flying Boats, RAF Air–Sea Rescue launches, used in ground stations, and in some ground radar vehicles. The first version of the receiver was the R1155, and later variants were designated R1155A, B, C, D, E, F, L, M, and N. A similar number of variants of the T1154 Transmitter were also produced.

The R1155 was a conventional supersonic–heterodyne type receiver (Superhet) using thermionic valves (called tubes in the USA), and covering frequency range 75 kHz to 18.5 MHz in five switched bands. The Wireless Operator could take Direction–Finding (DF) bearings by either visual means from his instruments, or by aural means from signals heard in his headphones.

The T1154 was a variable frequency, master oscillator/power amplifier type of transmitter and was capable of generating a Radio Frequency (RF) output power of 40-70 Watts on Continuous wave (CW) and 10-17 Watts on speech or Morse code Transmission (MCW), according to model.

By August 1944 the number of variants produced for the Receiver R1155 was reduced to just four types encased in aluminium or steel cases.

The T1154 and R1155 continued in use on various aircraft after the Second World War, through to the late 1950s, and Tom would have used this system on 271 Squadron flying Douglas Dakota DC3, the Vickers Viking of The King's Flight, and the Valetta on 10 Squadron, 24 Squadron, and the Far East Transport Wing V.I.P. Flight.

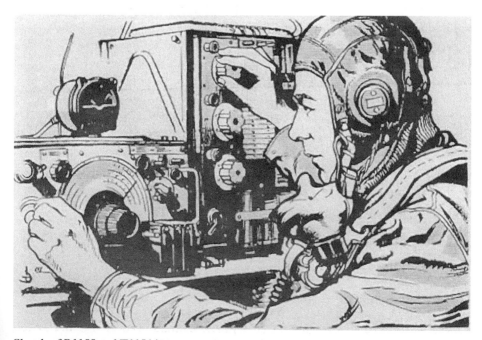

Sketch of R1155 and T1154 in use.

T1154 and R1155 at RAF Heywood Museum.

At the Yalta Conference on 4 November 1945, United States of America President, Franklin D. Roosevelt, and Great Britain Prime Minister, Winston Churchill, appeared to have decided in private that there was nothing they could do, short of war, to remove the Soviet Union, who were now unlawfully occupying countries in central and eastern Europe it had taken from the Germans during its advance into Nazi held Germany. Despite this, both leaders signed with Soviet Leader Marshall Josef Stalin, the document entitled, "The Declaration on Liberated Europe". This document provided for the restoration of democracy in the countries overrun by Nazi Germany.

Over the next forty years, Poland, Bulgaria, Czechoslovakia, Hungary, and Romania, would be independent only as far as they adhered to the Soviet Party line. These countries were to form Stalin's "Buffer Zone" against the threat of a renewed German invasion, and at the end of the Second World War there were a million "Red Army" troops stationed throughout Eastern Europe. The uneasy situation eventually hardened into a "Cold War" between East and West which would sometimes erupt into overt but limited confrontations. The Cold War was more often fought with weapons of propaganda, psychology, economics and subversive undercover operations as the competing ideologies of Western Capitalism and Soviet Communism vied to win over the peoples of the world.

The Iron Curtain

In March 1946, Winston Churchill, now out of office, coined a phrase that came to epitomize the western perception of the Cold War; during a speech in the USA, the former British Prime Minister spoke of an "Iron Curtain that was falling across the middle of Europe to the east of which lay total alien states controlled by Moscow". The "Free World" later realized this, too late to intervene.

One of the earliest "flashpoints" in the Cold War occurred in Berlin, Germany. By the end of the Second World War, the Soviet Red Army had reached the banks of the Elbe River nearly sixty miles west of the capital. Although Berlin was within the Soviet sphere of influence, the Allies shared the administration of the old German capital, dividing it into American, British, French and Soviet zones.

Tom had moved on from 271 Squadron during July 1946, this time posted to Comms Flight, 1 Wing, and on 3 August he was with MEDME Command (Mediterranean and Middle East) Headquarters, Cairo, on the V.I.P. crew to the Air Commander-in-Chief. By this time operational commands were being reduced and MEDME was still a command, though a subordinate one; it included Iraq, Palestine and Transjordan, Aden, East Africa, Egypt and the Sudan. Its Commander-in-Chief from February 1945 was Air Marshal (later Air Chief Marshal) Sir Charles Edward Hastings Medhurst, KCB, OBE, MC, and he resided in Air House, Cairo until March 1947, when he moved to new headquarters at Ismailia. The Royal Air Force presence in the Middle East at that time was to keep the Arab world out of the Soviet orbit and prevent them from becoming Allies of the ever growing dominance of the Soviet Union, and the new perceived threat of a potential Third World War.

The King's Flight Part One

King George V, the monarch who had seen in his reign the birth of air transport, the Royal Air Force, and organized aerial warfare, died peacefully in his sleep at Sandringham, as a result of a chill, on 20 January 1936. The next King, George his younger son, would also die at Sandringham some sixteen years later.

The personal flying unit subsequently became 'The King's Flight' on 21 July 1936, during the reign of King Edward VIII, who had been The Prince of Wales (Later The Duke of Windsor upon Abdication). It was charged with the duty of transporting members of the Royal Family by air, on short and long haul flights. From its birth until the outbreak of the Second World War, The Flight was based at Hendon, and on the outbreak of war it was moved to the less vulnerable site at RAF Benson in Oxfordshire, as a lodger unit of No 12 OTU. There was little use made of The Flight by the reigning monarch, HM King George VI during 1941, due to the lack of fighter protection, and it was disbanded and absorbed by 161 Squadron on 4 February 1942; and King George was transported by other aircraft, mainly those of 24 V.I.P. Squadron.

The King's Flight was descended from the personal flying unit established by HRH the Prince of Wales (later Edward VIII), in 1929 at Northolt, whilst his father King George V was the reigning monarch.

New Beginnings

Late in 1945, and after the war, it was represented to the King that in coming years, Royal travel by air over long distances, would be as natural as travel by car over short distances, so early in 1946 the King formally approved the reconstitution of The King's Flight, confirming Edward Fielden in the appointment of

Captain of The King's Flight (later Air Vice-Marshall, GCVO, CB, DFC, AFC). As his deputy and RAF Officer Commanding of the Flight, Fielden selected Wing Commander E.W. (Bill) Tacon, (Later Air Commodore CBE, DSO, LVO, DFC and Bar, and AFC and Bar). The King's Flight officially reformed on 1 May 1946, at RAF Benson in Oxfordshire; and it was hoped that it would be manned and equipped to establishment by 1 August, in preparation for the forthcoming Royal Visit to the Union of South Africa.

During June, twenty officers and one hundred and twenty airmen arrived at RAF Benson under OC Wing Commander Bill Tacon, who hailed from New Zealand. They were allotted a hangar which was in a filthy state. Offices, crew room, storage and aircraft

King George VI in his full-dress uniform as Marshal of the Royal Air Force.

space were sorted out. The oil and grease on the floors of the hangar and offices, which had been a servicing area for Mosquitoes, was scrubbed clean and washed down with high pressure fire hoses. The first of four Vickers Vikings, VL245, was collected from Wisley on 11 August 1946, and by January 1947 the remainder of the fleet had arrived.

The King's Flight, 1946: Aircraft, Crews and Staff - put to page 157

King's Aircraft-Viking VL246
Pilot Wing Commander E.W. "Bill" Tacon, DSO, DFC, AFC; *Second Pilot* Flight Lieutenant A.J. Alan Lee; *Navigational Officer* Flight Lieutenant Dennis Fawkes; *Signals Officer* Flight Lieutenant L.G.S. "Lofty" Reed, DFC.

Queen's Aircraft-Viking VL247
Pilot Squadron Leader H.F. Payne, AFC; *Second Pilot* Flight Lieutenant P.G. Tilbrook; *Navigational Officer* Flight Lieutenant A. Knapper, AFC; *Signals Leader* Flight Lieutenant D.J. Dartmouth.

Staff Aircraft-Viking VL245
Pilot Flight Lieutenant W.E. Welch; *Second Pilot* Flight Lieutenant A.E. Richmond; *Navigational Officer* Flight Lieutenant A.P. O'Hara, DFC, DFM; *Signals Leader* Flight Lieutenant P.H. McKenna, DFM.

Workshop Aircraft-Viking VL248
Pilot Flight Lieutenant R.J. Harrison; *Second Pilot* Flight Lieutenant E.B. Trubshaw; *Navigational Officer* Flight Lieutenant W.E. Boteler, DFC; *Signals Officer* Flight Lieutenant F. Myers, AFC; *Staff Adjutant* Flight Lieutenant L.T. Reid; *Chief Flight Engineering Officer* Flight Lieutenant A.A. Morley, DFC, DFM; *Ground Engineering Officer* Flight Lieutenant G.A. George Pearson; *Equipment and Accounts Officer* Squadron Leader H. Wright; *Engineer/Fitter* Corporal N.W.P. Southall; *Airframe Fitter* Leading Aircraftsman N.E. Thorn; *Engine Fitters* Aircraftsmen (First Class) G.F. Edginton and A. Edwards; *Maintenance Assistant* Aircraftsman (Second Class) P. Ferguson; *Radio Mechanic* Sergeant W.T. Clapperton; *Electrician* Sergeant T.E. Shore; *Instrument Repair* Corporal D.A. Dennis Sealey; *Aircraft Finisher* Sergeant E. Ward; *Safety Equipment* Corporal W.J. Brownlee; *Steward* Sergeant W.P. Jack; *Instrument Fitter* Flight Sergeant A.W. (Buzz) Cousins.

From 7 November 1946 to 3 January 1947, Tom was on a Signals Leaders Course at RAF Debden in Essex; and on 14 November 1946 he was given his Flight Lieutenant Seniority. During January 1947 he returned to RAF MEDME in East Africa as a Wireless Operator on return to his unit, but he was soon to be

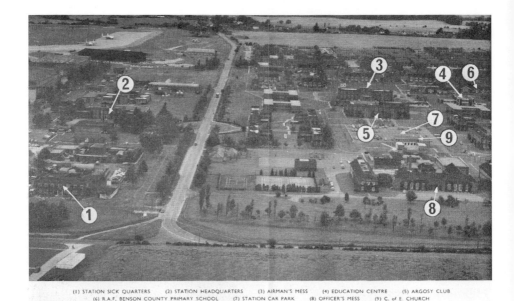

(1) STATION SICK QUARTERS   (2) STATION HEADQUARTERS   (3) AIRMAN'S MESS   (4) EDUCATION CENTRE   (5) ARGOSY CLUB
(6) R.A.F. BENSON COUNTY PRIMARY SCHOOL   (7) STATION CAR PARK   (8) OFFICER'S MESS   (9) C. of E. CHURCH

An aerial view of RAF Benson showing points of interest to new intakes.

Captain of the King's Flight Air Commodore E.H. Fielden together with Commanding Officer Wing Commander E.W. Tacon.

required elsewhere; on The King's Flight.

The four Vikings of The King's Flight took off from RAF Benson in late January, and with stopovers, eventually landed at Brooklyn Airport, Cape Town, South Africa.

Radio equipment carried in each of the four Vikings was respectively: (i) Command R/T; (ii) VHF TR 1430 very high frequency air-to-ground communication; (iii) MFHF Marconi 1154/55 lower frequencies air-to-ground communication; (iv) Radio compass; and (v) Radio altimeter. Radar equipment included, (a) Gee Mk II for obtaining "fixes" over selected areas; (b) Loran a long range variant of Gee which was to be used alternatively with (a) as necessary; and (c) Rebecca Mk III for providing a "homing beam" in

RAF Benson Crest. "Let Us Be Judged By Our Acts".

connection with beam approach when nearing a landing area. These items of equipment, together with the demands of what can be called the "domestic" side of the aircraft, had necessitated an enlarged and comprehensive electrical system, incorporating two six-kilowatt generators to handle the greater loadings. Whilst on the subject of communications, one might note the employment of a "house phone" system in the two Royal aircraft, a unique feature. Between each pair of facing seats is a telephone connected to the switchboard in the commodore's office; thus, by depressing the appropriate switches, any combination of the phones can be connected and one person may thereby talk to any other person or persons, without anyone having to leave their seat. In addition the commodore has intercom for communication with the flight-deck, galley, security officers, and the other aircraft of the flight.

The staff machine was to all intents and purposes a standard twenty-one-seater Viking, although sundry modifications were incorporated for the additional equipment carried. The fourth aircraft was virtually a flying maintenance unit, the interior being equipped with canvas bag racks for small parts stores and work benches fitted with vices, drills, grinders, etc. In addition, a Ben compressor unit and a Daganite starter trolley were carried, together with such bulky spares as a main undercarriage wheel and tyre, two tailwheels, oil cooler, etc. Four standard Viking seats are provided to starboard, at the rear of the flight deck, for the maintenance crew, and the commodore's station is opposite them on the port side of the fuselage.

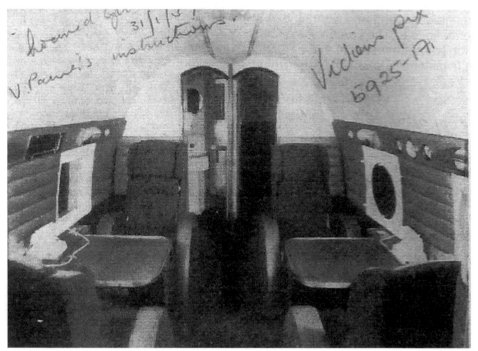

A view of the rear stateroom of VL246 looking aft.

Rear stateroom looking forward, showing wardrobes on bulkhead and seats incorporating Chair–chutes.

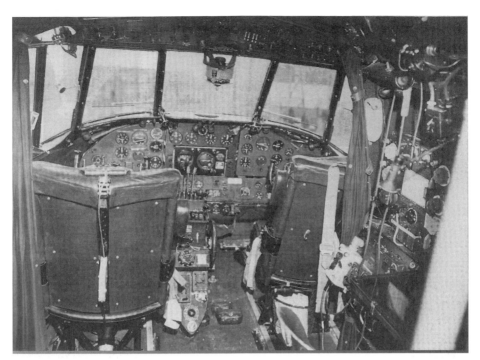

The flight-deck of VL247 The Queen's aircraft.

Viking VL247 The Queen's Viking seen in flight.

Vickers Viking VL246 The King's Aircraft photographed at RAF Benson on 23 January 1947.

On 1 February HMS *Vanguard* sailed from Great Britain, aboard were HM King George V1, Queen Elizabeth, HRH Princess Elizabeth, and HRH Princess Margaret.

The slower progress of the Royal Party obviated a problem that was to beset the aircraft crews soon after they had settled in at Brooklyn Air Station; this was the sudden outbreak of sickness among both the air and ground crews, there were recurrent problems finding the manpower to keep the Vikings serviceable and clean. There is no doubt that this was entirely due to the speedy change of climate that the personnel had suffered. Shortly after their arrival, all twenty officers were suddenly taken ill with dysentery, and Tom was sent from MEDME Command to supplement the Signals Officers strength until they regained full fitness. Tom, like the other members of The Flight, was kitted out with newly designed and manufactured tropical khaki, tailored from a beautiful soft material instead of the standard RAF issue.

A South African Air Force (SAAF) artist, Flight Sergeant Lowe, was asked to paint new crests on both sides of the noses of all four Vikings. He made stencils of a crest and painted it in oils. The crest differed from the simple "Crown and The King's Flight" scroll and was a larger round painting on the lines of a squadron plaque, with heraldic motifs, and he worked non-stop for a week.

HMS *Vanguard* arrived at Capetown, South Africa on 17 February and the Royal Family disembarked.

A personal recollection of the engineering on The King's Flight from Mr. A.W. (Buzz) Cousins, RVM, a former member of The King's Flight, who became Flight Sergeant i/c: "In 1946, whilst on embarkation leave to join an SDL team in Germany…I was recalled to an Air Ministry Board and posted to The King's Flight at RAF Benson, as the first Senior NCO to arrive and be greeted by Flight Lieutenant George Pearson, our Engineering Officer. Joining 'The King's Flight' from AM SDL in 1946, Wing Commander Bill Tacon arrived with aircrew members, and the ground crew arrived in droves. Flight Lieutenant Pearson had his hands full welding us into a team and preparing all trades for the projected Royal Tour of South Africa. Initially all trades were accommodated in small

Tom in his lightweight uniform. Photo by Wares.

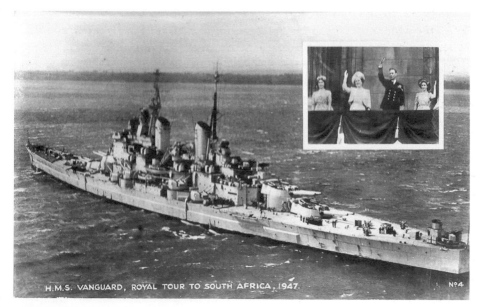

HMS Vanguard.

workshops in the hangar sides, but space was at a premium and 'ancillary trades', (instruments, electrical and radio), moved into a wooden hut placed behind the hangar. Our Vickers Viking Aircraft were all brand new and many bods attended courses at Vickers Weybridge, where the Vikings were built, resulting in good contacts being built with production, service and drawing office staff.

"The third aircraft to arrive was VL248, a 'Flying Workshop', fitted with workbenches, canvas racks of spare parts for all trades and boxes of tools. Being a 'tailwheel' aircraft it soon became evident that working on the benches at an angle of 15 degrees was a bit of a hazard and most of the instrument, electrical and radio spares disappeared into sections, to form the basis of a good servicing stockpile – saving the delay of indenting for and drawing spares from the station stores…Before departure to South Africa, we were all kitted out with newly designed and manufactured tropical khaki, tailored from beautiful soft material instead of the normal RAF issue (organized by Commodore Fielden), and had our photographs taken in civilian clothing we were to fly in, for civil passports to be issued to transit through Libya. We all flew to South Africa in our Vikings, via Libya, Heliopolis, Wadi Haifa, Khartoum, Entebbe, Salisbury and Pretoria, ending up at SAAF Base Brooklyn, Capetown, with four night stops on the way. Shortly after we all arrived safely at Brooklyn, a SAAF artist, Flight Sergeant Lowe, was asked to paint new crests on both sides of the noses of all five Vikings. He made stencils of a crest and did a marvellous job, painting in oils."

Buzz additionally sent me the following personal account:

Mr A.W. (Buzz) Cousins. R.V.M. (E.Eng. F.R.Ae.S. A.I.M.M.), member of The King's Flight and the Queen's Flight for five years from 1946 to 1952. RAF Flight Sergeant (Instrument Fitter) and Senior N.C.O. in charge, 1951.

"Although Tom and I shared the same experiences on the King's Flight during and after the Royal Tour of Southern Africa in 1947, we never met; the only 'Signaller' I knew personally was Flight Lieutenant 'Lofty' Reid, one of Wing Commander Bill Tacon's crew on the King's Viking, VL246. Nevertheless, I found this account of Tom's experiences on The King's Flight and beyond of great interest. Our contact on The King's Flight was limited by the social gap between the ground crew and the commissioned aircrews, until after the day I was appointed 'Senior Non Commissioned Officer In Charge' of the Flight, by Air Commodore 'Mousey' Fielding, captain of the flight. It was an unexpected overnight appointment and my first order from the Engineering Officer, Flight Lieutenant 'Chotta' Lamb, was, 'Chiefy, I want you to get all our Vikings polished like new pins, for a coming Royal Flight.' I organized all our ground crews into teams, allocated them to our five Vikings, issued them with tins of 'Brasso' metal polish, overalls and polishing rags and we all worked until sunset.

a twenty-three year old war experienced man. "Wares" had been demobbed after the Second World War on 28 August 1946 and had left Britain to seek his fortune in Southern Africa. He first worked in the Colonial Post Office Telegraph Department in Southern Rhodesia (now Zimbabwe) and Bechuanaland (now Botswana). It would be over a further fifty years before they saw each other again.

The Vikings performed faultlessly during the long tour, on various occasions carrying The King and Queen, Princess Elizabeth and Princess Margaret, to various parts of The Union; including Bechuanaland, Swaziland and Basutoland; and also to Northern and Southern Rhodesia.

One of the reasons that the Royal Family so relished their visit to South Africa was that the four of them were together. The King was as yet in good health, Princess Elizabeth, already in love, would marry Prince Philip that November; and the King and Queen were at the apex of their popularity.

The three month long Royal Tour saw the ordering of eight ivory-painted air-conditioned saloons by South Africa from Britain, three of which were built to Blue Train sleeping car standards, while the remaining five were special saloons for use by the Royal Family and Field Marshal Jan Smuts, the South African Prime Minister. During part of the tour the Royal Train was used for touring the huge expanse of the isolated African townships, including Mafeking and Bulawayo on 17 April.

The five flights of the Royal Family were from Bloemfontein to Bulfontein (30mins) and return; from Pretoria to Pietersburg (1 hour 20mins) and return; and from Pretoria to Salisbury (2 hours 50 mins). The King and Princess Margaret travelled in the King's aircraft, and The Queen and Princess Elizabeth

The four original Royal Vikings on tour in South Africa in 1947 Tom Clark is believed to be the one on the right of the centre group of officers.

The King's, The Queen's and the Royal Household Vikings on tour in South Africa in 1947.

The King and Queen and the two Princesses walking from the Vickers Vikings on their return to Bloemfontein airfield from the Orange Free State Game Reserve.

"The next morning I had a surprise, Wing Commander Bill Tacon, our boss, walked into the hangar followed by his white overall clad air crews, came to meet me and said, 'Please allocate a Viking to us "Chiefy" to give you all a hand!!!' and I nominated VL 247, The Queen's Viking. This had never happened before. They worked with gusto and 'Brasso', but I soon noticed that some aircrew had left 246 and had spread to other aircraft, working with my ground crews and this proved to be a great fillip, to morale and team spirit, from then on.

"After a couple of years of hand polishing, and our Vikings were always highly polished, a lot of corrosion was found on the fuselage sides and underbelly – boffins from Vickers Weybridge arrived and diagnosed that our 'polishing' had eaten through the hard anodic layer on the 'Alclad' sheet aluminium skin and all the aircraft were progressively returned to Weybridge to be re-skinned!

"I decided to introduce some long awaited innovations to The Flight; 'Duty Crews' of engine and airframe NCO's and 'erks' normally accompanied our Vikings on Royal Flights to handle refuelling, cleaning, chocks, drip trays, steps and other sundry items. I asked our senior fitter, Sergeant Hardiman, to train all other tradesmen to handle such work, so they could take a turn at 'Duty Crew' and travel the world, and all the 'Gash Trades' appreciated the new travel opportunity.

"I found Chris Clark's book about his father Tom's experiences in life and in the RAF to be as interesting as another book I would also recommend 'A History of The King's Flight and The Queens Flight, 1936–1995' (ISBN 1-903953-32-4) and recommend both books to Ex RAF ground and aircrew, wherever they have ended up."

Buzz Cousins 15 November 2010.

On the evening of the Royal arrival, 17 February, Table Mountain was floodlit, and a civic firework display was given at Greenpoint Common in honour of the Royal Family. During the Royal Tour, and during the visit to Cape Town, Princess Elizabeth and King George VI went to the top of Table Mountain by cable car, accompanied by South Africa's Prime Minister, Field Marshall Jan Christiaan Smuts.

In so vast a country, aircraft supplied the only means of covering anything like a representative cross-section, for not only were there statesmen and officials to meet, but also a certain amount of sightseeing to be enjoyed. On 28 February, the Royal Family visited Port Elizabeth by train.

The first time that the King's Flight flew The King on the Tour of South Africa, was on 8 March, when he and Princess Margaret were flown from Bloemfontein to Bulfontein, and return; on the return flight he sat in the co-pilot's seat. During the second week of March in Bloemfontein, the Royal Family piled into their Royal Vikings for a quick picnic in the Free State Game Reserve.

During April Tom met his brother, James "Wares", in Salisbury (now Pretoria), after ten years absence, from when James was still a schoolboy; James was now

Tom and Wares Salisbury 1947.   Another shot of Tom and Wares.

in the Queen's. The two Princesses were taken for a one and a half hour flight over the Cape Peninsula in the King's aircraft from Brooklyn Airport. In addition, General Smuts was flown twice, once from Capetown to Pretoria, and Sir Evelyn Baring the High Commissioner to South Africa, on three occasions.

The four Vickers Vikings completed more than 160,000 miles flying without incident, save for when The King was being flown near Pietersburg, the aircraft collided with a snake bird and the nose of the aircraft was dented. In addition, Tom told me of an amusing moment which occurred during one of these flights. HRH Princess Margaret, then aged nineteen, and romantically connected to Group Captain Peter Townsend, CVO, DSO, DFC and Bar, Equerry to King George Vl; asked permission to enter the flight deck to get a closer look of the panoramic view of the ground. She stood in front of Tom's Signaller/Navigator position and between the pilot and co-pilot; just at that time the pilot banked left and HRH fell backwards and landed in Tom's lap. Embarrassed, and apologetic she got up, and said, "Oh I'm so sorry Officer!" Tom replied, "I can assure you that the pleasure was all mine Ma'am."

During the time that The Flight was stationed at Brooklyn, Wing Commander "Bill" Tacon received, and accepted, an invitation for the whole Flight to visit a winery at Stellenbosch, in the hills about fifty miles east of Capetown. Everyone, including Tom, boarded the fleet of three buses which took them to the venue, they all had a most interesting and enjoyable day, visiting the vineyards, sampling the wines, joining a string of local natives, singing and dancing naked as they did the conga round and round in great vats, stomping grapes into juice, sampling more wines; eating lunch, sampling more wines and getting thoroughly wrecked before travelling back in the buses which were full of crates of wine to sample! Everyone had a marvellous day, with Sunday to recover.

Three of the Vickers Vikings returned to RAF Benson whilst The Royal Tour was still going ahead, the King's machine having covered 7,500 miles in fifty-four hours; leaving Capetown at 1230 hours on Friday, 25 April, it reached Benson at 0632 hours on the following Sunday, and at 0751 hours on Monday, 28 April, it took off again for South Africa. It was to be present at an air display in Johannesburg on 3 May and was scheduled to fly 15,000 miles in five days. The Queen's aircraft (VL247) left Capetown at 0600 hours on Friday, 25 April and landed at Benson at 0154 hours on Monday, 28 April and the staff aircraft (VL245) left Capetown at the same time and landed at Benson at 0154 hours on Monday, 28 April, VL245 left Benson again for Capetown at 0900 hours on Tuesday, 29 April and VL247 at 0800 hours on Wednesday, 30 April.

After their return to Benson during early May, the Vikings were regularly used by members of The Royal Family, excluding The King, whose health was deteriorating due to his tuberculosis and removal of a lung infected with cancer; and Princess Elizabeth, as Heir to the Throne, was increasingly used in formal Head of State occasions. On 10 July 1947, King George V1 announced the engagement of "the Princess Elizabeth to Lieutenant Phillip Mountbatten, RN", adding that he had "gladly given his consent". The couple had been unofficially engaged for some time, and the official announcement had been scheduled for 15 July but had leaked out.

During September 1946 Flight Lieutenant Arthur Patrick O'Hara was appointed to be a Navigator on the King's Flight, after an illustrious career with 214 and 109 Squadrons during the Second World War and a stint on 147 Squadron, post-war. In the spring of 1947 he formed part of the crew of the No. 3 aircraft carrying the Royal Household staff. At the end of 1947, he left the RAF to become an Air Traffic Controller with the Civil Aviation Authority.

Prince Philip and Princess Elizabeth lived for two years, between 1949 and 1951, in the Maltese hamlet of Gwardamangia, at the Villa Gwardamangia (or Villa G'Mangia), which Louis Mountbatten (Phillip's Uncle), Earl Mountbatten of Burma, had purchased in about 1929. The winter of 1947 was the most severe in living memory, and little use was found for the Vikings as there was little flying in Great Britain during this time.

Tom was also involved in flying HM Queen Elizabeth (The Queen Mother), HRH Princess Margaret, and HRH the Duke of Edinburgh, for most of 1947. At various times between 1946 and 1953, the Duke of Edinburgh was stationed in Malta (at that time a British Protectorate) as a serving Royal Naval Lieutenant. Also during the prelude to the forthcoming Royal Wedding, the work of the King's Flight called for a considerable number of journeys to and from the continent, in order to collect and return the many Royal guests who would attend. The Royal Wedding was on 20 November 1947, the marriage of HRH Princess Elizabeth to

HRH Prince Phillip; this brought some glitter and cheer to the austerity of post-war Britain, which was still suffering rationing. At the ceremony he was given the title by the King, of Prince Philip Duke of Edinburgh.

On 11 November 1947, Tom was at RAF El Hamra in Egypt, on Supy duty with MEDME Command (Mediterranean and Middle East Command). On 25 November 1947, he was at 101 Personnel Dispersal Centre at Uxbridge for Release "A", and left the Royal Air Force on 9 March 1948. One memorable occasion in 1948, before he left Benson, was a visit to the Flight by the *Punch* Magazine cartoonist Mr Pat Rooney. He was preparing drawings of many of The Flight, which eventually resulted in a full "centrefold" in an issue of *Punch*. He presented many of his original drawings to members, including one to Tom which later took pride of place at our home in Dersingham.

After eighteen months as a "civilian", Tom was hating the lack of excitement and variety in his life, so when the Berlin Siege occurred he volunteered his services and flew with 47 Squadron from RAF Topcliffe.

Post Second World War Russian Occupation of Berlin

It was nightfall on 2 May 1945 when the Russian occupation of Berlin became complete. Then, after three years of uneasy confrontation, all road and rail links between the city and the west were severed by the Soviets, and the Berlin Airlift began. For ten months it was only the efforts of the RAF, the USAF and a variety of civil airline contractors, which enabled the Western-occupied sectors of the city to survive. Enormous tonnages of food, fuel, and other supplies, were flown into the beleaguered city in an endless stream of aircraft operating around the clock in all weathers. They were constantly harassed by Russian fighters and fifty-four aircrew gave their lives.

The Berlin Airlift was preceded by nearly three years of constant tension and sniping by Russians against the Western Allies in an attempt to drive them out of West Berlin and Western Germany. They used a variety of tactics including searches, blocking transportation of even basic supplies to West Berlin, and intimidating West German civilians. This followed the Western Allies announcing a plan to unify their Zones of Occupation in Western Germany. This announcement alarmed the Soviets and at midnight on 23 June 1948, the Russians cut the electrical power to the Western Sectors of Berlin, and at six o'clock on 24 June, they severed all road and barge traffic to and from the city, and at the same time they stopped the transfer of all supplies from the Soviet Sector.

From that date the Western Sector of Berlin was under siege, and the only route remaining open to the Western Allies were the three air corridors leading from the Western Sectors of Germany to the western controlled Berlin Sectors. Each corridor was twenty statute miles wide, extending vertically from ground level to 10,000 feet. Two terminated in the British Zone and one in the American

EASTERN BLOC AREA
BORDER CHANGES
1938 TO 1948

- ▦ USSR 1938
- ▦ Annexed or Expanded SSRs
- ▢ Satellite States
- ▢ New Satellite State Land
- — 1938 Borders
- — New Borders

KARELO-
FINNISH
SSR
RSFSR

ESTONIAN
SSR

RUSSIAN
SFSR

LATVIAN SSR

LITHUANIAN
SSR

RFSFR

BYELORUSSIAN
SSR

REP. OF
POLAND

GERMANY
(Soviet-
zone)

UKRAINIAN
SSR

CZECHOSLOVAK
REP.

MOL-
DAVIA
SSR

REP. OF
HUNGARY

ROMANIAN
PEOPLE'S
REP.

FEDERAL
PEOPLE'S
REP. OF
YUGOSLAVIA

PEOPLE'S
REP. OF
BULGARIA

PEOPLE'S
REP. OF
ALBANIA

Zone. The two British corridors ran over relatively flat country, but the American Corridor crossed over ground rising to 3,000 feet over much of its length. To supply West Berlin, the Americans had only one hundred C-47 transport aircraft in Europe, and the RAF could add one hundred and fifty, mostly Dakotas with a few Avro Yorks. This meant that against the daily requirements of 13,000 tons of food for Berlin, the USAF, and RAF between them, could probably airlift in only 700 tons at the outside. Some American military advisors cautioned a less aggressive stand over Berlin, while they flew to Britain to find out the British attitude towards the Soviet move. They were surprised when the British Secretary of State for Foreign Affairs, Ernest Bevin, informed them that the Cabinet had voted not to sanction a withdrawal from Berlin, and that the RAF transport aircraft were already flying in supplies under "Operation Plainfare".

The British Government's viewpoint was that the situation would be back to normal in a few days, once the Russians had made their gesture. On 25 June, US President Truman ordered that all resources were to be channelled into forming a viable airlift organization. Bases at Waterbeach and Oakington in Cambridgeshire were initially used by RAF Transport Command, they mainly used Dakotas that flew to Wunstorf, which soon became heavily congested. This situation was further exacerbated with the arrival of Avro York; however, temporary steel planking was laid out to expand unstable areas. During 5 July the transport force was augmented by ten Short Sunderland Flying Boats from 201 and 230 Squadrons, which operated a shuttle service from a temporary base at Finkenwerder, on the River Elbe, west of Hamburg, to the Havel Sea (Lake Havel) adjoining Gatow Airfield. As the ongoing situation developed, more and more resources were thrown into this massive daily, long term operation. Hastings and other load bearing aircraft were also used throughout this time.

It was through a 16 Squadron Association Newsbrief that I came across Tom's involvement with 47 Squadron during the Berlin Airlift as a volunteer: 16 Squadron 1939-1945, Newsbrief 18 April 2001. Flight Lieutenant J.M.R. "Taff" Jones… "He was very pleased to recognize himself in the photograph of five 'sprogs' of the 16 Squadron Signals Section in Amiens in 1940, sent in by Tom Clark. This resulted in a long telephone conversation between them, their first contact for sixty years. They discovered that after the war, Tom was in 47 Squadron at RAF Topcliffe when 'Taff' was a Wing Signals Officer there, and they were both with Transport Command during the Berlin Airlift." There is a gap in Tom's Service Record from March 1948 until September 1949, so he must have enlisted as a volunteer during the Berlin Emergency.

After the war, 47 Squadron was sent to Java to restore peace there, before disbanding briefly in 1946 and a month after, reforming in Palestine. The squadron returned to the UK, firstly to RAF Dishforth and then RAF Topcliffe, becoming the first operational Hastings C.1 Squadron during November 1948. During the Berlin Airlift, the squadron moved as a detachment to RAF Schleswig in South Jutland in Germany, some 70 kilometres from the Danish border, and north of Kiel. There, together with 279 Squadron, they maintained and operated twenty-three Hastings, along with four civilian carriers. The air base had underground fuel storage tanks capable of storing 160,000 gallons, and in addition it had a very good loading area which could handle sixteen aircraft at a time, and was only a short distance to the rail yard which could handle three trains. The Hastings was rushed into service because of the Berlin Airlift, with No 47 Squadron replacing its Halifax A Mk 9's in September-October 1948 and flying its first sortie to Berlin on 11 November 1948. The squadron was later supplemented by 297 and 53 Squadrons. Over 3,000 sorties were flown by 47 Squadron in the seven months it was assigned to the operation, mainly transporting coal to the beleaguered city. The thirty-two Hastings deployed delivered 55,000 tons of supplies for the loss of two aircraft. The squadron returned to RAF Topcliffe on 22 August 1949, until disbandment in the middle of November 1950.

The Handley Page Hastings had a normal crew of five or six and was powered by Bristol Hercules radial engines, yielding a maximum speed of 354mph, an initial climb rate of 1.030ft per minute to a service ceiling of 26,500ft, and a range of 4,250miles. The wingspan was 112ft 9in, length 80ft 9in, height 22ft 5in and wing area 1,408 sq ft. Thus equipped, the Hastings could offer a 20,311lb payload with an empty weight of 49,415lb and 80,000lb loaded.

Here are some first-hand accounts of those days: "I still recall flying in and out, fifteen minutes on the ground, a quick coffee and then off again. On some days we would do four or five trips, but thankfully that soon reduced to two or three", said a veteran of 263 trips, Sir John Curtiss. "For me it was something worthwhile; having been in Bomber Command it was very much better delivering food than bombs and we felt we were doing something important as indeed it turned out we were." His sense of achievement was shared by former 99 Squadron Sergeant John Whitlock; "At the time I thought I was just doing my job – there was a problem and we, the British Forces, helped solve it. It is only looking back that I realized just what a remarkable feat it was." And remarkable it was. But the demand to keep the constant stream of aid flowing relied on the aircraft being serviceable at all times, and placed a significant strain on the engineers. Men like John Holden from Tyne & Wear, who saw themselves as just doing their jobs. The former 47 Squadron Flight Mechanic said; "The job had to be done and you just did

47 Squadron Motto: "Nili nomen roboris omen". "The name of the Nile is an omen of our strength".

it. Basically we were keeping them ready for flying, making sure the tyres were inflated and the de-icing was working because it was heavy winter. 47 were flying coal into RAF Gatow which was a vital commodity; if you had coal you could

RAF Hastings aircraft being loaded with supplies during the Berlin Airlift.

keep warm and keep factories going. We just did the job and I never heard anyone complain or moan."

On 4 April 1949, the West put the final nail in the Soviet Union's "divide and conquer" policy. The Articles, plainly stating that an attack on any one nation, or its representatives, would be considered an attack against them all. Article 6 of The Treaty stated: "An armed attack on one or more of the Parties is deemed to include an armed attack…on the forces, vessels or aircraft of any of the Parties, when in or over these territories (i.e. territories under the jurisdiction of any of the Parties in the North Atlantic area north of the Tropic of Cancer) or any area of Europe in which occupation of any of the Parties were stationed on the date when the Treaty came into force." This prevented the Russians from taking West Berlin by force, as it would have involved a war with all of its Western Allies. The Russian blockade of Berlin had failed lamentably, and left the Russians in a dubious position. With the fall of China to communism, the Russians could afford to lose the Battle for Berlin, and on 4 May the four powers, Russia, Britain, France and the United States of America, reached an agreement. All restrictions imposed on traffic to and from Berlin by all parties were to be removed on the fourth anniversary of the end of the Second World War, 12 May 1949. On 8 May, the Parliamentary Council in Bonn adopted a constitution for the new Federal Republic of Germany. The Soviet response was the creation of the German Democratic Republic in East Germany, during the following month.

Crash of Hastings TG611

On 16 July 1949, Hastings TG611 of No. 47 Squadron, from RAF Topcliffe, had just completed unloading at Tegel Air Base in Berlin and was returning to West Germany. On take-off the aircraft was seen to climb steeply to around 150 feet until it was almost vertical. As the port wing dropped, power was reduced, and level flight almost returned, but the wing dropped again and the aircraft dived into the ground and was destroyed. The cause was found to be the elevator trim tab, which had been turned to the fully back position. The Hastings was out of RAF Gatow near Bergen, Germany. The crew members were Flying Officer Ian R. Donaldson, Sergeant Joseph Toal (Glider Flight Regiment), Navigator 1 William G. Page, Signaller 11 Alexander Dunsire and Engineer 111 Roy R. Gibbs age twenty-three. All five perished. The United States crash crew at Tegel attempted to rescue the crew of TG611 and were commended by Air Commodore J.W.F. Merer. One of the crash crew was Pete Semanick, who describes the incident: "Our crash crew was in front of the flight line fire station waiting for our relief to replace us for the next shift (24 hours on duty – 24 hours off duty). Several Hastings had been grounded overnight at Tegel due to bad weather. We were able to overhear all radio transmissions with tower and aircraft crews. The aircraft started their engines and asked for taxi approval. Approval was given and the aircraft started their way to the end of the runway. The first aircraft asked for permission to take-off and tower granted this request. As the aircraft went rolling down the runway and immediately became airborne, all engines quit firing and the aircraft nosed over and crashed right across the ramp from our fire station. Our fire crews were already in our trucks and responded as soon as we saw what had occurred. There was not much fire damage due to our quick efforts of fighting the fire. I was on the first truck at the scene and my partner and I used our hand lines dispensing high pressure water and foam extinguishing agent. In a second or two we observed a dead crew member in our approach path. My partner couldn't stand the sight and passed out, which left me alone to fight the fire. We were only eighteen years old and this was our first crash with casualties. I am seventy-seven years old (written in 2008) and even though this was 1949 I can still see the body there on the ground."

Chapter Seven

"Rejoining; By Royal Approval; And Far Out"

RAF 10 Squadron; 24 Squadron; The King's Flight (2) and Far East Transport Wing

Tom was recalled after the Berlin Airlift on 26 September 1949, and was given a Short Service Commission as Flight Lieutenant, General Duties Signals Branch, at RAF Biggin Hill, on Supy to Recall, and his seniority was re-established as from 2 June 1948, as though he had never left the service.

On 19 October 1949, he was posted to 10 Squadron, Signals, as a Signals Leader, and attached to RAF Waterbeach in Cambridgeshire; the squadron had recently arrived there from nearby RAF Oakington. Waterbeach was a late expansion scheme airfield just prior to the Second World War and was built on farmland at Windfold, north of Waterbeach Village, and adjacent to the A10 trunk road, some five miles north of Cambridge. The low lying location in the Fens necessitated concrete runways, a perimeter taxiway and hardstandings. The squadron had been part of Bomber Command throughout the Second World War, and changed to Transport Command at the end of the war. It then had four years flying Dakotas to India, and then in Europe, taking part in the Berlin Airlift. In the four months that Tom was with the squadron as a Supy Signals Officer he was involved with further V.I.P. Flights ferrying various politicians and diplomats here and there; a lot of whom had been European exiles during the war and who had fled to Britain to escape being interred or killed. He stayed with 10 Squadron until 20 February 1950, when the squadron was disbanded. He then transferred to 24 Squadron, also at Waterbeach, but in days the squadron moved to nearby RAF Bassingbourn; as Waterbeach's runways were due to be re-structured in the March, the base having changed its status from Transport to Fighter Command, and brought in two Meteor Squadrons. We lived in Officers Married Quarters at Waterbeach, but I recall nothing of our short time there, being less than five years old.

This squadron had a long history of Royal Flying and V.I.P. Transport Flight. It also operated Winston Churchill's personal aircraft during the war; and flew King George VI in the Prime Minister's personal Avro York, LV633 "Ascalon", on the two longest Royal Flights thus far, when they flew him from RAF Northolt, to Tripoli and back, in June 1943 and from Northolt to Naples and return in July and August 1944. By mid 1944 the squadron changed roles to become a transport support unit flying Dakotas and was involved with courier, evacuation, ambulance and communication flights to the Continent, Gibraltar, Malta and later India. After the war, 24 Squadron received a Douglas Dakota MKIV, KN386, which had been selected for the King in June 1945, but after that the King had little occasion to fly for many months and the aircraft was used for general V.I.P. duties.

The squadron had left RAF Hendon in February 1946 for Bassingbourn, where it absorbed No. 1359 V.I.P. Flight in June, and operated Avro York and Avro Lancastrians; it was also designated a Commonwealth Squadron, with crews from various Commonwealth countries joining the squadron. It was a nomadic squadron, moving from base to base. Although it had a V.I.P. role, it still became involved in the Berlin Airlift, flying Handley Page Hastings.

Here is a narrative article from an ex 24 Squadron Wing Commander from New Zealand:

"I joined 24 Commonwealth Squadron in July 1949, as a Wireless Operator and one of the RNZAF crews which would replace the tour expired New Zealand crews due for repatriation. After a short refresher course at Waterbeach we moved on to Lubeck to join the other Commonwealth crews. At the end of the airlift we returned to Waterbeach, just in time to move with the squadron to Oakington… As the other two pilots had no experience on York aircraft, two crews were posted to Topcliffe for conversion training. The

Motto "Rem Acu Tangere" "To Hit The Mark".

two Wireless Operators did not go to Topcliffe as at this time, I had over one thousand hours on York aircraft and the other Wireless Operator had six hundred hours on Mosquito aircraft, we did our category exams on the squadron… By the time our original two crews returned to the squadron with nine categories, W/O J and I had completed trips to Canada and the United States, South Africa and New Zealand, plus a couple of trips to Singapore and Australia. I left the squadron at the end of January 1950."

A pilot who had been with the squadron on the Avro York from April 1947 until January 1950, and who was at Bassingbourn, was Alex Wickes, although he and Tom did not serve there together, their paths met later from 1952 until 1954, when Alex was a Squadron Leader Wing Pilot with the Far East Transport

Motto "In Omnia Parati" "Prepared For All Things".

Wing and Tom was his crew Signaller (This is covered later in the book).

When Tom joined 24 Squadron, as a Signals Leader, they had just moved to RAF Oakington from RAF Bassingbourn on 24 February 1950. They were operating Douglas Dakota, Avro York C 1, and Vickers Valetta C1. The 24 (Commonwealth) Squadron operated the V.I.P. element of the UK Valetta force at Oakington and received its first two aircraft (C2, VX577 and C1, VW849) the same month; its role was special flights and the carriage of V.I.P's. It also participated at the Farnborough Air show that year when it flew VW849 in the fly-past of more than 200 aircraft, including Transport Command's other aircraft, York, Dakota and Hastings. The Squadron's Commanding Officer up until March 1950 was Wing Commander P.A. Lombard, DFC, and from March to December 1950 it was Wing Commander Charles Frederick Read, DFC, of the Royal Australian Air Force. (He later became Air Marshal Sir C.F. Read, KBE, CB, DFC, AFC.) In a six months operation, mainly V.I.P. work, the squadron flew senior Army and RAF personnel on tours of the Near East, the Canal Zone, Germany, and the UK. The Valetta's association with 24 Squadron was short-lived and later the squadron moved to RAF Lyneham, in Wiltshire. In November 1950, it replaced its ageing Yorks and Dakotas with Avro Hastings, these they flew for seventeen years, before equipping with C-130 Lockheed Hercules in 1968. The squadron is now known as XXIV Squadron, currently operating, Hercules C4's and C5's to date.

Again Tom's stay was short lived with 24 Squadron, and on 22 June 1950, Tom rejoined His Majesty's King's Flight, for a further two years and four months.

I contacted The National Archives for flight records of The King's Flight and was informed, after a search, that the relevant documents were not stored there and to try the Air Historical Branch. Again after a thorough search I was informed that no papers from The King's Flight had been lodged there. I then contacted The Royal Archives at Windsor Castle with a negative result:

As a result of this I then contacted The Queen's Flight Association and was informed by Chris Harrison, the Member Secretary, that after a search, they too did not have the missing

Hastings C.1A TG527 of No 24 Squadron

material. However, Chris was determined to get to the bottom of the matter and paid a visit to RAF Benson, and together with a colleague, Mike Prendergast, who works there, found the Royal Vikings log books in dusty boxes where they had lain for nearly sixty years. Mike then took the books home and waded through them, photocopying all entries appertaining to Tom's presence on board each aircraft. If it had not been for the efforts of Chris and Mike, then the following nine pages, in the main, would not have been published here; and the contents of the Royal Flights lost for all time. Thank you both for your endeavour and for helping to make Tom's story complete.

On 22 June, Tom was thrown straight in at the deep end with a Training Flight in Vickers Viking VL 233, with Wing Commander Scott (Pilot), Flying Officer Jenkins (Navigator), Flight Lieutenant Davies (Signaller), Tom (Supernumery Signaller), and Flight Lieutenant Toogood (Flight Engineer). They left RAF Benson with The King's Flight servicing crew at 2359 hours and arrived at RAF St Eval, Cornwall at 0445 hours on the 23 June. They then left St Eval at 0540 hours and arrived in Gibraltar at 1205 hours, then after a day's rest they left Gibraltar at 1005 hours on 24 June and arrived in Malta at 1530 on the same day. On 25 June they returned from Malta to Benson, leaving at 2330 hours and arriving at 0730 hours on 26 June; a journey of some eight hours duration.

Wing Commander E.W. "Bill" Lamb, MVO, RAF (retired) served two tours as Senior Engineering Officer, the first as a Flight Lieutenant from 1 June 1950 until the 1 June 1952. He remembers:

"In 1950 The King's Flight was equipped with five Viking C2 aircraft, two of which were specially equipped and used exclusively for Royal Flights (VL246 and VL247). Two aircraft were standard commercial twenty-two-seat passenger

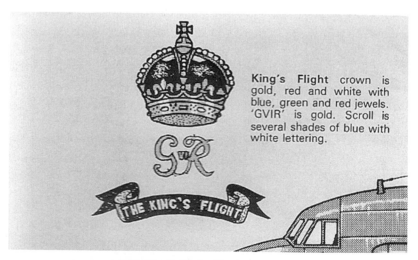

King's Flight crown is gold, red and white with blue, green and red jewels. 'GVIR' is gold. Scroll is several shades of blue with white lettering.

The King's Flight Crest 1936-1952.

RAF Benson Crest.   The Queen's Flight Crest 1952–1995.

aircraft and were used for support and training flights (VL232 and VL233). The
fifth aircraft (VL248) was fitted out as a workshop, but by 1950 was 'mothballed'
in storage. Externally, all the aircraft appeared alike and were maintained to the
same high standard. Parachutes were carried for all passengers and crew; two
eight–man dinghies were fitted in the upper rear of the engine nacelles. The fuel
tanks were crash proof and bullet proof to the same pattern as the Wellington
bombers; the Viking wings and engine nacelles were in fact to the Wellington
design of geodetic construction.

"The flight deck provided for an aircrew of four; a Pilot and Flight Engineer at
the dual controls and Navigator and Signaller at a sideways-facing desk. A crew
lavatory and the galley with Steward's position were aft of the flight deck, as was
the rearward-facing seat for the Captain of The King's Flight.

"The Royal aircraft were kept in a state of basic readiness at all times as the
engineering staff were given only short notice, usually less than twenty-four hours,
of a Royal Flight. When a Royal Flight was notified, the aircraft was serviced to
schedule requirements and then fully air-tested. The 'social engineering' was then
carried out to ensure that the aircraft was immaculate both inside and out. The
aircraft finish was bare unpainted aluminium and the whole exterior surface was
hand–polished with metal polish and dusters. Not surprisingly, some skin panels
had to be replaced over the years. All personnel took part in polishing, including
clerks, typists and drivers, some sixty men in all; the whole task took about 200
man hours. The undercarriage and radio aerials were chromium-plated and this
saved a lot of cleaning. There was never a problem with the chromium plating
peeling off, as had been forecast by RAE. The hangar was unheated and dimly lit

by small ceiling lights. Considered opinion agreed that the winter in RAF hangars extended from 1 September to the following July. Certainly condensation was a major problem, especially when it came to polishing aeroplanes, and the only alternative to wet floors was to keep the doors open and endure the blast. Aircraft servicing was also carried out with hangar doors open. When preparation was completed, the aircraft was inspected by the Engineering Officer and the Flight Sergeant i/c Flight (only one Flight Lieutenant and one Flight Sergeant in 1950). This took about an hour and included checking documentation, fuel-state, appearance, correct flags, panels secure etc. There was no insurance factor applied in checking engineering work as the Captain's policy was 'one man one job' and the full responsibility that went with it. This policy extended to one Pilot being considered quite enough, Second Pilots were not normally carried, although the aircraft had dual controls.

"While the aircraft exterior was being polished, the three Stewards prepared the interior and loaded the cutlery, glass and crockery into special racks. Catering supplies were prepared by the same Stewards in the galley in the hangar. The Stewards were in fact Batmen/Waiters who were paid one shilling and sixpence a day (seven and a half new pence) flying pay. Food was a problem, as rationing was strictly observed by the Royal Family; in 1950 bread was rationed and the meat ration was ten pence (four new pence) worth per week. Eggs were sometimes unobtainable and the King enjoyed a four-minute egg! In an unpressurized

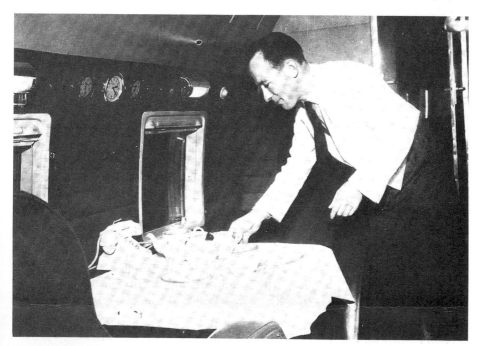

Sgt Griffiths a Steward of The King's Flight laying a table in VL 246.

aircraft the temperature of boiling water varies with altitude, but such was the engineering expertise available that the galley displayed a graph showing the boiling time of a 'four-minute egg' at various altitudes. Incidentally, the egg was boiled in the hot-water geyser, but it was washed first so the tea was not polluted.

"The embarking or disembarking of the Royal family was attended by personnel of The King's Flight as far as possible. Placing steps against an aircraft door may seem a simple enough task, but a combination of local aircraft workers and nervous officials was a recipe for embarrassment. The steps hitting the doorframe with a resounding thud, or being positioned a foot clear of the threshold were experiences which led the Captain to direct that we do it ourselves. For aircraft positioned at London Airport a 'steps party' was sent from Benson. While away from the base, the Flight Engineer and the Steward became expert in quickly assembling the dismantled steps carried in the hold. One near-miss occurred on an overseas tour when the local airport manager had special, hydraulically adjustable steps flown in from Cairo. The suspicious engineer required a full dress rehearsal, and as the airport manager stepped from the aircraft, the steps gently subsided amidst a fountain of hydraulic fluid. When an aircraft returned from a flight, it was prepared to a basic readiness state without delay, no matter what time of day or night it was. The fuel state was brought up to two-thirds full only, to prevent fuel having to be unloaded if the maximum disposable payload was required on the next flight. All galley equipment was pre-prepared but stored in the hangar. Dust-sheets were placed on the furniture and floor, and all doors locked.

"During 1950 and 1951, probably due to the prolonged illness of The King, there were only ten or twelve Royal Flights per month, which resulted in each Royal aircraft flying about 200 hours per year. The other two aircraft flew about 400 hours per year on training and support flights. The life of main components between major servicing or factory overhaul was; Viking airframe and associated components, 800 hours; wheels and tyres 200 landings. It was realized that the level of aircraft utilization would result in the two Royal aircraft taking four years between major servicing, whilst the two support aircraft would take only two years. The situation would soon arise where the support aircraft would have a better modification state than the Royal aircraft and would have newer components fitted. A decision was made as a matter of internal policy that all 'lifed' components on the two Royal aircraft would be removed at half-life and fitted to the two support aircraft, where the remaining life would be used prior to overhaul at the normal time. Higher authority was not consulted, and it was never the intention that components supplied to The King's Flight should only be used for half the normal life. However, this policy was subsequently adopted by the Air Ministry (MOD) as one of the additional safety and reliability measures to be applied to The Queen's Flight aircraft."

On 26 May 1950, Princess Elizabeth presented the King's Colour to the RAF in Hyde Park in His Majesty's absence, as his illness had worsened. Nearly three months later on 15 August 1950 Princess Elizabeth gave birth to her second child, a daughter, Princess Anne, at Clarence House, the new London home that she and her husband had moved to on 4 September 1949. And on 27 September that year, she was appointed a Counsellor of State during The King's illness.

As a family, we lived in Officers Married Quarters at Crowmarsh Gifford, near Wallingford, and during July 1950, a second sibling, another sister, was born.

During August 1950, the Private Secretary to His Majesty King George VI advised Australian authorities that the King, Queen Elizabeth (later The Queen Mother), and Princess Margaret, would tour Australia in early 1952. This tour would be in place of the proposed tour of 1949 which was cancelled, and was to have been a more limited and less demanding tour due to the state of the King's health. Australian Prime Minister Menzies stated on 5 September 1950, that "the fact that the King's health has improved to such an extent as to enable His Majesty even to contemplate a visit to Australia is in itself a matter for intense satisfaction and rejoicing."

On 1 September 1950, Tom was Signaller on The King's Aircraft, Viking VL246, with Wing Commander Roy Scott as Captain and Pilot, Flight Lieutenant Jenkins, Navigator, Flight Lieutenant Toogood, Flight Engineer, and Sergeant Griffiths, Steward. They flew HRH the Duke of Edinburgh from London to Luqa in Malta, via Le Var in Southern France, and they returned to Benson via Gibraltar and Lisbon on the 5 September.

On 9 October 1950, it was announced from Buckingham Palace that The King, on advice of his doctors, would not carry out an intended visit with Queen Elizabeth (later The Queen Mother) to Australia in 1952; and their place would be taken by Their Royal Highnesses, Princess Elizabeth and The Duke of Edinburgh.

On 18 October 1950, Tom was again a Signaller on VL 246, The King's Aircraft, together with Air Commodore Sir Edward Fielden as Captain and crew of Scott, Jenkins, Toogood and Griffiths, together with Aircraftsmen Simmons and Giddy for embarking and disembarking the aircraft. Again the Royal passenger was His Royal Highness The Duke of Edinburgh, this time they flew from Benson to Malta via Nice to collect HRH and flew him home on the 19 October.

On 30 November 1950, Princess Elizabeth left behind a fog bound London Airport, her two and a half month old baby daughter Princess Anne, and two year old son Prince Charles, on board Viking VL 247 bound for Malta and en-route to stay with her husband Prince Philip; Tom was her Signals Officer.

On 1 December 1950, Tom was the Signaller on board VL 246 with Sir Edward Fielden, Roy Scott, Flight Lieutenant K. Jenkins, Flight Lieutenant W.E. Toogood, and Sergeant Griffiths. They collected Her Majesty The Queen (Queen Mother) from RAF Marham during her stay at Sandringham, and flew her to London; the following day they flew HM back to RAF Marham to resume her holiday.

On 15 December, during the morning, the same crew as above flew HRH the Princess Margaret in VL 246 to Malta via Nice. The crew stopped over in Malta, and on 18 December they flew Their Royal Highnesses the Princess Elizabeth and Princess Margaret from Malta to Castel – Benito, near Tripoli in Libya, returning that afternoon.

I started my first primary school at Crowmarsh during January 1951 and during October 1951, a further sibling, a third sister, was born.

On 19 March 1951, Tom was a Signaller on VL 246 with Sir Edward Fielden, Roy Scott, Flight Lieutenant Jenkins, Flight Lieutenant Hallam as Flight Engineer, and Sergeant Griffiths and Leading Aircraftsman Simmons as Stewards. They flew HRH The Princess Elizabeth from London to Malta via Le Var and on the return flight, without their royal passenger, flew back via Rome on the 20 March.

From March to May 1951 Princess Elizabeth frequently stood in for her father at public events and visited Greece, Italy and Malta by King's Flight; with Tom as Signals Officer.

King George VI and Queen Elizabeth (The Queen Mother) still attended some official functions, including visits to Balmoral and The Highland Games. On 13 May 1951 there was a rare occasion when HM The King, HM The Queen, HRH The Princess Margaret, and Group Captain Peter Townsend were flown in the same aircraft by the crew of Fielden, Scott, Jenkins, Tom Clark, Hallam, and Griffiths, in VL 246 from London Airport to RAF Dyce in Aberdeenshire, for their spring stay at Balmoral and the Highland Games.

Tom had a photograph, on the back he had written "Receiving Queen Elizabeth RAF Dyce 1951." In the photograph Tom is on the left, standing next to the Royal car, and HM Queen Elizabeth is being presented to Group Captain Roy Scott.

On 3 June 1951, Her Majesty The Queen (The Queen Mother) and HRH The Princess Margaret were flown from Aldergrove Airport Belfast to London Airport in VL 246 by Sir Edward Fielden, Roy Scott, Jenkins, Tom Clark, Hallam and Griffiths.

On 20 July 1951, Roy Scott, Jenkins, Tom Clark, Hallam and Griffiths collected HRH The Duke of Edinburgh in VL 246 from Malta and flew him to London.

On 18 September 1951, HM The Queen and Their Royal Highnesses The Princess Elizabeth and The Duke of Edinburgh were collected from RAF Dyce and flown to London Airport by Sir Edward Fielden, Roy Scott, Jenkins, Tom Clark, Hallam, Griffiths and Simmons. On 22 September they flew HRH The Princess Margaret from London Airport to Dyce.

Later that year, the first crossing of the Atlantic by air was made by a member of the Royal Family. From 8 October to 12 November, Princess Elizabeth and Prince

THE DAILY MAIL, TUESDAY, MAY 22, 1951

THE
ROWN
-25-

The Proud Blue Line

THE King's Flight was in action again yesterday when their Majesties, with Princess Margaret, flew back home from Balmoral.

Above is a photograph of officers of the Flight taken beside the King's Viking aircraft. They are, from left to right: The Adjutant, Flight Lieut. K. G. Sharp, D.S.O.; Flight Lieuts. D. Gray, A. W. Hallam, D.F.C., F. W. Gray, K. Jenkins, E. Brewin, F. H. Pennycott, S. N. Sloan, D.F.C., C.G.M.; Wing Commander R. C. E. Scott, A.F.C. and Bar, chief pilot of the King's Flight; Flight Lieuts. R. C. Churcher, D.S.O., D.F.C. and Bar, T. B. Clark, K. G. Hampson, D.F.C., and Flight Lieut. E. W. Lamb, the engineer officer.

This body of young men, and the technicians under them, make of the King's Flight an absolutely self-contained unit which is probably the most efficient in the world. It is stationed at Benson Aerodrome, near Oxford.

Normally, when the King is flying, the crew consists of Air Commodore E. H. Fielden, C.B., C.V.O., D.F.C., A.F.C., Captain of the King's Flight, the pilot, navigator, signaller, engineer, and steward.

A copy of the original photo from The Daily Mail Archives.

Members of The King's Flight aircrews pose in front of The King's Viking 21st May 1951 Flight Lieutenant Tom Clark is 3rd from the right Group Captain Roy Scott is 5th from the right and Flight Lieutenant Bill Lamb extreme right.

Receiving The Queen Mother.

Phillip, went on a tour of Canada, in BOAC Stratocruiser "Canopus". The Royal Party visited Newfoundland: St John's. Prince Edward Island: Charlottetown. Nova Scotia: Springhill, Truro, Sydney, and Halifax. Quebec: Montreal, Quebec City, Saint-Hyacinthe, Rimouski, and Drummondsville. Ontario: Ottawa,

Brockville, Royal Military College of Canada in Kingston, Trenton, Toronto, Niagara Falls, Hamilton, St Catherines, Windsor, Fort William, North Bay, and Kapuskasing. Manitoba, including Winnipeg, Saskatchewan, including Regina, Alberta, including Edmonton and Calgary and British Columbia, including Victoria and Vancouver. The Royal couple then visited the President of the United States, Harry S. Truman, in Washington, DC. On that trip, the Princess carried with her a draft Accession Declaration for use if the King died while she was out of the United Kingdom.

On 17 January 1952, Her Majesty Queen Elizabeth (The Queen Mother) was collected from RAF Marham during her Christmas stay at Sandringham, and flown to London Airport and return in VL 246 by Wing Commander Roy Scott, Commodore; Squadron Leader R. Churcher, Captain and Pilot; Flight Lieutenant K. Jenkins, Navigator; Flight Lieutenant Tom Clark, Signaller and Stewards Sergeant Whitehead and Leading Aircraftsman Simmons.

In 1952 came the ill-fated and re-scheduled Royal Tour of Australia and New Zealand, via East Africa and Kenya, which left England on 31 January 1952, with Princess Elizabeth and The Duke of Edinburgh on board representing HM The King; they were seen off by His Majesty who looked pale and drawn and obviously seriously ill. So extensive was the programme of visits due to be made during their Australian tour, that only air travel would have made their itinerary practicable. Between 1 March and 1 May they were scheduled to be flown some 6,000 miles round the Australian continent by The King's Flight. They landed at Nairobi on 1 February, and on 3 February, The Royal party arrived at Sagana Hunting Lodge in Nyeri, in the foothills of Mount Kenya, some 100 miles north of Nairobi, and spent the night in Treetops Hotel.

The King Is Dead King George VI 1936–1952

King George VI, aged fifty-six, died in the early hours of the morning on 6 February 1952, during his winter sojourn at Sandringham, Norfolk – the place of his birth. He had suffered from ill health for some years and had a lung operation the year before. He died following a heart attack and lung cancer, his under-valet found him at 0715 hours when he took him tea in bed. It was at Sagana Lodge that the Princess received the news of the death of her father on 6 February 1952; that same day she left Entebbe, Uganda, by air for London, arriving at 1630 hours on the 7 February.

Long Live The Queen. Queen Elizabeth II, 1952 – to date

Her Majesty Queen Elizabeth II has already reigned for longer than any other Monarch before her, apart from Queen Victoria who reigned for sixty-three years and seven months; and she continues to give first class service to her Country and

Commonwealth. She comes from a long line of female longevity and long may she reign over us.

After news of her father's death reached her, the new Queen and The Duke of Edinburgh immediately postponed their tour, and set off for Entebbe airport in Uganda. From there the flight to London Airport, a distance of 4,127 miles, took twenty hours. On her arrival at 1619 hours on 7 February, the new Queen was met by Winston Churchill, The Duke of Gloucester, Anthony Eden, Clement Attlee and other Privy Councillors.

On 6 March 1952, the late King George VI's sister, The Princess Mary of York the Princess Royal, was flown from Zurich to London Airport in VL 246, by Scott, Churcher, Jenkins, Tom Clark, Hallam, Flight Lieutenant G. McCarthy, Supr' Pilot, and Sergeant Whitehead as Steward.

On 6 June 1952, Her Majesty Queen Elizabeth (The Queen Mother) was flown in VL 246, from London Airport to RAF Dyce and Balmoral, by Sir Edward Fielden, Flight Lieutenant Churcher, Flight Lieutenant Jenkins, Tom Clark, Flight Lieutenant H.J. Redding, Flight Engineer, and Leading Aircraftsman Simmons, Steward.

On 21 June 1952, the same crew as above, flew Their Royal Highnesses The Duke and Duchess of Gloucester from London Airport, to Manston airport in Kent, and return. On the same date they flew The Princess Mary of York the Princess Royal, from London Airport to Aldergrove Airport in Belfast, and return, and on 25 June, flew her from London Airport to Eglinton, City of Derry Airport and return.

On 5 July 1952, The Queen's Aircraft VL 247, flew on a proving flight from RAF Benson to Oslo, Stockholm, Helsinki, to Copenhagen, and return to Benson. The nine man crew consisted of Air Commodore Sir Edward Fielden; Wing Commander Roy Scott as Captain; Squadron Leader R. Churcher as second Pilot; two Navigators, Flight Lieutenant D. Gray and Flight Lieutenant K. Jenkins; two Signallers, Flight Lieutenant Tom Clark and Flight Lieutenant R. Manning; Flight Lieutenant J. R. Coates as Flight Engineer and Corporal Naylor as Steward.

On 21 July 1952, VL 247 was used by Sir Edward Fielden, Flight Lieutenant Churcher, Flight Lieutenant H. D. Rafferty, Flight Lieutenant Tom Clark, and Flight Lieutenant H. J. Redding as Flight Engineer, to fly HRH The Princess Margaret from Exeter to London Airport.

On 25 July 1952, VL 247 was used to transport HRH The Duke of Kent from London Airport to Copenhagen, and on to Helsinki. The ten man crew consisted of Air Commodore Sir Edward Fielden, Squadron Leader Churcher as Captain, Flight Lieutenant McCarthy as Pilot, Flight Lieutenant Kirby as Navigator, Flight Lieutenant Rafferty as second Navigator, Flight Lieutenant Hannah as Signaller, Flight Lieutenant Tom Clark as second Signaller, Flight Lieutenant Redding as Flight Engineer, Flight Lieutenant Lake as second Engineer and Sergeant Naylor as Steward.

On 1 August 1952, The King's Flight was re-named The Queen's Flight, and on 8 August, the crew of VL 246, comprising of Air Commodore Sir Edward Fielden, Squadron Leader R.E. Churcher (Captain and Pilot), Flight Lieutenant M.D. Rafferty (Navigator), Flight Lieutenant Tom Clark (Signaller), Flight Lieutenant E.E. Lake (Flight Engineer), and Sergeant Whitehead (Steward) flew Her Majesty Queen Elizabeth II from London Airport to Edzell in Angus, Scotland.

The last time that Tom flew on The Queen's Flight was on 5 October 1952, when the crew of Wing Commander Scott, Flight Lieutenants Churcher, Rafferty, Tom Clark, Lake and Sergeant Naylor as Steward, flew Air Commodore Sir Edward Fielden and Group Captain Peter Townsend from RAF Benson to Edzell, and then flew HRH The Duke of Edinburgh from Edzell to RAF Marham.

The Korean War

Far East Transport Wing of the Far East Air Force (FEAF) incorporated 48, 52, 110, Far East Communications & 41 New Zealand/Australia Squadrons. It was established at HQ FEAF, Changi on 1 January 1952, and lasted until 15 February 1956.

The situation in Korea was beginning to stabilize some twenty-eight months into the war and was on its way to a peaceful settlement when Tom was posted to HQ Far East Air Force (FEAF) on 12 November 1952; some eight months before the end of that war. He was transferred to Far East Transport Wing on 16 November 1952, and from 15 December that year operated as a Qualified Signals Leader on a Valetta of Far East Transport Wing. The Wing Pilot was Squadron Leader Alex Wickes (who I remember later in Singapore still flying with Tom, see later). The Valetta flew in a V.I.P. Flight role, transporting the Commander-in-Chief of FEAF, Air Marshal Sir Clifford Sanderson, Commander-in-Chief, 11 June 1952 to 12 November 1954; or his deputy, and other V.I.P.'s, from FEAF HQ at Changi in Singapore to the far flung areas of the Far East Air Command, including Hong Kong, India and Japan.

During 1952 and 1953 Air Commodore R.C. Field was AOC of HQ RAF Hong Kong and AHQ.

Crest of RAF Kai Tak.

The Vickers Valetta was the military version of the Viking which Tom had been on previously, with the King's Flight. The 158th Viking became the prototype Valetta, and first flew on 30 June 1947. The Valetta differed from the Viking fundamentally, in being fitted with more powerful engines, a strengthened floor and large loading doors. The Viking and Valetta provided the basis of the Vickers Varsity; the only difference between the Varsity and the Valetta was the position of the third wheel. The Varsity had a nose wheel, and the Valetta a tail-wheel. The Valetta was based on the wartime Wellington bomber, designed by Barnes Wallis, and incorporated the Wellington's fuselage and engines, and the first of its type entered service as a replacement for the

Crest of Far East Air Force. (Transport Wing).

Dakota. The only external difference between a C1 and a C2 V.I.P. Valetta was the faired in tail-cone of the V.I.P., compared to the blunt end of the C1. The C2 V.I.P. version, of which nine were built, in the series VX571-580, could carry up to sixteen V.I.P.'s, thirty-six parachutists, or light vehicles such as land rovers. It was known affectionately as the "Flying Pig" because of its tubby appearance. Tom was also engaged in an air support, supply, and transportation role, operating from RAF Kaitak in Kowloon, Hong Kong and RAF Changi in Singapore, at the foot of the Malaysian Peninsula.

Far East Transport Wing helped the essential supply links between Singapore, Hong Kong and Iwakuni in Japan.

Squadron Leader Alex Wickes joined Far East Transport Wing on 23 October 1952 as a Wing Pilot, flying Valetta, York and Harvard. After familiarization and standardization, with Squadron Leader Taylor and Flight Lieutenants Coulson and Savage. Alex then flew as first pilot with his own crew and made repeated journeys to and from Kai Tak in Hong Kong, to Clark Field in the Philippines, Kai Tak – Saigon-Changi, Changi-Negombo- in Sri Lanka, Changi – Bangkok, Tengah-Kuala Lumper-Ipoh in Malaya, as well as local flights, Changi-Seletar. Tom joined his crew as Signaller in December 1952, and became a regular member flying with Alex. Group Captain Roulston, formerly a Second World War Commanding Officer of 55 Squadron in North Africa was the Wing Commanding Officer.

The following two photographs, taken by Tom in 1953, clearly shows that the RAF regularly flew over the Republic of China's territory during that troubled time. The first is of Wing Pilot Squadron Leader Alex Wickes flying a Valetta over Taiwan, formerly named Formosa, during 1953.

In the second photograph, the Island of Taiwan is being overflown and clearly visible below the starboard engine of the Valetta.

Author's note: The Island of Taiwan is seventy-five miles from the Chinese mainland and was at the time the base for the new fledgling Republic of China Government. Other aircraft which the crew flew in included Avro Anson, Douglas Dakota and Avro Hastings.

On 18 May 1953, Alex and crew flew with V.I.P. Commander-in-Chief of Far East Land Forces, General Sir Charles Frederic Keightley, GCB, GBE, and DSO, together with Lady Keightley and the GOC Malaya, Lieutenant General Hugh Charles Stockwell, GCB, KBE, DSO and Bar from Tengah Air Base Singapore to Kuala Lumper and Ipoh, in Valetta WJ499 (Return Flight 26 May). In the meantime, on 24 May, he flew Air Vice-Marshal Frederick Rudolph William (Fred) Scherger, KBE, CB, DSO, AFC, Commander of Commonwealth Air Forces in Malaya, and Argentinean General Juan Peron, from Tengah to Kluang in Valetta VX523, as part of Operation Commodore.

The Queen's Coronation, the fortieth monarch since William the Conqueror, took place on Tuesday, 2 June 1953, amid great public rejoicing. It was over a year since The Queen's Accession, but the ceremony required months of planning and respect for the Royal Family on the passing of King George VI and of Queen Mary on 24 March 1953, Her Majesty's grandmother, and King George VI's mother, who also died of lung cancer.

Tom's caption reads "Hong Kong 5 metres from China 1953" Tom is on the right and standing next to Alex Wickes, other crew members unknow.

Cocos Islands.

Crew taking refreshment, Officers Mess RAK Kaitak 1952, Tom is on the right next to Alex
Wickes the other crew members unknown.

Tom and the other two, photo taken by Alex Wickes.

On 28 August 1953, the crew flew the British Minister of Supply Mr Edwin Duncan Sandys, from Kuala Lumpa to Kallang in WJ499, and on 31 August General (later Field Marshal) Sir Gerald Walter Robinson Templer, KG, GCB, GCMG, KBE, the High Commissioner of Malaya and Lady Templer, from Bayan Lepas to Kuala Lumper.

On 7 September the crew flew from Changi to Djakarta and then on to the Cocos Islands.

On 3 October the crew again flew General Gerald Templer and Lady Templer, this time from Bayan Lepas – Kuala Lumper, Changi. From 3 November until the 20 November they were paratrooping in Valetta WD159.

On 4 December 1953, Tom received his Flight Lieutenant Royal Air Force Permanent Commission from Her Majesty Queen Elizabeth II. He had sat his intensive examination to pass in four stages, whilst with The King's Flight. In March 1951 a "C" Partial Pass. September 1951 a "C" Partial Pass. March 1952 a "C" Partial Pass and a "C" Pass during September 1952. He would receive his signed illuminated framed scroll dated 5 October 1954. It reads:

Elizabeth II, *by the Grace of God* OF THE UNITED KINGDOM of GREAT BRITAIN and NORTHERN IRELAND and of HER OTHER REALMS AND TERRITORIES, HEAD OF THE COMMONWEALTH, DEFENDER OF THE FAITH, To Our Trusty and well beloved **Thomas Buchanan Clark** Greeting:
We, reposing especial Trust and Confidence in your Loyalty, Courage, and good Conduct, do by these Presents Constitute and Appoint you to be an Officer in Our Royal Air Force from the Fourth day of December 1953. You are therefore carefully and diligently to discharge your Duty as such in the Rank of Flight Lieutenant or in such other Rank as We may from time to time hereafter be pleased to promote or appoint you to and you are in such manner and on such occasions as may be prescribed by Us to exercise and well discipline in their duties such Officers, Airmen and Airwomen as may be placed under your orders from time to time and use your best endeavours to keep them in good Order and Discipline. And We do hereby Command them to Obey you as their superior Officer and you to Observe and follow such Orders and Directions as from time to time you shall receive from Us, or any superior Officer, according to the Rules and Discipline of War, in pursuance of the Trust hereby reposed in you.

GIVEN at Our Court, at Saint James's
The Fifth day of October 1954, in the Third Year of Our Reign
By Her Majesty's Command

The Korean War was the first armed confrontation of the Cold War and set the standard for many later conflicts. It created the idea of a limited war, where the two superpowers Russia and America would fight in another country, forcing the people

A Vickers Valetta.

Valettas at RAF Kai Tak Kowloon Hong Kong 1954.

A busy RAF Kai Tak with Valetta, Hasting, Dakota and Sunderland aircraft in the bay.

The airport buildings.

in that nation to suffer the bulk of the destruction and death involved in a war between such large nations. The superpowers avoided descending into total war with one another, as well as the mutual use of nuclear weapons. It also expanded the Cold War, which to that point had mostly been concerned with Europe.

The Malayan Emergency

110 Squadron Crest. "Neither Fear nor Despise."

Whilst the Korean War was underway, disruption had already begun on the further southern Peninsula of south-east Asia, that of Malaya.

No. 48 Squadron was the "founder member" of modern Changi; ever since 1946 when it was reformed from the former 215 Squadron it had operated from Changi, initially with Dakotas, then from 1951 with Valettas. In addition to its routine task of operating transport routes throughout the Far East, the squadron became heavily involved in the anti-communist operations in Malaya, operations which lasted from 1948 until 1957. The main task was supply dropping, a task which, in the difficult terrain and weather conditions of the area, cost the squadron four

52 Squadron Crest. "By Sweat and Blood."

48 Squadron Crest. "By Strength and Faithfulness."

aircraft and their crews during these years. The squadron's first child, the Far East Communications Squadron, continued to operate from Changi too, flying aircraft similar to those of 48. In 1952 it received the first V.I.P. Hastings and retained some of its Valettas until at least the mid 1960's.

No. 52 Squadron deserves a place in the Changi history story, for it operated there for twelve years, including the whole of the Malayan Emergency. It had re-equipped with Douglas Dakotas for general transport duties in India, and in 1947 the squadron moved to Singapore during the start of the Malayan Emergency, and were engaged in supply drops to jungle troops, mainly SAS and other security forces. Valettas replaced the Dakotas in June 1951, which were flown until the squadron disbanded in April 1966.

No 110 Squadron reformed in June 1946, moved from Kai Tak, Hong Kong, to Changi in Singapore in July 1947, from then on it "hedge-hopped" between there, Kuala Lumpur and Seletar until July 1951. When, together with 81 and 84 Squadrons, also flying Dakotas, and converting to Valetta C1 between October 1951 and April 1952; it again moved to Changi where it did continuous service until December 1957 when it was disbanded for a period of eighteen months. The squadron continued to provide transport and supply drops, and communications support to the security forces in Malaya. One of the squadron's Vickers Valetta was VX525 "H".

So this was the situation when Tom joined FEAF in the middle of November 1952, in the air support role of Korea, until its end; and then he was also involved

The SS *Empire Trooper.*

in the Malayan Emergency, in a V.I.P. role, still flying the Commander-in-Chief of FEAF and other V.I.P's.

During a cold day in January 1954, Mum, Dad (Tom), my elder half- brother and four sisters and me, as well as the family car; set sail on HMS *Empire Trooper*" from Southampton, bound for Singapore. Our journey would take us through the Bay of Biscay and to the Straits of Gibraltar, past the "Pillars of Hercules" between Gibraltar, and Spain to the north, and the Jebel Musa in Morocco, to the south, which separates Europe from Africa at the division of the Atlantic Ocean and the entrance to the Mediterranean Sea. We docked at Gibraltar, and went ashore whilst the ship was taking on fresh supplies of food, water and fuel.

We then sailed across the Mediterranean, bound for Malta and en route to Cyprus, before docking at Port Said in Egypt, and on through the Suez Canal to the Gulf of Sucz and the Red Sea, stopping at Aden. We then headed out across the Gulf of Aden into the vast traverse of the Indian Ocean and on to our next stop at Colombo, Ceylon (Sri Lanka).

The last leg of our journey was through the Straits of Malacca and the Straits of Sumatra, between Malaya and Sumatra, before our final destination, Singapore. Our home for the next fourteen months would be 55, Lloyds Leas Officers Married Quarters, Changi. It had been a new-build ambitious project, comprising of officer's, senior NCO's and airmen's married quarters on a new site opposite Selarang Barracks, extending as far south as Tanah Merah Besar Road. It had been named after Sir Hugh Lloyd, Commander-in-Chief in the late 1940s. Between 1950 and 1953 a new primary school was built, its new assembly hall replacing the pre-war generating plant repair shop.

Around the time of our arrival in Singapore, there was a fatal crash of a Vickers Valetta C1 WJ494 on the 21 February 1954. It was on a single engine approach to RAF Changi when it lost height, contacted trees, crashed and caught fire. The aircraft was serving with the RAF Far East Transport Wing; three of the twelve on board died.

As an eight year old, my life was idyllic in a jungle covered tropical island, roughly the size and shape of the Isle of Wight; but with a population then of over one million. Changi airfield looked out over Changi Creek and had a village of many shops at its door. The exchange rate was 32 Malay dollars to the Pound Sterling.

RAF Changi Crest. "We Shelter Many Empty."

Headquarters of the Far East Air Force were situated at the eastern end of Singapore Island in handsome red-roofed buildings, delightfully situated on a slight eminence a few miles from Changi airfield, commanding a magnificent view overlooking the eastern channel leading to the Johore Straits and the estuary of the Johore River. The grounds were pleasantly laid out with tropical trees – the red blossomed "flame of the forest", the yellow-flowering cassia, the handsomely tall, laurel-like-leaved garcinia, the drooping and less brilliantly yellow-blossomed casuarinas, banana and papaya trees; and for shrubs the purple bougainvillea, delicate oleander, jasmine and deeply-scented frangipani. These trees and plants Tom would have revelled in, looking at his future "civvie street" employment. The air was hot, and the atmosphere sticky with the humidity of a rainy, low-level tropical island. Singapore has much the same climate and temperatures all the year round, which vary from 93°F daytime, to 78°F at night, and there is an absence of cool nights. Singapore and Malaya lie below the atmospheric inter-tropical convergence zone and during spring there was a regular weather sequence. During the day there would be a clear morning with hot sunshine, clouds beginning to build up around eleven, probably thunder and rain or a continuance of build-up until the afternoon; then about four or five there would come a deluge, followed by an evening of thunder muttering in the distance, or perhaps a final rainstorm before the night became fine and clear.

RAF Changi taken from the air 16 April 1954.

RAF Changi looking from Lloyds Lees Married Quarters.

One of the bungalows on Lloyds Lees Estate this one housed the Bradley family.

However, life for the services was far from idyllic, and the RAF squadrons using Dakota and Valettas, supported the Army Counter-Insurgence operations in Malaya by providing communications, dropping troops and supplies, landing of supplies, delivering leaflets and the evacuation of casualties. The squadrons also flew in supplies for the SAS in the jungle, did valuable reconnaissance work and launched air strikes against the communist led insurgents.

Mum in the lounge of 55
Lloyd Leas seated by our Hong
Kong carved Cocktail Cabinet
and Malay wood carving.

Wing Commander "Jimmy" Neville Stack (later Air Chief Marshall Sir Neville Stack, KCB, CVO, AFC) was made Commander of FEAF Transport Wing in 1954; he had been a Flying Officer on 201 and 204 Flying Boat Squadrons from 1939 to 1945, and was on 201 Squadron when Tom joined them in 1940.

On 14 March 1954, the crew of Valetta VX485 was Alex Wickes, Pilot; Flight Lieutenant Duncombe, Navigator and Flight Lieutenant Tom Clark, Signaller. They flew the station commander and party from Changi to Labaun, then part of British North Borneo, and on 16 March did the return flight. On 27 March Alex, Tom and Flight Lieutenant Perkins as Navigator flew in VX526 Paratrooping and Continuation Training. Then on 29 March the crew consisting of Alex, Tom and Flight Lieutenant McCormack as Navigator, flew in VX485 on an air test. On 30 March· the same crew and aircraft flew from Changi to Labuan and on to Clark Field; the following day they flew from Clark Field to Kai Tak, Hong Kong. On 1 April they flew from Kai Tak to Kadena, Okinawa, Japan and on to Iwakuni.

I remember one lunchtime during 1954, at the Officers Mess at RAF Changi, as a nearly nine year old, sipping a half-pint glass of "Tiger" beer and lemonade shandy, together with Tom and Alex Wickes, who were drinking copious pints of Tiger and Carlsberg alternatively, when they decided to take me up "for a spin" in one of the Transport Valettas. We all climbed on board with Alex as pilot, Tom

Map showing Japan, Korea and China.

as co-pilot and me in the Navigator bucket seat behind. Alex taxied the aircraft and took off from Changi, and in no time we were flying and circling over the Malayan jungle and mangrove swamps off the coast of south-west Malaya. It was quite an exciting and exhilarating experience for me and I felt very privileged.

Sir Clifford Sanderson was superseded as C-in-C of FEAF on 12 November 1954 by Air Marshal Sir Francis Fressanges, KBE, CB, who remained in post until the 13 July 1957.

At a press conference in Singapore given by Air Marshal Sir Clifford Sanderson, on the occasion of his handing over command of FEAF to Air Marshal Fressanges, it was stated that, in the event of Malaya being attacked, British air defence could be doubled in three or four days. It was also said, that in an emergency, British jet bombers could pour into the network of new and strengthened airfields in the Far East; that Malaya's potential air strength was now greater than ever before; and that co-operation between the RAF in Malaya and the USAF in the Philippines had recently been considerably strengthened.

FEAF was controlled by a Commander-in-Chief with its headquarters at Changi RAF Station on Singapore Island. The RAF's main task in the Far East was to defend British interests at key points which were still under British direct control. Secondly, our air and shipping routes through the Indian Ocean and

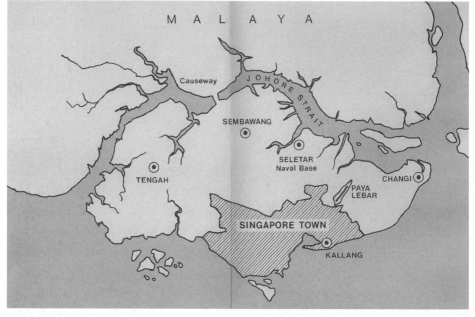

Map showing area Author went "for a spin".

Some of the shanty type shops in Changi Village.

the Pacific had to be protected, and assistance with air search and rescue (not, of course, confined to British ships and aircraft in distress) given where necessary. Thirdly, our air contribution to SEATO and the commonwealth strategic reserve in the Far East was made by FEAF. Fourthly, active support had been and was continuing to be given, to the police forces in Malaya in their campaign against communist terrorists, which had been ongoing since 1948. Fifthly, training was carried out of Malays, Chinese and Indians who joined either the RAF, or the

The Author and his four sisters on the veranda.

China–Town Singapore City.

Changi Beach Singapore.

The Author and his two eldest sisters at Changi Beach.

The Airmen's swimming pool at Changi with the RAF Hospital in the background.

The Officer's Swimming Pool.

Malayan Auxiliary Air Force. Finally, the integration of RAAF and RNZAF commanders, squadrons and units within FEAF should be stressed – for this co-operation benefitted both Australia and New Zealand in their national defence and also Britain, with its worldwide commitments.

In a later statement, Air Marshal Sir Francis Fressanges, Commander-in-Chief FEAF said: "In the fight against communism in South-East Asia, the Far East Air Force plays a vital and indispensable part. There are two main facets of our activities in this area; first, the provision of air support for the emergency operations against the communist terrorists in Malaya, and secondly, the contribution towards the overall defence effort of the allied treaty organizations of SEATO and ANZAM. The most active role of the Far East Air Force is an operation against the communist terrorists in Malaya. Since the emergency began, we have achieved considerable success by a direct offensive with bombers and ground attack aircraft. However, our main task continues to be that of air support and air supply to the ground forces. Without this support, they would be unable to operate effectively against the enemy in the deep jungles of Malaya. The task of air supply in the difficult conditions of terrain and weather in Malaya is a highly specialized one. Our transport aircraft are required to maintain garrisons in jungle forts which are inaccessible except by air. Troops must be flown into and out of advanced bases deep in the interior; supplies must be dropped under

Loading a jeep through the cargo doors of a Valetta C1.

Three views of one of the few remaining C2 Valettas in existence VX580.

all weather conditions, and casualties evacuated. Specially equipped 'voice' and leaflet dropping aircraft are employed in the psychological warfare against terrorists. All these tasks must be carried out with the highest degree of efficiency if our ground forces are to maintain the pressure against the enemy which has produced such good results during the recent past…"

Tom would also become involved in the parachute dropping of troops into the jungle, dropping supplies to British SAS and other soldiers deep in the Malay jungle; and he was also involved in the Psychological Warfare Operations, where leaflets and broadcasts were prepared in simple vernacular language for distribution to the scattered villages and estates where the majority of the sympathetic Chinese and Min Yuen lived. Leaflets were usually dispatched from a supply-dropping aircraft, like the Valetta, and Dakota. Throughout the campaign, leaflets remained the chief medium for disseminating information and propaganda to the insurgents in the jungle and to the Min Yuen.

General Service Medal with Malaya Bar Awarded for Campaigns and Operations that fell short of full scale war.

During February 1955, Air Commodore W.H. Kyle, CB, CBE, DSO, DFC, ADC, became AOC Malaya and assumed the acting rank of Air Vice-Marshal.

For his individual role in Malaya, Tom was awarded the General Service Medal (1918) (ER version) with clasp "Malaya", engraved "FLT LT T B CLARK RAF". He did not qualify for a Korea Medal, as he flew less than the required thirty sorties to and from Korea during his time at Kai Tak from 16 November 1952 to the end of hostilities on 27 February 1953.

Whilst we were in Singapore, on Good Friday during April 1955, my grandfather, and Mum's Dad, John (Jack) Stringer died suddenly of a heart attack, and Mum and Dad made arrangements to go back to Britain to be with my grandmother, Florence.

At the end of April 1955 we flew back to Britain. It took three days in total with a flying time of some thirty-three hours! We had left Singapore on a hot balmy night and landed at night at a foggy and freezing cold old England airfield; no change from when we had left some fifteen months before. We flew from Changi to Blackbushe Airport near Camberley on the Surrey/Hampshire border, in a Handley Page Hermes flying at 9,000feet via Bangkok; Calcutta; Delhi (overnight stop); Karachi; Bahrain; Cairo (landing/refuelling); Nicosia; Rome (overnight stop).

Chapter Eight

"Air Signaller Examiner & Instructor; Air Electronics Officer"

Following the death of his father–in–law, and my grandfather, "Jack" John Stringer, on Good Friday, 8 April 1955 and our return to England, Tom was deplaned on 4 May and on disembarkation leave from 5 May until 11 June 1955.

Tom was then placed on the instructors complement at the Air Signallers School at RAF Swanton Morley in Norfolk, as an examiner, from 20 June. That year, fed up with being in various married quarters, Mum and Dad bought a house at "Excelsior" 8 Brook Road, Dersingham, whilst he was on accrued leave from 12 June until 1 July 1955 and we moved in, lock, stock and barrel. It would become the family home for the next fifty years, until my parents' death during 2005.

"Excelsior" the Clark family home 1955-2005.

Flying Training Command Crest.
"Through Toil To Supremacy".

RAF Swanton Morley, Station Motto
"Steadfast To Serve".

Tom, in the meanwhile, commuted to Swanton Morley in our black Austin, DPY50. At Swanton Morley his job was as an examiner, on the new type Morse code with Flying Training Command (FTC).

Here is an extract from a former "Red Arrows" pilot, Tony Cunnane, of his experience at Swanton Morley on an Air Signaller Course when he was a corporal, whilst Tom was an instructor there:

"I was a student on AS39 Course at the Air Signallers School at RAF Swanton Morley in 1956 as the courses were beginning to run down with the decreasing requirement for air signallers. Until we arrived, new courses had been starting every two weeks. However, the next course to start after us was AS41, a month later, and the final courses were AS45 and AS48. In the meantime, officers were arriving to start the first Air Electronics Courses, but they were kept well away from us. The school was renamed the Air Electronics School on 1 April 1957, but then closed down at the end of 1957 and moved to Hullavington. We on AS39 were the first to learn Morse code by a new method. Up until this time, the combination of dots and dashes that make up the Morse code had to be learned by various old-fashioned but well-tried methods. Instructors, the world over, swore by their own favourite method and so there were many different ways of trying to simplify the learning process. Under the earlier teaching system, once the letters, numbers, punctuation signs, and the various other special symbols, had been learned, it was just a matter of gaining speed until students reached, or failed to reach, the all important twenty-two words per minute required to qualify as an Air Signaller. Under that old system most students had temporary mental plateaux at around eight, twelve, and eighteen words per minute. Quite why those particular speeds were stumbling blocks, no-one seemed to understand. Some students could never progress beyond four or eight words per minute and left the course for pastures new. Those who failed to reach twenty-two words per minute were given further training and another test. If they failed again at twenty-two words per minute, they failed the course. I eventually passed the official tests sending Morse code at twenty-eight words per minute and reading at thirty words per minute, and I was jolly proud of those results.

"In the RAF's new system that was first used on my course at Swanton Morley, the individual Morse characters were played to us at the equivalent of twenty-two words per minute from the outset. So in Lesson 1, when most of us did not know a single Morse symbol, we listened on headphones to code generated by a punched tape machine, watched the instructor write the corresponding letter on the blackboard, and then wrote the letter down in our note books. Initially there was a seven second gap between each character, so we had plenty of time to listen, watch and write. We learned the symbols by the association between sound, sight and writing – and it worked. We did not need to know "p" was dot-dash-dash-dot; all we needed to know was the particular sound that represented the letter P.

"The instructor uttered not a single word during the entire lesson because the system was supposed to be suitable for use with any language. New characters were introduced with each new tape until we knew them all. In subsequent tapes the gap between the characters was steadily reduced, until eventually, we were reading Morse at true twenty-two words per minute. To give you an idea of how fast that is, just try writing down, legibly, sentences when someone is reading them to you at twenty-two words per minute. It is not easy! Signallers' logs, being legal documents, had to be perfectly legible."

Author's Note: During this time I remember Dad (Tom) bringing home a large reel-to-reel tape recorder with all sorts of strange bleeping on it; he would also often tune into Long Wave Radio Band on the wireless and tape it, and then try and impress us with what Russian and other Warsaw Pact broadcasts were saying and he would be talking in a strange tongue, i.e. "dah, dah, dit, dit, dah". It was all above us kids.

Back to Tony Cunnane and the Air Signaller Course: "The instructors, mainly former Second World War Wireless Operators of one sort or another, were initially as sceptical about the new system as we students were. Each tape lasted for a mind-boggling forty minutes and there were forty-nine of them – why forty-nine rather than fifty we never asked or discovered. I have to admit that as we progressed, the gaps between symbols began to seem interminably long. At about sixteen words per minute I had enough time to write the letters down immaculately instead of my usual scrawl. Indeed, in one lesson at about sixteen words per minute, I wrote the entire forty minute sequence down twice on separate pieces of paper as it was being transmitted, just for the hell of it – and still got zero errors. When our instructors reverted to send the Morse code manually instead of the machine, they would occasionally misspell words deliberately, or introduce grammatical errors, to catch out any of us who had been tempted to read ahead. A missed letter counted as one error, but a wrong letter counted as two, and a few of those made all the difference between a pass and a fail. One of our instructors was a former Polish Air Force Signaller and when he lapsed into Polish Morse there was absolutely no way we could have read that ahead! We used to get our own back by cheekily pointing out that his pronunciation of English left a lot to be desired! After the completion of the Air Signaller's Course at Swanton Morley, the few of us who graduated were faced with a wait of several months because there was a blockage in the system which meant that we couldn't immediately be phased into Operational Conversion Units (OCU)."

The "V" Bombers, Avro Valiant, Victor and Vulcan carried the small British Independent Nuclear Deterrent. Powered by four Avon 204 engines, the Valiant had a top speed of just over 550mph. Air Chief Marshal Sir Lewis Hodges (A Second World War SOE Pilot), had helped to pioneer the "V" Bomber which gave Britain an aircraft which had the capability of carrying nuclear weapons for its small Independent Nuclear Deterrent. The United States developed their B52 Second World War bombers from propeller to jet engine to fulfil their nuclear carrying offensive aircraft. Air Chief Marshal Hodges commanded the RAF "V" Bomber Operational Conversion Unit at RAF Gaydon, and later was Commanding Officer at RAF Marham. The first Valiant B had entered service with 232 Operational Conversion Unit in June 1954, which became 138 Squadron at RAF Gaydon, Warwickshire, in January 1955. The squadron then moved to RAF Wittering and became fully operational in July 1955. Wittering had been home to the RAF's slowly increasing stockpile of nuclear weapons since 1953 and now finally the RAF had bombers and bombs in the right place.

In 1956 both RAF Marham, and RAF Honington, were prepared for V-Force operations, and five more Valiant squadrons were formed, No 214 Squadron, No 207 Squadron, No 148 Squadron, No 49 Squadron and No 7 Squadron.

On 21 January 1956, 214 Squadron reformed at RAF Marham in Norfolk with Valiant B1's, the first of the "V" Bombers. 207 Squadron disbanded on 27 March 1956 and reformed on 1 April with Valiant.

Stuff Of James Bond Facts Stranger Than Fiction

Sir William Hayter, Britain's Ambassador to the Soviet Union, suggested to the British Government that they invite Nikita S. Khrushchev, the head of the Soviet Communist Party, and Nikolai A. Bulganin, the Soviet Prime Minister, to make a visit to Great Britain. During six days, in March 1956, the Soviet Union TU-104 aircraft was parked and cordoned off at London Airport Central and few people were permitted to look inside. From the comments of the officially privileged, it was possible to present a fair picture of the aircraft's interior. The general impression was that finish and workmanship was first rate, but that the styling was somewhat rococo. Accommodation was arranged for fifty with one main cabin for twenty-eight aft, and four small V.I.P. Pullman-type saloons. There was no dominant colour scheme (again typically Russian), much woodwork including dark polished frames around each window. The cabin width was more than eleven feet and there seemed to be plenty of space for at least seventy tourist passengers. Two lavatories accessible via separate washrooms were right aft (as in the Comet) against the pressure bulkhead.

From Russia With Love

During April 1956, Nikita Khrushchev and Marshall Nikolai Bulganin visited Britain under the disguise of a Diplomatic Mission, aboard the Soviet Cruiser "*Ordzhonikidze*".

Military Intelligence (MI6) recruited Commander Lionel "Buster" Crabb – a former Second World War Royal Navy diver and holder of the "George Cross"- to try and find more information about the propeller and underside of the Russian ship; this was of a new design that Naval Intelligence wanted to find out more about. During the previous year, Crabb had investigated the hull of the Soviet ship "*Sverdlov*" in order to evaluate its greater manoeuvrability, on that occasion he had found a circular opening at the ship's bow and inside it a large propeller which could be directed to give thrust to the bow.

On 17 April 1956, Crabb and A.N Other, took a room in the Sally Port Hotel in Portsmouth, to await the arrival of the "*Ordzhonikidze*" and on the 19 April, after the Soviet ship had berthed, he dived into Portsmouth Harbour and his MI6 handler never saw him alive again. Meanwhile, Crabb's companion, and the chief police detective for the area, took away all of Crabb's belongings and tore out the page in the hotel registration book where they had written their names.

On 19 April 1956, the same date as Commander Lionel "Buster" Crabb went missing, Tom was recategorized to Air Electronics Officer.

On the afternoon of Monday, 23 April (St George's Day), Khrushchev, Bulganin, and Georgy Malenkov, left Claridge's Hotel by limousine complete with police motorcycle escort and laid a large five foot high wreath of white lilies and red flowers at the foot of the plinth of The Cenotaph. The inscription read. *"From the Government and the Peoples of the Soviet Union to Eternal Memory of the Gallant Warriors of Great Britain who together with the Gallant Warriors of our Country gave their lives during the First and Second World War in the common struggle for Peace and the Security of Nations".* They went on to Buckingham Palace, where they met HM Queen Elizabeth II, (just two days after her thirtieth birthday) and then called at 10 Downing Street where they saw Prime Minister Sir Anthony Eden; upon leaving, Russian Ambassador Jacob Malik shook hands with Eden and later the Russian Party entertained the British Government and Opposition Leaders at the Soviet Embassy in Kensington Gardens. They then went to London Airport, where they inspected a British Overseas Airways Corporation Bristol Britannia under the guidance of Sir Miles Thomas, who told them that next November the aircraft was likely to visit Moscow with the Sadler's Wells Ballet Company on board.

Air Electronics Officer half brevet.

They then flew in a British European Airways Vickers Viscount to Birmingham where they visited the British Industries Trade Fair and then had a luncheon. Bulganin sat with Prime Minister Eden in the centre; Khrushchev sat with Lord Privy Seal, Rab Butler, and Andrei Gromyko with Harold Macmillan, the Chancellor of the Exchequer, and Hugh Gaitskell, the leader of the opposition (the Labour Party). Jacob Malik sat with John Selwyn Lloyd, the Foreign Secretary. In an after-luncheon speech, Mr Khrushchev claimed that the Russians would have a guided missile that could deliver a hydrogen bomb warhead anywhere in the world; and that Tupolev was building a turboprop aircraft to carry 170 passengers, and another two-engine jet airliner to carry forty-seven at 850km/hr (over 500mph). Later that day, they flew from Birmingham by British European Airways Viscount and landed at Royal Air Force Marham, situated near Swaffham in Norfolk, at 1600 hours. In the party, which included Marshall Nikolai Bulganin and Nikita Khrushchev, were Andrei Gromyko, Foreign Minister, Jacob Malik, Russian Ambassador to Britain, Mr I.V. Kurbachov the Russian Nuclear Scientist and Mr A.N. Tupolev the Russian aircraft designer and pioneer of Soviet Military and Civil Aircraft.

The Soviet party were received by the Secretary of State for Air, Mr Nigel Birch, and the Station Commander Sir Lewis Hodges (A former Second World War Special Operations Executive Pilot) and other senior officers. Hunters, Canberras and Valiants were lined up on the tarmac as the Viscount taxied in. The visitors watched from the control tower balcony as Marshall Bulganin gave the signal for a mass take-off. They were entertained by an impressive air display. A mass start, and rapid take-off, by twenty-eight Hawker Hunters, this was followed by a fly-past of twelve Avro Valiants and sixteen Canberra B.6s. The highlight of the display was the formation aerobatic demonstration by four Hawker Hunters of 43 Squadron, the Fighter Command aerobatic team led by Flight Lieutenant P. Bairstow. They went through the full range of manoeuvres, changing formation frequently the whole while. Then followed a fly-past comprising of twelve Avro Valiants, twenty-four Hawker Hunters and sixteen Canberras. The Soviet Leaders seemed deeply impressed and Mr Tupolev commented enthusiastically on the standard of the flying and asked many searching questions about the aircraft. An invitation to attend the Russian Air Display later in the summer was extended to senior RAF officers. The Soviet party then toured the living quarters of the base and was shown one of the Married Quarters before returning to London in the Viscount.

Tom was on duty at Marham having been specially handpicked from his instructors job in Air Electronics at nearby Swanton Morley, to keep an eye on the Russian Party, and Mr Tupolev in particular, to prevent them from obtaining classified secret and sensitive technology and other information on RAF aircraft, and in particular, the Valiant "V" Bombers; and had been briefed in order to placate them with performance and agility details, which could be released without compromising Britain's advanced Nuclear Air Capability.

An eye-witness account from an RAF Marham-Memory of that day: "The Cold War was at its peak during our time at Marham, but the Soviet heads, Khrushchev and Bulganin decided to make a diplomatic visit to Britain. They expressed a desire to see an RAF station, and Marham was chosen. On the day of the visit, squadron personnel were on parade at the side of the airfield, with the Canberra aircraft parked each side of the taxiway. The visitors landed in a well polished Viscount, which taxied to the end of our line. They alighted and were met by the Group Captain and Squadron CO's. They climbed into an open top car accompanied by their own bodyguards and a couple provided by the camp. The selection process was 'anyone done any boxing?' A Londoner colleague, named W, stuck his hand up and was volunteered! An unforgettable moment followed:

"As the visitors' car passed along and in between the aircraft, the 'start engines' command was given from the Control tower. In those days the Rolls Royce engines were cartridge started through a small turbine in the spinner. These sounded like cannon firing, and as the first 'shots' were fired the distinguished guests threw themselves on the floor and their bodyguards jumped up and brandished pistols, which had been hidden up to then. It could have been the start of World War Three, but as the realization of what was happening sank in, peace prevailed, and the aircraft soon took off and gave their usual spectacular display."

During their stay, the Russian Leaders experienced travelling on a British steam train and were carried in the Pullman Royal Carriage, "Perseus".

Six days later, on 29 April, "The shit really hit the fan" when British newspapers published stories about Commander Crabb's disappearance during an underwater mission. M16 tried to cover up the espionage attempt and on the same day, the Admiralty announced that Crabb had vanished whilst taking part in trials of secret British underwater apparatus in Stokes Bay. The Russians answered by releasing a statement stating that the crew of the "*Ordzhonikidze*" had seen a frogman near the cruiser on the 19 April.

Some fourteen months after Commander Crabb's disappearance in Portsmouth Water, on 9 June 1957, a decomposed body in a frogman's suit was found floating off Pilsey Island, close to West Wittering, in the mouth of Chichester Harbour, some ten miles to the east of Portsmouth Harbour, minus its head and hands, making it impossible to identify (Remember DNA testing did not come about until nearly thirty years later, during the mid 1980s). His former wife inspected the body and was unsure if it was Crabb. Pat Rose, his girlfriend, claimed it was not him, and former friend Sydney Knowles said the body failed to have a scar on the left leg, which Crabb had. The coroner recorded an open verdict but announced that he was satisfied the remains were those of Crabb.

Tom remained as an Air Electronics instructor at Swanton Morley, and on 1 April 1957, the unit title changed to the Air Electronics School. There, and later at Hullavington, his job would be teaching untrained Air Signallers, Air Electronics Officers and Air Signallers on the Advanced Air Signallers Course.

Then came the dawn of satellites, the first of which, would be launched by the Soviets in 1957, and which would be able to spy on lands from outer space. On 4 October 1957, Russia won the first round in the "Space Race"; the Russian news agency Tass stated that "Sputnik One" had been launched into space; the first man-made object to leave the earth's atmosphere. The satellite weighed 180lbs and circled the world every ninety minutes at a height of 560 miles. I remember as news broke on television, Dad (Tom) and I went outside, and were able to see the object circling from east to west and marvelled at the achievement. "Sputnik One" transmitted information via radio signals to Soviet scientists for three weeks, these signals fascinated both radio enthusiasts, including Tom, and western scientists. The following month "Sputnik II"was launched, with a Russian dog called "Laika" aboard, which allowed Russian scientists to learn much about the prospects for human space travel. In December 1957, the US programme suffered a setback when a rocket carrying their first test satellite into space, exploded. On 1 February 1958, The United States of America successfully launched its first satellite called "Explorer". There then followed a "Tit for Tat" race of successive US and Soviet launchings until 12 April 1961 when Major Yuri Alexeyevich Gagarin was fired from the Baikonur launch pad in Kazakhstan, Soviet Central Asia in the space craft "Vostok" (East) and became the first human being in space. He orbited the earth for

108 minutes travelling at more than 17,000 miles per hour. The following month, on 5 May, Rear Admiral Alan Bartlett Shepherd became the first US Astronaut to orbit the earth in "Freedom7", and thereafter both the super-powers got caught up in the race for the first man on the moon; which culminated some eight years later with the flight of Apollo 11, in July 1969.

On 23 December 1957, RAF Hullavington became the Air Electronic School and remained so until 14 January 1962. During January 1958, Tom moved to the Air Electronics School at RAF Hullavington, in Wiltshire, on a Signals Category Flight with Flying Training Command (FTC). We, as

RAF Hullavington Crest.

a family, joined him in Officer Married Quarters and I attended Bremilham Secondary Modern School at Malmesbury. At RAF Hullavington we lived in a spacious four bedroom officers house on the base. As far as I was aware at the time, it did not appear from the outside to be much of an operational flying base, it looked rundown, with elderly and obsolete aircraft littered about the place; including York, Vampire, Dakota, Anson and Varsity.

I didn't have a clue to what Tom's role was there, until very recently when I stumbled across an article written about Special Operations. Tom, who was a trained and experienced Air Signaller of some twelve years standing and an Air Electronics Officer of some two years, was evidently an instructor on the Advanced Signaller's Course. Then after a year, he moved back to RAF Watton as a Signals Leader, to "front end" NCO radio operators under 90 Group Signals and later flew in Comet, Canberra, Lincoln and Varsity aircraft, on 51 Squadron and Development (Dev) Squadron.

History Of COMINT ELINT & SIGINT Flights

Throughout the Cold War, RAF and other NATO countries routinely conducted flights along the borders of Warsaw Pact countries to gather Electronic Intelligence (COMINT or ELINT), these activities were described as "Radio Proving Flights". The purpose of these flights was to allow the intelligence community to build up a picture of the Soviet Union air defences, upon which RAF Bomber Command could then base their operational plans. The RAF flights were initially undertaken by No 192 Squadron from RAF Watton using five specially equipped Lincoln B2 aircraft. These were later supplemented by Washington RB–29's.

A Brief History Of RAF Watton

After the Second World War, as previously covered in earlier chapters, there was now a new potential enemy in Eastern Europe, and so the silent war would continue; albeit at a slower pace. Flight Sergeant Bob Anstee flew the first colonial ELINT operations against communist insurgents in Malaya just after the Second World War in a specially adapted Lancaster bomber known as "Iris", which could listen in to the guerrilla's radio transmissions.

RAF Watton Crest.

A new organization, the Radio Warfare Establishment (RWE) was to be created within the RAF. The nucleus of RWE's Flying and Servicing Wing would be formed from air and ground crews of the recently disbanded 192 Squadron, with Halifax aircraft which had been part of 100 Special Duties Group.

Initially RWE was based at RAF Foulsham in Norfolk; its Headquarters, Technical and "Y", or Signals Intelligence Wings, were formed from the Bomber Support Development Unit (BSDU) at RAF Swanton Morley, also in Norfolk. The BSDU had been formed in the spring of 1944 as an integral part of 100 Group, for the purpose of developing and testing the RAF's radio warfare equipment. It was now to be disbanded and absorbed into the RWE and permanently based at RAF Watton, also in Norfolk, and began to arrive on 21 September 1945; where they continued the development and training of radio warfare techniques.

"Y" Wing, a highly classified Signals Intelligence Gathering and Collating Unit (SIGINT) also took up residence on the base, this unit was a major part of the Air Section of the Governments' "Y" or Intelligence Service (Government Code and Cipher School), which monitored both domestic and foreign signals intelligence. "Y" Wing was tasked with both ground based and airborne signals intelligence gathering, and monitored the extracted information from both domestic and foreign signals traffic and the perceived threat from Eastern Europe. Several aircraft, referred to as "Y" aircraft, were attached to this unit to carry out its various airborne SIGINT tasks and Communications Intelligence

(COMINT). Important amongst these tasks were communications monitoring, and monitoring and recording of radar emissions with the purpose of being able to develop countermeasures against these radars.

Commanded by a Wing Commander, "Y" Wing also had a responsibility for the training of both airborne and ground based Intelligence Intercept Officers, otherwise known in the trade as "Special Operators" or "Spec Ops". Using information gained from various intelligence sources, mainly by "Y" Wing, Watton was to play a major role in the ongoing research and development of radio/electronic warfare equipment, both airborne and ground based. Radar calibration squadron, including 527, also arrived at Watton during November 1945. In 1946, 527 Squadron was absorbed into RWE's Flying Wing as a Calibration Flight.

Central Signals Establishment (CSE)

In the twelve months since its formation, the Radio Warfare Establishment had seen its responsibilities and tasking increase and proliferate, as well as its work in the secret world of radio warfare and in particular "countermeasures". It had been given the responsibility for the RAF's Ground Controlled Approach Service, a "talk–down" system for landing aircraft in poor visibility and would be carrying out radar and communication calibration.

Added to this was the additional tasks concerning RAF Air Traffic Control, airfield landing aids, and the installation, maintenance and calibration of Radio Navigation Aids (RNA).

To recognize and cope with these increased responsibilities, a new umbrella organization was to be created on 21 September 1946, which was to become known as the Central Signals Establishment (CSE). RWE's functions and the tasks it had carried out were to be absorbed into the CSE. The CSE's initial remit was:

1. In respect of Radio Counter Measures (RCM) and Tactical "Y" Signals Intelligence matters, to keep abreast of developments in air warfare and radio techniques in peacetime. (The term Tactical "Y" refers to the gathering

RAF Central Signals Establishment Crest
The Crest features a hawk's lure and bears the Motto "Ars Est Celare Arten" meaning "The Art Is To Conceal The Art".

and collation of Signals Intelligence (SIGINT) for the purpose of producing Radio Counter Measures (RCM).)

2. To study the possible countermeasures against developments at home and abroad.
3. To be the means by which the Air Staff would be kept abreast of the possibilities of Radio Counter Measures (RCM) and Tactical "Y" as offensive and defensive weapons.
4. To maintain a "Y" Section to ensure the development of the technology, and provide intelligence for, Radio Counter Measures (RCM).
5. To produce prototype equipment for Radio Counter Measures (RCM) and Tactical "Y", and ensure the development and trials of all Radio Counter Measures (RCM).
6. To ensure that British equipment possessed maximum immunity from enemy Radio Counter Measures (RCM).
7. To ensure the training of personnel for Radio Counter Measures (RCM), "Y" Section, and Ground Control Approach.
8. To be responsible for the installation and maintenance of radio navigational aids.

The main thrust of the Central Signals Establishment (CSE) work was still to be Radio/Electronic Warfare.

After the war the RAF's Electronic Intelligence ELINT role had been run down. The first sign of its revival came in September 1948 when a Lancaster and a Lincoln aircraft from Watton, each fitted with a camera and modified as a Signals Intelligence SIGINT prototype, flew to the Habbaniya British base in Iraq. From there they flew several eight-hour SIGINT sorties listening to Soviet signals traffic.

During 1948, Research Squadron was brought about from Research Section and continued to use Development or more commonly referred to as, "Dev", Squadron, to carry out airborne testing and trials of special equipment that Research Squadron produced. "Y" Wing's flying unit, "Y" Squadron, became Monitoring Squadron and was used to eavesdrop on signals traffic for intelligence purposes anywhere in the world. A new unit was formed and given the title Radio Counter Measures (RCM) Squadron. Both "Dev" and RCM Squadrons had within them, both air and ground operating units. All three of these new squadrons were under the control of Technical Wing.

During 1949, further aircraft of CSE, probably Monitoring Squadron, were based at the RAF airfield of Habbaniya in Iraq; they were at work gathering Russian signals intelligence in the Middle East. In December 1948, CSE was awarded its own crest, and presented by the AOC 90 Signals Group.

During 1950, within Technical Wing, RCM Squadron and Monitoring Squadron merged to form a new unit Radio Warfare Squadron and operated in two flights, these were RCM Flight and Monitoring Flight. During the latter half of 1951, 192 and 199 Squadrons were used in the Electronic Warfare Intelligence Gathering role, and on a regular basis, 192 Squadron began what was officially termed "Navigation Exercises" under the control of 90 Signals Group. These flights were in fact, Signals Intelligence (SIGINT) gathering sorties to monitor Communist Bloc communications traffic and radar emissions, the results of which would be analysed by "Y" Wing at Watton.

192 Squadron Crest.

On 15 June 1951, No 192 Squadron was reformed at the Central Signals Establishment, RAF Watton, in Norfolk, for Radar Counter Measures (RCM), Operational Signals Research (OSR), and Electronic Counter Measures (ECM) activity. Its main role was to "listen in and record" Warsaw Pact electronic activity. The squadron was eventually equipped with six Lincoln B2 aircraft that had been specially converted to use in the ELINT role. Five of the Lincolns used by 192 Squadron were:

Registration Squadron	Letter
SS715	53
SX942	L
SX952	(Not Known)
SX980	54
WD130	61

The six specially equipped Lincoln were used for over fifteen years by 192 Squadron in a Signals Intelligence gathering role, but no official details of these activities have ever been made public.

On 12 April 1957, Watton's first De Havilland Comet, XK 663, arrived at the Special Radio Installation Section in No 3 Hangar and commenced fitting out for 192 Squadron's monitoring task on 23 April, and it was to be the biggest modification job that had ever been attempted by the RAF up until that time. When the fitting out was eventually completed the aircraft would be designated as a Comet C2(R). At about the same time Canberra WT305 was to be fitted to BMk6 (RC) standard for 192 Squadron. Watton's second Comet, aircraft XK659, was delivered on 12 July 1957. Until the two Comet aircraft were ready for service, 192 Squadron would undertake no further signals tasks; every effort was made to prove the Comet installation and clear both aircraft for operations at the earliest moment.

The end for 192 Squadron aircraft – the Washington – came in December 1957. By then, the maintenance situation had deteriorated to the point where it was considered unlikely the aircraft could successfully complete a sortie without some major unserviceability. As a result, all three operational aircraft were stood down. Luckily, the Washingtons replacement, the Comet R2 was nearly ready for operations. In the end only two months were lost in the changeover, the Comet flying its first operational ELINT sortie in February 1958.

The remaining three RB29 Washingtons were flown to Aldergrove for disposal after a ceremony to mark their departure. They had given six years valuable service and had witnessed Soviet radars and voice communications increase in sophistication, from the simple VHF bands in the early 1950s, to the stage where an advanced surveillance system was needed by the RAF. The four Washington aircraft and their crews had faithfully monitored, recorded, and brought home evidence of the Soviet advances in radar and communications technology. As previously outlined, it was a Washington of 192 Squadron that returned to Watton with the first evidence that Soviet fighters were being equipped with Airborne Intercept (AI) Radar. It was not without great risk to them that the crew had obtained a twenty second recording of this new radar, given the NATO codename "Scan Odd". Most of 192's missions were sensitive and simply called Air Ministry Operations and given the title AMO and a number; no more detail than that.

In August 1958, No 192 Squadron was renumbered 51 Squadron and took delivery of seven Comet R MK 2's, taking over the ELINT role from the Lincoln and Washington. In addition to the front crew of two pilots, a navigator, an air signaller and a flight engineer, up to ten specialists were carried in the main cabin of the aircraft where they operated the monitoring and recording equipment, much of which was manufactured in the USA.

RAF Signals Command.

51 Squadron Crest.

There was a ten channel TR 1998 VHF Transmitter for military frequencies, and a 140 channel STR 12D to cover the whole of the civil frequency range. Also fitted, were special radio and radar aids, twin ADF's, ILS, Gee, Loran, (All sophisticated Navigation Aids) Eureka MK 7 (Transpoding Radar System) with BABS (Beam Approach Beacon) and map based cloud warning radar displays.

The squadron initially took delivery of three Comet 2CR aircraft: XK663, XK655 and XK659. These had square passenger cabin windows with twelve racks of special equipment in the passenger cabin. Each rack had a double bench seat, so it had a maximum accommodation of twenty-four; most racks required just one operator. These aircraft were only half pressurized so all on board needed oxygen. The other Comet 2 aircraft that were used by the squadron were all ex Transport Command and their passenger cabins left empty. These were used for "front–end" crew training and delivery of urgent spares and mechanics to any of the "Special Comets" anywhere abroad.

XK663 was burnt out in a hanger fire in June 1959 (see later) and much later was replaced with XK695, which had oval cabin windows.

The ELINT and SIGINT flights all took place over friendly or neutral territory, or over international waters – no penetration of Warsaw Pact airspace was involved. The main area of operations for the RAF during the 1950s and 1960s were the Barent Sea, the Baltic, the Black Sea and the Soviet/Iran border. The Prime Minister was sent a copy of the proposed monthly programme of flights for his approval. Once this was obtained, Ministry of Defence and Foreign Office officials then carefully planned each individual flight and final authorization rested with the Secretary of State for Defence. The principles governing these flights were:

1. Aircraft approached no closer than thirty nautical miles to Soviet or Satellite territory (American rules allowed twenty nautical miles and forty nautical miles in the Arctic (to allow for weather changing contours).
2. Except in the case of West Germany, aircraft were not permitted to overfly the territory or territorial waters of friendly or neutral countries whilst engaged in these operations without the concurrence of the competent authorities in the countries concerned.
3. No more than four aircraft were used together in the same operating area.

4. Daylight operations were limited to single aircraft.
5. Single aircraft operating by day or night were not permitted to make a direct "provocative" approach to the coast or border and had to fly broadly parallel to the coastline.
6. Operations involving more than one aircraft had to be normally flown in conditions of total darkness and in any case under conditions of the light of no more than "half moon".

The American Intelligence Community also ran their own electronic intelligence gathering operations during the same period, utilizing the Boeing Stratojet RB-47, the USAF electronic countermeasure reconnaissance aircraft. The American Government submitted a monthly list in advance to the British Government detailing when an RB-47 intelligence gathering flight was planned from a British base, such as Brize Norton, Sculthorpe or Lakenheath. A copy of the RAF monthly programme was also forwarded to the American Government. Radio Proving Flight Coordination Meetings also took place on a regular basis between British and American officials.

RAF Flights were usually conducted with two aircraft, a Comet R MK2 and a specially equipped Canberra, also from 51 Squadron. Typically, the Canberra would fly a profile that would attract the attention of Warsaw Pact radar defences, allowing the Comet to record the transmissions. This would usually involve the Canberra flying at low-level below radar cover towards the target area, and then, as the aircraft neared the minimum distance they could approach to the Warsaw Pact boundary, it would suddenly climb rapidly into radar cover, alerting the air defence radars. Meanwhile, the Comet would sit back at higher altitude, flying parallel to the boundary, listening in and recording the frequencies and transmissions of the radar, and radio transmissions, used by the air defence forces. Direction finding equipment on-board the Comet would also enable the location of the radar and transmitters and missile stations to be determined. However, flights were conducted throughout in strict radio silence, to maintain an element of tactical freedom and surprise, whilst concealing the identity of the aircraft from the Russian Defences. Radio silence was only broken in an emergency or to recall the aircraft. The job of the Comet and Canberra was to fly along air corridors adjacent to Warsaw Pact Countries and others sympathetic to Russia; locating new radar and Surface-to-Air Missile Sites (SAM). This is fully expanded later in the book during 1961, when a Special Operator describes the setup at RAF Watton in the early 1960s.

In the latter part of 1958, RAF Watton also played host to an American CIA reconnaissance unit operating the Lockheed U-2 aircraft (see later). This unit operated out of No 2 Hangar for a period of time amid very high security – American as well as RAF; Gary Powers was one of the pilots there at this time.

Also during that period, both Comet aircraft were flying for equipment calibration, in preparation for operational tasking in February 1959, whereby they commenced operational flights immediately, beginning with the first "Border" signals intelligence monitoring flight by an RAF Comet. By the end of February 1959 both Comets had completed operational ELINT electronic intelligence tasks. Two navigators were carried to increase accuracy; the emphasis on navigation was highly important because not only were accurate navigation skills required to identify the exact location of radar/radio transmitters in Warsaw Pact territory, but also for ensuring that aircraft did not stray off course. The British approach was slightly different to the USAF. The RAF aircraft had a much larger crew, usually with at least one, and more often three, COMINT 1 linguists. The USAF 55th SRW, based at RAF Brize Norton, rarely had more than one linguist aboard. If COMINT was required, a separate COMINT aircraft with linguists was used. On the Comets, provisions were made for ten operators and twelve ground crew passengers to help deploy overseas detachments. The primary operating positions 1, 2, and 3, were provided with AN/APR-9 receivers; the Comets carried a great deal of American equipment modified with British plugs and accessories.

Dan Honley, a Canberra pilot who joined the squadron in 1957 and converted onto Comets recalled:

"Micky Martin was Group Captain (Ops) and would always brief us on operations – Air Ministry Operations. These were done at the time of no moon, usually over several days. We would have very carefully laid out routes. We flew along the peripheral; we flew up to the Sea of Murmansk, often out of Bodo. For the Baltic we flew out of Watton and for the Black Sea it would be Cyprus. We would also go to the Middle East. I did some missions in the Middle East. With the Soviets we would stand-off and one or two Canberras would come in and stir up their defence. Often they would start below radar level and pop-up near the Soviets. We never intruded into their airspace or over flew. We used to keep twenty/thirty miles off. We thought the Americans took losses because of their poor navigation; I had two navigators, once we nearly went the wrong way. One of the Russian speakers in the back would tell us what their ground controller was doing. Our ELINT equipment also told us what radar was on us. They would sometimes send MiG's up to intercept us. We could tell which radar was onto us and whether it was height or tracking radar. Then as the MiG approached we would see which radar they were using. If they got their firing radar on us we got the hell out. I was never shot at but I once got pursued and jinked and evaded right down to 700 feet. The only time I know of a 51 Squadron Comet being shot at, was one that got warning shots from the Turkish Air Force. That aircraft was forced to land at Incurlik and stayed there for two hours; someone had not been notified".

Chapter Nine

"Flying High; Lying Low; Going To And Fro"

During the late autumn of 1958 we moved back to our house at Dersingham, and on 17 November, Tom was posted to the Central Signals Establishment at RAF Watton as a Qualified Signals Leader and Air Electronics Officer; he subsequently flew with 51 Squadron and later Development ("Dev") Squadron as a "front end" Signaller.

De Havilland Comet XK655, the third Comet to eventually be added to 192 Squadron's strength, had arrived on 24 March 1958, to undergo conversion to C2 R status in No 3 Hangar. The aircraft was delivered to the squadron in the following month, bringing the squadron up to its Comet establishment; this would be the aircraft that Tom would be a "front end" Signaller Radio Operator in during 1959. This aircraft started its life as a DH-106 Comet 2, plate 06023 Mk2a, and was registered with BOAC (British Overseas Aircraft Corporation) as G-AMXA and was first flown on 27 August 1953. It was then shown at the Farnborough SEAC the following month as the first production aircraft with Rolls Royce Avon 502 engines. It concluded its flight trials with a convincing demonstration of long range characteristics when John Cunningham, the Chief Test Pilot for DeHavilland, covered the 3,064 miles from London to Khartoum, non-stop in six and a half hours on 22 January 1954.

BOAC considered the Comet 2 series the first variant able to serve routes to South America and ordered twelve aircraft, these being built on a new production line at Hawarden, outside Chester. The fuselage was increased from the Mk 1

BOAC Comet 2 G-AMXA Later RAF Comet XK655 Tom's aircraft.

by three feet, seating layout was for forty-four passengers and the fuel capacity was 7,000gals. The first production aircraft, G-AMXA (aka XK655) made its maiden flight on 27 August 1953, and in January 1954 it began a four-week trials programme, first in Khartoum, then Johannesburg. Once back at Hatfield, C of A trials were continued until 8 April 1954, when all Comets were grounded.

G-AMXB was the first civilian Comet aircraft to go to the RAF, and was later allocated the serial number XK669 that year and joined 216 Squadron at RAF Lyneham during 1956. In 1955, modifications were made to G-AMXA, at Marshalls of Cambridge, to the secret 2R electronic intelligence gathering ELINT version, and it was allocated the serial number XK655, and joined the fleet at RAF Watton. During its time with 51 Squadron it was detached to Cyprus and Sharjah in the United Arab Emirates. It was in fact the first jet airliner to land at Sharjah and it is a fitting final resting place for its nosecone. The aircraft, when in use with the RAF, was known as a "Spook", and it patrolled at low-level along the sensitive border areas of Eastern Bloc countries with experimental surveillance and radar equipment, and frequently called at Sharjah for refuelling. It was used by 51 Squadron from 21 August 1958 until 1 August 1974.

During 1959 Tom made at least three flights in Comet XK 655 on ELINT and SIGINT sorties as a "front end" Signaller and may have also flown in XK659. Around the same time, a SAM Missile Base was also established at Watton; these were there to protect the "V" Bomber Force bases in Britain and would be operated by RAF crews from bases in the UK.

XK655 was later sold by the RAF to the Strathallen Collection in Scotland and then scrapped in 1990 when that museum closed. The Cockpit of XK655 was placed on the roof of Gatwick Airport in 1995, it remained outside and deteriorated over the next ten years; it was then given to the Sharjah Museum and has been fully restored in its former BOAC livery.

Below is the interior of a passenger transport C2 Comet of 216 Squadron at Lyneham. The crews had to have at least a "B" (above average) classification; in the case of a 51 Squadron "Spyflight" Comet the crews had to have "A" (Excellent) classification. Tom's Signaller position is shown at E. In the 51 Squadron Comet type, the passenger seats were removed for the Special Operator positions facing the windows.

Comet C.2 floor plan: A, captain; B, co-pilot; C, engineer; D, navigator; E, signaller; F, sub-division into seven freight bays. Rails are shown for a twelfth row of seats, forward.

CDC74 Comet XK655 in the early 1960's.

Comet XK655 taking off.

Interior of XK655 showing Captain, Co-Pilot and Flight Engineer position. Tom sat in the Radio Operator position situated behind the Flight Engineer position

Comet XK659 at an overseas base during 1959.

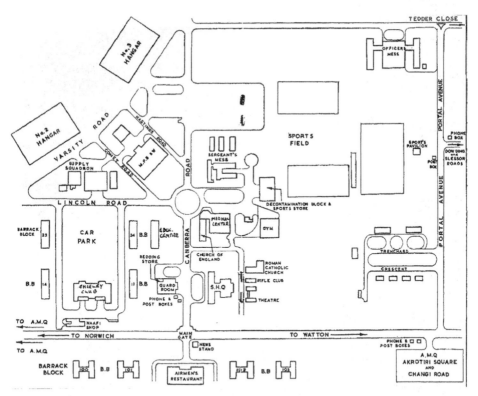

A sketch plan of RAF Watton.

Britain was a major centre for ELINT operations, especially for the entire Western Sector of the Eastern Bloc, beside No. 51 Squadron at Watton, as mentioned previously, the USAF 55th SRW worked out of Brize Norton. One USAF crew member recalled:

"We worked with the RAF in developing systems for the Comet quite often; I flew on the Comet from time to time; we had RAF people, who came and flew with us."

On 29 May 1959, Air Commodore S.D. Melvin took over Command as Commandant CSE, from Air B.D. Commandant Nicholas who had been CO in November 1958; he left to take up a position in NATO.

XK659 taking off from Watton on a sortie during the early 1960s.

Here is a recollection from SAC Peter Clarke who was an Air Traffic Controller posted to Watton from May 1959 until December 1961: "Watton was, in those days, part of Signals Command; there was only one other station in that Command, that being at RAF Tangmere.

"The aircraft at Watton were in 51 Squadron and the CO was Wing Commander Rake. They consisted of two or three Comets, a few Lincolns, a Varsity or two, a Hastings, a few Canberras and a Meteor. The work done was of a secret nature; to the extent that when we arrived the SATCO told us to forget some of the things we had been taught at Shawbury regarding the rules of filing flight plans and so on. When an aircraft was due to fly, all the Air Traffic Control (ATC) were told was that the so-and-so would be taking off at a given time and would be away for a given number of hours. No flight plans were filed with ATC. Obviously as time went on we gradually formed our suspicions as to what they were up to – but we rarely mentioned it to anyone (Official Secrets Act we thought). These suspicions were confirmed to a degree when we sometimes received a call from the Air Defence people at Bodo (north Norway) – 'Are any of your aircraft in the air?' We were not allowed to answer; and always referred the call to the Wing Commander or the Station Commander.

"It did get somewhat boring when a Lincoln took off early in the evening and, although that was the only aircraft in the air, we had to remain on duty until it returned, which could have been in the early hours of the following morning, or even almost breakfast time! Our suspicions as to what they did were reinforced to some extent when the U2 was at Watton for a short period with Gary Powers. What an incredible aircraft that was! It had a tandem undercarriage and when it came to rest after landing it tipped onto one of its wings which had special 'skid' pieces on for that purpose. Each time it took off it did so with minimal warning to the Control Tower and returned with similar lack of warning. If no other aircraft were in the air we just had to wait!! Where it went to or came from we never knew – only guessed. Another interesting situation I remember was a call from London Air Traffic, 'Any of your bloody aircraft in the air?'

"'Sorry we will have to refer you to the CO.' They thought that was extremely strange, and got, shall we say, quite rude. Sometime later we found out that one of the planes had been dropping 'window' out over the North Sea; the wind changed and blew it all toward London and blocked out London Approach Radar. Window was, of course, used for jamming Radar!!!

"One night there was all sorts of commotion when one of the hangars caught fire. We found out the next morning that the thing had burned out completely with one of the Comets inside it. Those Comets were full of all sorts of electronic wizardry (at least by the standards of those days)."

I contacted Peter Clarke for any further information that he may have regarding Tom's time at Watton, and he sent me an E-mail reply on 18 June 2010; in it he says: ".... 51 Squadron was very much 'off limits' except for those guys who worked there. As you probably know whatever went on over there with Comets, Lincolns and so on was very much on the secret list. Even us lot in Air Traffic never knew where they went when they took off, nor what they got up to in the air, though we did sometimes find out through various means – all unofficial. We suspected that some clandestine work was done when the aircraft went off, but we were never told. If we ever got a call from any organization outside the RAF (and sometimes inside it) asking about our aircraft, we always had to refer them to Wing Commander Rake the CO, or, failing that, the Station Commander. Having gone through six weeks of trade training at RAF Shawbury, the first thing we were told on arrival at Watton was to forget what we had been told in the way of operating Air Traffic Control – such was the nature of the happenings at Watton...."

Here is a first-hand account from Peter Oakley who was a Special Operator on the same Comet XK655: "Training courses for 51 Squadron Special Operators lasted twenty weeks and were held at the ECM School at CSE Watton. My course was held from Dec 58 to May 59. A tour on the squadron was usually of five years duration. I have been to the Records Office at Kew yesterday (5 Feb 2009) to review the Operational Record Books of 51 Squadron from 1959 to 1964. I was looking at particular dates that I had listed in my own flight log and started in the ORB for June 1959 because I had started Operational Flying with 51 Squadron at that time; prior to that, I had flown in a Varsity training aircraft while I was training to be a Special Operator. I came across the name of a Flight Lieutenant Clark, who was a 'front end' Signaller who flew one sortie that I was on board, on 1 June 1959 on a AMO (Air Ministry Order) Flight, which was a 'crawl' along the East/West German border. He and I flew again on 11 June on another AMO, in Comet XK 655, the Captain was Flight Lieutenant Davies and the duration of the flight was four hours thirty minutes, which was my second operational sortie. During September of the same year he again flew as a 'front end' Signaller in the Comet with me. Shortly after this time the requirement for a radio operator on the flight deck was removed and voice communications en route were carried out by the pilots".

WJ640 English Electric Canberra B2
51 Suadron operated the Canberra from August 1958 until October 1976

Other aircraft that Tom would have flown in, seen at Watton. Above English Electric Canberra B2 WJ640 and below Vickers Varsity WJ940.

The Squadron had a heavy overseas detachment commitment and the availability of a Hastings for transport support was useful.

During June 1959, Wing Commander Rake was Commanding Officer of 51 Squadron and Squadron Leader C.D.C. Briggs was CO of Development Squadron.

As previously mentioned, on 3 June 1959, De Havilland DH-106 Comet 2R, registration XK 663, was written off (damaged beyond repair) at RAF Watton. In the early morning a fire erupted in No 4 Hangar, an ELINT aircraft of 51 Squadron was destroyed. An exhaustive investigation was carried out by the SIB (RAF Provost Special Investigation Branch) and an inquiry headed by a Group Captain. The fire was believed to have been started by an inspection lamp which had been left switched on in the Comet's under floor servicing bay. This very serious accident left 51 Squadron with only two Comet aircraft to carry out its highly classified tasking. It appears obvious to me now, that the results of the Comets' missions were passed on at the highest level to the Military Intelligence M16, the Government Communications Headquarters (GCHQ), The Pentagon, the USA Government, and the CIA, in order for the U-2 to overfly the new Russian sites and photograph them; and that RAF Watton and 51 Squadron were working "In Tandem" with the CIA; which made Tom's role highly sensitive and secret.

Government Communications Headquarters (GCHQ) moved to Cheltenham in 1952, from its former Second World War premises at Bletchley Park, where it had been responsible for breaking secret codes, including the German "Enigma" Code. During the "Cold War" it was involved in Signals Intelligence (SIGINT) gathering and decoding. CSE Watton worked closely with GCHQ. During 1959 and 1960, RAF Watton had visits from certain personnel based at GCHQ, their identities were deleted from the Station ORB Diary.

On 1, 5, 11, 16 and 26 June 1959, Tom was "front-end" Signaller on Comet 655 with 51 Squadron, and on 17 June a Signaller on Lincoln 130 with Development Squadron. So it shows that he had a roving role within CSE Watton.

Date	Aircraft Type & Number	Crew	Duty	Time Up	Time Down	Details of Sortie or Flight
		Sgt. Thomas E.L.				
		F.Sgt. Metcalfe G.				
12-6-59.	Lincoln 130	Flt. Lt.R.L.Matthews	Cont.Trg.	15.10.	16.10.	D.C.O.
		F.Sgt. Ore D.J.	Tangmere and			
		F.Sgt. Wheeler M.P.	Return			
		Sgt. Humphrey A.				
		Sgt. Harrison				
15-6-59.	Lincoln 685	Flt.Lt.M.G.Read	Gilbert	10.10.	13.10.	D.C.O.
		Flt. Lt.E.W. Watkin				
		M.E. Coveney R.D.				
		M.S. Arnold J.				
		Sgt. Humphrey A.				
15-6-59.	Lincoln 359	F.Sgt. Croft H,	Air Test	14.00.	14.35.	D.C.O.
		F.Sgt. Cresswell K.N.	Cont. Trg.			
		M.E. Milligan T.P.				
		F.Sgt. Ganson W.E.S.				
		Flt. Lt. R.G. Gray				
		Cpl. Purves				
		Cpl. Barrel				
17-6-59.	Lincoln 132	Sqn.Ldr.C.D.O.Briggs	Gilbert	08.55.	14.15.	D.C.O.
		F.Sgt. Ore D.J.				
		F.Sgt. Wheeler M.P.				
		F. Sgt. Walker B.				
		F.Sgt. Lucks R.F.				
17-6-59.	Lincoln 130	Pg.Off.A.E.Whitaker	Gilbert	09.10.	14.10.	D.C.O.
		Flt.Lt. J. Watt.				
		F.Sgt. Rockey R.				
		Flt.Lt. Clarke				
		Flt. Lt. T. Every				

17 June 1959, Tom is Signaller on Lincoln 130.

During July 1959, 51 Squadron's Canberra Mk2's left the squadron, during their time there the BMk6 (RC) Canberras had sported very unusual and non-standard Canberra noses. Instead of the usual clear view nose with bomb-aimer's vision panel, these aircraft wore nose cones of varying shapes, usually long and pointed, with occasional "warts" to house sensors, scanners and aerials for their special equipment.

From 23 to 25 July, "Dev" (Development Squadron) flew all of its Lincolns in support of Exercise Matador, an annual UK Air Defence Exercise. The Lincolns were employed in making ECM (Electronic Counter Measures) at radar installations, such as Boulmer, Neatishead and North Coates.

On 26 July 1960, Tom flew in Lincoln 359 with pilot, and new Officer Commanding Development Squadron, Flight Lieutenant D. Dacre and others, from Luqa in Malta to RAF Idris in Libya, and on 27 July from RAF Idris to Gibraltar and the 29 July from Gibraltar to Watton.

From 8 to 31 August 1959, Watton's runway was closed for resurfacing and therefore there was no flying activity from the station, including 51 Squadron flights during this period, and most personnel took leave. In September 1959, Flight Lieutenant J.A. Brothers, of 51 Squadron put an appeal in *Flight* magazine for any information on the squadron, as he was compiling a history of it.

The year ended with one of Dev Squadron's Lincolns being wrongly identified as a Lancaster suspected of gun running, being forced down onto a French airbase by French Fighters. Having realized their error, the French Air Force entertained the Lincoln crew in style before they continued their journey to Watton.

On 3 February 1960, an official visit to CSE Watton was made by the new Secretary of State For Air, the Right Hon. Julian Amery MP and he was met by the AOC in Chief Signals Command, Air Vice-Marshal Sir Leslie Dalton Morris, KBE, CB. Mr Amery visited "Dev" and 51 Squadrons and their crews, and also Research Section and Installation Flight. At this time Squadron Leader O.A. Lines was Commanding Officer of Development Squadron.

DATE	AIRCRAFT TYPE & NUMBER	CREW	DUTY	TIME UP	TIME DOWN	DETAILS OF SORTIE OR FLIGHT
9.9.60	Varsity	Flt.Lt.Dean	+Pilot	09.10	11.20	Spec.Operator Training
	L.686	Flt.Lt.Warren	Nav.	14.00	15.45	Land Watton
		F.S.Neville	Sig.			
9.9.60	Canberra	Flt.Lt.Craig	Pilot	11.20	12.45	Form: Practice
	J.984	F.S.Cassely	Nav.			
9.9.60	Canberra	M.P.Harris	Pilot	11.20	12.45	Form: Practice
	H.642	F.S.Ballantine	Nav.			
9.9.60	Varsity	Flt.Lt.H.Broadley	Pilot	14.00	15.00	C/T
	F.576	M.S.Schofield	Sig.			
9.9.60	Varsity	M.P.Handbury	Pilot	15.05	15.45	Watton - Benson
	J.940	Flt.Lt.Yeldham	Nav.			
		F.S.Kennedy	Sig.			
9.9.60	Lincoln	Flt.Lt.Dacre	Pilot	10.05	14.25	Navex
	685	Flt.Lt.Proctor	Nav.			
		Flt.Lt.Tylee	Sig.			
		F.S.Payne	Eng.			
9.9.60	Lincoln	F.S.Miller	Pilot	10.05	13.40	AA Demo.Bude.
	359	M.N.North	Nav.			
		F.S.Taylor	Eng.			
		F.S.Shilling	Sig.			
		F.S.Lucks.R.	S.O.			
		F.S.Perkins	Eng.			
		Flt.Lt.Clarke.T.	Sig.			

Tom shown as Signaller (2) on Lincoln 359, 9 September 1960.

By October Dev Squadron's Canberra force had increased to three aircraft, but a fatigue life of 1,700 hours imposed on the squadron's Lincolns effectively reduced the Lincoln force to three aircraft. This meant that the squadron's immediate tasking could not be carried out with insufficient aircraft on strength.

1961

On 20 January 1961, John Fitzgerald Kennedy became the thirty-fifth President of The United States of America, replacing Dwight Eisenhower, the previous leader of fourteen years. Kennedy was informed by the CIA (Central Intelligence Agency) of a plan for American backed Cuban exiles to invade Communist Cuba and extract the Communist Leader, Fiedal Castro and restore Democracy to the island. On 14 April, US planes bombed Cuba's airfields and two days later 1,400 Cuban exiles arrived at the "Bay of Pigs" in five merchant ships and led an attack on the Communist Regime. However, this democratic led invasion force was a total failure, with all invaders being killed, wounded, surrendered or captured.

On 20 February 1961, Air Commodore J.C. Miller assumed Command of CSE Watton as Air Vice-Marshal Sir Leslie Dalton Morris relinquished his post upon taking up the appointment of AOC in Chief, Maintenance Command. The AOC in Chief Signals Command was Air Vice-Marshal A. Foord-Kelsey, CBA, AFC, BA and he paid his first visit to Watton on 16 March. There would be a further change of command in June when the next AOC in Chief for Signals Command, Air Vice-Marshal W.P.G. Pretty, CB, CBE, was appointed.

As a direct result of the Sunderland Flying Boat crash of August 1941, and exacerbated by constant ack ack fire in Italy during 1944; during February 1961, Tom was admitted to the RAF Hospital at Ely in Cambridgeshire for a delicate eye operation. This in those days was a finite art; and it involved the complete removal of the diseased lens of his left eye and removal of a cataract from the right eye lens. After the operation Tom had sand bags placed around his head to stop movement which would have resulted in delicate stitches breaking; and thus he was in this position for some six weeks, followed by convalescence, light duties, and was then discharged. He later received a War Pension upon retirement due to the loss of one eye.

By this time, a secure nationwide system of passing radar data from place to place had been developed and was being put into service. The data was passed by means of microwave transmissions through strategically placed secure data–link towers in "line-of-sight" with at least two other adjacent masts. One of these towers had been under construction at CSE Watton and was completed in July 1961. Its closest companions were at Stoke Holy Cross near Norwich, and at Downham Market.

The Berlin Wall

Most people expected the City of Berlin to be the starting point for a Nuclear War. Since the end of the Second World War it had been divided into an Eastern Occupation Zone controlled by the Soviet Union and East Germany and a Western Zone controlled by the USA, Britain and France. East Germans regularly crossed the border into the more affluent Western Sector to escape the severe communist control and food and other rationing as well as deprivation. On 12 August 1961, the Soviet Union and East Germany decided to stop the defections and began to build the "Berlin Wall" around the Western perimeter; thus dividing the country into two, physically as well as ideologically; anyone then trying to cross east to west was shot. This wall would last for the next twenty-eight years, before being pulled down in 1989.

On 2 October 1961, Tom returned to Central Signals Establishment at Watton and was Supy for Admin Duties until his medical category was regained, and he appears to have been on 51 Squadron and Development Squadron ground establishment. A little bit of light is thrown on this as Peter Oakley recalls: "I recall seeing a tall officer wearing an eyepatch attending 51 Squadron Briefings."

At the time, 51 Squadron's aircraft complement was the two Comets XK655 and XK659, its Canberra B Mk6 (RC) s, WT305, WJ775, WH698, and the Hastings TG530 "Iceni", which Dev Squadron had borrowed for a while. No 3 Hangar at Watton was Special Installations Flight where the special equipment was changed or updated.

On 21 October 1961, Comet C2R XK655 of 51 Squadron was detached for a visit to the United States of America, at Strategic Air Command and Forbes Air Force Base, having been flown there via Keflavik in Greenland and Goose Bay in Canada. The object of the visit was to exchange information of Electronic Counter Measures (A means of disrupting an enemy's radar or communication systems formerly known as Radio Counter Measures) and associated subjects. Aboard XK655 on this visit was the Commandant CSE Air Commodore Miller, together with specialists and representatives from the Air Ministry, Signals Command, the Central Reconnaissance Establishment at RAF Wyton, Cambridgeshire, and GCHQ. The aircraft returned to Watton on the 29 October.

The following month the same aircraft was involved in an "Incident" whilst leaving an operational area. Peter Oakley was a Special Operator attached to 51 Squadron and was on board XK655 at the time: "During a series of four 'Radar Flights' from Akrotiri we had completed the last leg over the Black Sea and then proceeded to fly south to overfly Turkey at about 40,000 ft. Having departed the surveillance area the Special Operators had closed down their equipment and were completing their written logs. I switched my intercom to listen to the front end crew. Wing Commander E.M. Sparrow was the captain, and Flight

Lieutenant Phil Walker was co-pilot, there was some discussion going on as a Turkish jet fighter had appeared, and was flying on our port wing tip. I lifted my window blind and could clearly see the irate pilot gesticulating with his right hand and pointing downwards in quick jerks! I got his message straight away! The captain held his southerly course and height, while the co–pilot was trying to contact Incirlik airfield (where we knew there was a USAF presence) by radio. The fighter then dropped back some hundreds of yards, and as I watched, I saw flashes from his gun ports as he cleared his guns! I rapidly relayed this information to the captain who would not have been able to look that far aft. The fighter then accelerated and came alongside again and when he was level with us he jinked the nose of his fighter to starboard and fired a short burst across our bow! The Comet shook as we flew through the disturbed air.

"Phil Walker immediately said 'I really think we ought to descend now, sir' and the captain pushed the nose down and throttled back the engines. We were now in radio contact with Incirlik and the American voice from there said that the Turks insisted that we should land there! Otherwise, they would send another fighter to intercept us. (The original had left us to refuel.) We descended and following instructions by radio, landed at Incirlik. We followed an air traffic vehicle to a remote part of the airfield and shut down the engines. The vehicle took the Wing Commander away and the remainder of the crew were left inside the aircraft. We had noticed about fifty shadowy figures surrounding the aircraft (it was now dark) and assumed they were armed guards. After about thirty minutes, these figures melted away, and we reckoned that we were unguarded. Although the co-pilot wanted us to stay within the aircraft, a number of smokers wanted to climb down the rear door ladder, which we did. Later, the captain returned with news that the Turks were now full of apologies and wanted to supply some fuel which he had accepted. After refuelling we got airborne again after two hours thirty minutes on the ground! It was just a short leg of an hour back to Akrotiri. Our ground crew were pleased to see us as they had not been told anything of the delay.

"When we went on detachment the Comet always took three pilots. The reason for this was to have one pilot on the ground each time we carried out an operation from the base we were visiting. If anything did go wrong during a sortie the 'on the ground pilot' would know the current procedures and who to contact. He would also be in possession of sealed instructions covering most eventualities. Flight Lieutenant Bill Bonnar was the 'on the ground pilot' on this occasion. (He later returned to command the squadron in 1972 to 1975 as a Wing Commander.) In the original squadron records, the Incirlik incident is dismissed as a diversion."

The following narrative mirrors later flights undertaken that Tom would have been involved with during 1959, as a "front end" signaller, on Comet XK655.

Number 51 Squadron in the 1960s By a Special Operator

"Early in 1961, after three tours of flying on numbers 230 Squadron (Flying Boat), 220 Squadron, and 205 Squadron (Shackleton), I was on a ground tour at RAF Hullavington as an Instructor, teaching u/t (Under Training) Air Signallers, u/t Air Electronics Officers and Air Signallers on the Advanced Air Signallers Course. I had been instructing for about eighteen months when a notice appeared on Station Routine Orders (SRO's), asking for volunteers who had completed at least two flying tours, and the Advanced Course, to apply for training as Special Operators on squadrons under the direct control of 90 Group (Signals). No details of what the job would entail were given, but initially all applicants were required to attend RAF Watton for interview, assessment and suitability. If successful, and subject to security clearance and a decompression check, you would then be posted to RAF Watton for a five-year tour… About two months later I received notice that I had been accepted for training and was given a posting date and joining instructions for the Special Operators Training Section at RAF Watton.

"When I arrived at the Sergeants Mess at Watton, I met four other SNCO's who were also joining the course, and the following day, after completing our arrival on the station, we went to the Training Section and were joined there by the one officer who completed our course. The six of us were the only personnel on the course and we were told that on completion we would be posted to No. 51 Squadron, which was equipped with two Comet MK 2R aircraft, and six Canberras. Our course was scheduled to last twelve weeks, the first six being in the classroom and the last six flying in the section's two Varsity aircraft. We settled in to the mess and for the first two weeks were pounded with radar theory. We still did not know what our job was eventually going to be and members of the squadron who lived in the mess were not at all communicative about what they did on the squadron. There was another squadron based at Watton, No. 115, and they were equipped with Avro Lincolns. We soon learnt that the Special Operators on that squadron were operating radar jamming equipment and that most of their flying was conducted against the various Early Warning Radar Stations around the coast of Britain.

"At the end of our two weeks of radar theory, we were informed that provisional security clearance for us had been received and we were introduced to the equipment that we would be operating in either the Comet or the Canberras. This was all American equipment and for the next four weeks we learnt block diagrams, frequency coverage and how to use all the different black boxes. We now knew what we would be doing, as the equipment was all receivers, capable of analysing radar signals from metric radars through 'L' Band, 'S' Band, 'C' Band, 'X' Band up to 'J', 'K' and 'Q' Band. In other words, virtually the complete radar spectrum as it was then. The equipment was also capable of direction finding on individual radars and we were taught how to plot the positions of these radars on a chart showing the aircraft's course and timing points.

"We learnt how to measure 'Pulse Widths', 'Pulse Recurrent Frequencies' (Pulse Repetition Rate) and scan patterns using the equipment and how to recognize different types of radar from the 'Audio' patterns of the PRF's. We also learnt that the radars we were most interested in were all from the Soviet Bloc and we spent hours listening to tapes of different Soviet radars until we could almost recognize individual types of radar from their scan patterns and PRF's.

"At the end of our six weeks in the classroom it was time to put all our training to the test in the Varsity aircraft. We would take off from Watton and head out to sea, and then fly a course parallel to the eastern coastline, searching for, and direction finding any radars that we intercepted. Because of its small size, one of the Varsity aircraft was fitted out for 'L' and 'S' Band radars and the other for 'X' Band. Most of the early warning radars were in 'L' and 'S' Band and we were soon producing plots that gave an accurate position for each of the Early Warning Radar sites. It took us about two hours to fly from Watton to the North of Scotland, so we would land at RAF Kinloss for lunch and to refuel and then do the same thing on the return trip. This would allow the six of us to work in pairs, one doing the search and the other the direction finding and then to swap over so that we all spent an equal amount of time on all the equipment. In the Varsity equipped for 'X' Band, we would fly up the centre of the country, again landing at Kinloss for lunch, or down to St Mawgan in Cornwall. The following day would be spent plotting and analysing all our results. Also fitted in each aircraft, was a tape recorder that was capable of recording the audio from all the radars that we intercepted, and by playing these tapes through the laboratory equipment we could check just how accurate our airborne analysis was.

"After four weeks of flying we were all becoming quite expert working in the Varsitys and we were then told that for the next two weeks we would be detached to RAF Gutersloh in Germany and that whilst there we would fly parallel with the ADIZ (Air Defence Intercept Zone), and would be able to listen to and plot the Russian radars sited over the East German Border. These trips were called 'Baby Crawls' and were our first insight as to what we would be doing in the Comet and Canberras once we were assimilated on the squadron. As our trips in the Varsitys were only flown at eight thousand feet we could not look very far into East Germany, but in the 'X' Band Varsity we did manage to record our first Russian AI (Air Intercept), radar from an East German fighter patrolling the border.

"We returned to Watton on the Wednesday of the second week, and on the Thursday morning we had a complete wash–up on everything that we had done throughout the course. We were told where our weaknesses and our strengths lay, and we were shown our confidential reports that would be passed on to the Special Operations Leader on the squadron. One of the other members of the course had been recommended for specialization on 'X' Band radars. In the afternoon we were visited by two men from the Ministry, who informed us that we all had our security clearance upgraded to that necessary to work on the squadron, and we were given a lecture on the need for security and what would be expected of us regarding security on the squadron. On the Friday morning we were taken to No 51 Squadron hangar and shown over the two Comets (XK655 and XK659) and the Canberras, and how all the equipment was laid out in each aircraft. We were told to report to the squadron after lunch for interviews with the Squadron Commander and the Special Operations Leader and to collect our security passes for the hangar. The interview with the Squadron Commander was very brief, mainly to welcome us to the squadron and wish us well in the future, but the interview with the Special Operations Leader was much more in depth, he went through everything that had been written on our confidential reports and how he thought our future on the squadron would progress. He agreed that I should specialize on 'X' Band radars and said that, whenever possible, I would be paired up on that position. After our interviews we went to the crew room where a barrel of beer and food had been laid out to welcome us.

Operational

"Our first few flights in the Comet were training flights, mainly to familiarize us with the layout of the equipment in the aircraft and the way the whole system worked. Because of the aerials that were mounted on the skin of the aircraft, and carried in the canoe suspended below the fuselage, the aircraft was only cleared for partial pressurization.

"Consequently, when the aircraft was at thirty-seven thousand feet the cabin pressure was around twenty-five thousand feet. This meant that as we climbed through ten thousand feet we had to go on oxygen and remain on oxygen until we descended at the end of the flight. There were twelve positions in the aircraft, six down each side, and each position could accommodate two persons. In addition to the operators there was also two supervisors who looked after the tapes and all the recording equipment. The front-end crew was the normal Transport Command of two pilots, two navigators, a signaller and an engineer. Our training flights were very similar to those that we had flown in the Varsity, except that we would take off from Watton, fly up the East Coast to the North of Scotland, then down to Land's End and then back to Watton; a round trip of approximately six hours. This was done for a purpose, as most of our operational flights were between six and seven hours in duration and we needed to get used to working on oxygen for that length of time.

"After about four weeks of just flying on training trips on the Comet, we were included on the crew list for our first operational sortie, which was a 'Crawl' down the full length of the ADIZ and back, and was primarily to update the positions of known radar sites and to find any additional sites that may have been put in place. I was doubled up on 'X' Band position and our brief was to search for Fire-Control Radars that were associated with SAM (Surface-to-Air Missile) sites as well as monitoring the AI (Airborne Intercept) frequencies for Eastern Bloc aircraft. We were also told to record any new signals that we might hear during our search that emanated from the east. The day after landing we would plot all our results on a chart provided by one of our navigators and the positions obtained would be compared against previous results. The Canberras were used mainly for these flights against specific targets, as well as being used jointly with the Comet as 'probes'. Some flights from base were carried out over the Baltic Sea. We would leave Watton and climb to thirty-seven thousand feet and cross Denmark, heading between Sweden and Germany, to about twenty miles from the Polish coast; then north, to remain twenty miles off the coast towards Finland. We would then reverse course and pass just twelve miles east of Gotland (Latvia). We would usually pick up our first AI (Airborne Intercept) as we passed north of Poland, and as we moved north-east and then north we would pick up an escort of one or two Soviet Fighters. (Usually MiG-17's or MiG-19's, but occasionally MiG-21's and Yak-28's.) As we proceeded further north our escort would change and we would check carefully that no attempt was being made to 'box' us in.

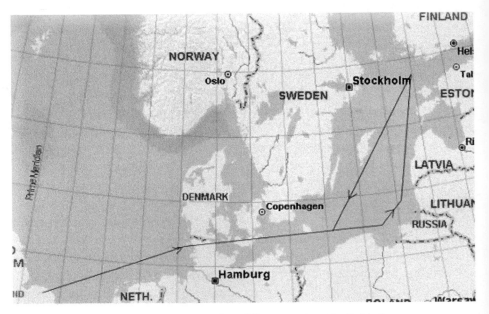

Squadron Special Operator Flight route from Watton out into the Baltic Sea.

"The squadron operated very loosely as two flights. When one aircraft was away on detachment, the other would carry out all the base duties and training. One of these duties was a three-day detachment to Bodo, north of the Arctic Circle, in Norway. This was the 'land of the midnight sun' and for nearly six months of the year our trips to Bodo would be in daylight, irrespective of the time of day and likewise for the other six months of the year would be in complete darkness. Transit to Bodo was undertaken covertly, and the aircraft was parked in the secure aircraft park, away from prying eyes. Only one trip was flown from Bodo and the timings for this trip were varied each month, both during the winter and summer months. Our route varied slightly each time and only one pass was ever made, and we were under radar surveillance from the Norwegian radar situated at North Cape, at the very top of Norway, for the whole trip. The Americans, who also carried out this type of radar reconnaissance with B-47 aircraft had lost one of their aircraft (believed to have been shot down), on an earlier occasion in this area, but that aircraft had reversed track at the northernmost point and was returning on a reciprocal track when it had disappeared from the Norwegian radar.

"Murmansk was the headquarters of the Soviet Northern Fleet and many of our intercepts were of ship borne radars, but Novya Zemlya (Arkhangelsk) was one of the main Soviet testing grounds for new SAM systems and new Fire Control Systems, (the other being the Sevastopol Peninsula in the Black Sea), and was a source of many new intercepts.

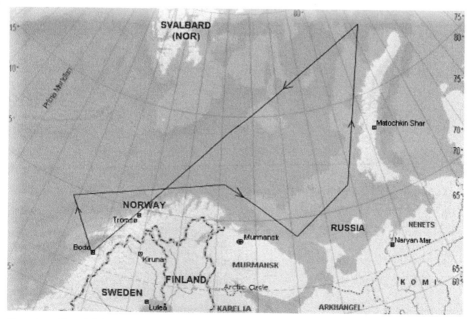

Squadron Special Operator Flight Route from Bodo past Murmansk.

"Whenever we flew from Bodo on this route there was always a flurry of activity from the Soviet radar sites and we were regularly acquired by fire control radars and by the search elements of the SAM sites but there was very little air activity and Soviet fighters never intercepted us. We heard the occasional AI, but it was always at long range and of a type that we knew. Occasionally the SAM radars would lock onto us but only for brief periods. We were convinced that they quickly recognized what we were up to and closed everything down once they were convinced that we were no threat to them.

"During the winter months the outside air temperature at high altitude was in the region of −50° C and because of the partial pressurization, inside the aircraft wasn't very much higher. For these trips we were issued with Arctic Parkas and fleecy lined underwear to wear under our flying overalls, but even with these, it was extremely cold working in the aircraft. The floor of the aircraft got so cold that if any hot coffee was spilt on the floor it turned to ice almost immediately. We used to hook our feet up on top of one of the black boxes under the rack to try and obtain a little warmth from the equipment. It wasn't very much but it did provide a little bit of comfort. We were always glad, after we had landed, to soak up the heat in the sauna in the mess. Our accommodation with the Royal Norwegian Air Force was excellent. All the buildings were double-glazed and heated by steam from a central boiler house. The blankets for our bedding were contained in a linen cover and this was our first experience of duvets. Food was another thing! The Norwegians seemed to live on a diet of fish and cod liver oil. They put cod liver oil on their cornflakes at breakfast, and lunch was always a fish dish. For dinner there would be fish soup, followed by either a fish or reindeer main course and a sweet that was usually mostly raw yoghurt. We managed to convince the powers that be to allow us to eat in the airfield restaurant, where we could obtain the kind of food that we were more used to at home. As we were only there for three days it wasn't too much of a hardship and the results we obtained were well worth the small inconveniences. The Norwegian servicemen made us very welcome in the mess and provided we weren't flying that night they treated our visits as an excuse for a party. They also organized outings for us during the summer months to show us the splendour of some of the local fjords and visits to local villages where the main occupation was woodcarving. During the winter months everywhere was icebound, but a few of the more hardy members of the squadron did try their hands at sledging and skiing.

"Our main detachment every other month was to the Middle East. We would fly as a normal Transport Command aircraft from base to El Adem in Libya, but from there we would transit covertly to Akrotiri in Cyprus. We would spend three to four weeks in Cyprus, but sometimes, we would deploy to Teheran for a few days, or to Sharjah in the Trucial Oman States. Our trips from Akrotiri were mainly conducted over the Black Sea, with the occasional flight flown against the Soviet radars sited in Egypt. Our trips from Teheran were all flown over the Caspian Sea. The Sharjah flights were all working transit trips, made so that we could look along the northern and southern borders of Iraq. Separate sorties were flown along the eastern border. By far the most productive of any of our flights were those flown over the Black Sea. We would take-off from Akrotiri and climb to height, crossing Turkey under diplomatic clearance, and then follow a course skirting Georgia, St Avropol, Ukraine, Romania and Bulgaria, and across Greece back to Cyprus. The timings of these trips varied, by night and by day, and were flown in both clockwise and anti-clockwise directions. Similarly, the flights along the Egyptian and other Arab countries' borders were varied in time and direction, but were never flown on a Friday, as this was their Sabbath.

"One of the security requirements of the squadron was that we were not allowed to tell anyone where we were going on detachment, including our wives, but they soon got to know as we would pack KD (Khaki Drill), for our trips east, and cold weather clothing for our trips to Bodo. Also, we were not supposed to write home until we had been away for three days, and letters from the wives had to be delivered to the squadron headquarters for onward posting to us. As we were normally briefed for a detachment a good week before we left, the wives knew where we were going, so used to write to us c/o the mess at Akrotiri. During the summer months at Akrotiri nearly all our spare time, when we were not flying, was spent on the beach during the afternoons and in the bar in the mess in the evening. The mornings were spent recovering from the after effects of the previous evening and normally meant a walk to the NAFFI Shop, which had its own café, for a pint of ice-cold milk. In the winter, although the weather was still warm compared to the UK, trips were organized to take us up to Mount Troodos, where we could borrow skis and sledges and try our hands at winter sports. January was always a good month to go to Akrotiri as it was the height of the citrus fruit season, and for a pound, it was possible to buy a basketful of tangerines, oranges and grapefruits from the local plantation to bring home. Cigarettes and spirits were rationed, but as we lived in the mess and were temporarily on the strength of the station, we had no problems getting our Duty Free allowances to bring back with us.

"Sharjah was situated about ten miles north of Dubai and the RAF detachment was built around an old fort that was used by the 'Cable and Wireless' personnel who ran the airfield. During the summer months the temperature rose to over 120 coupled with a humidity of 100 per cent. Our ground crew, who travelled with us, were only allowed to work outside on the aircraft for a maximum of twenty minutes at a time because of the heat and humidity, and we spent most of our spare time in our air-conditioned accommodation until the sun went down and it was comfortable to venture out. The big problem came when we were scheduled to fly in the heat of the day. A mobile air cooler would be fed into the front door of the aircraft and kept running until after we had started the engines and were ready to taxi. But even with this, by the time we had taxied to the runway, we would all be like grease spots until we had started to gain height. Then, as we climbed, the temperature would drop rapidly, until at height, we would be putting on extra clothing to get warm. During the winter months it was still very warm during the day but the humidity was less and at night the temperature dropped to almost zero.

"Sharjah was a very small Muslim town ruled over by the local Sheikh. No alcohol was allowed to be taken off the base, but the Sheikh regularly visited the mess in the Fort with several of his wives, completely covered from head to toe no matter how hot the weather, and always left with a crate of spirits. The town was 'off limits' to us on a Thursday as this was the punishment day and all punishments were carried out publicly in the Town Square. We were always glad to leave and get back to Cyprus. Fresh water in Sharjah was only for drinking, all showers and washing was with salt water and we found the only way to get a lather was by using either shampoo or a local soap called 'Vel'.

"After I had been on the squadron for about eighteen months one of the specialists 'X' Band Operators was posted and I moved into his slot permanently. I had thought that after a year of requesting, it would be a move to the Canberras, but the Special Operations Leader said that I would be better employed on the Comet. I did fly the odd sortie, but only when I was covering for one of the regular operators who was on leave. My partner and I quickly developed our own system of working together so that our task was achieved without the need for a lot of intercom chatter between us, which allowed more time for recording, and direction finding."

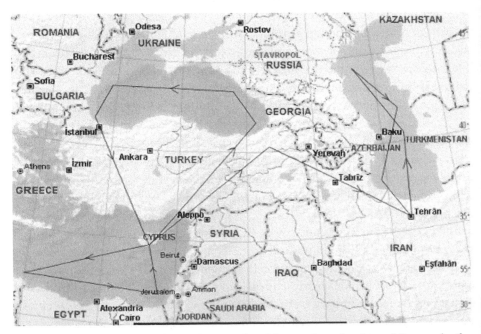

Squadron Special Operator Flight Routes along the northern borders of Iraq and other Middle East locations.

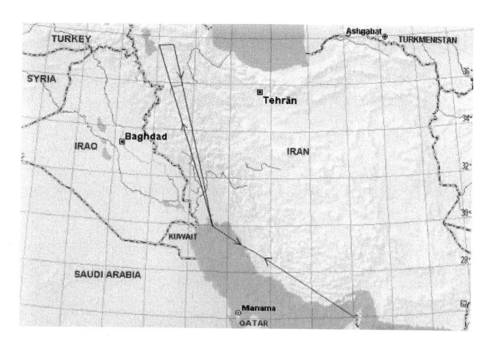

Another Special Operator, Air Electronics Operator who joined 51 Squadron at Watton during 1961 and left at Wyton during 1965 was Flight Sergeant Stanley Haddock. He regularly flew on XK655 and XK659 and he says:

"The subject aircraft were quite unique. They were prototypes for what was an intended production run of Mk II Comets for BOAC. They retained the notorious 'square' windows of the Mk 1 and were of similar appearance. The original De Havilland Ghost engines (centrifugal flow) were replaced by Rolls Royce Avons (Axial flow). I believe the reduced skin thickness, which was blamed for the in-service, explosive decompressions at Elba, was retained, and was further weakened by numerous slot aerials, needed for 51's specialist work. Wisely, the RAF imposed strict restrictions on the use of the aircraft's pressurization system, allowing only 'half altitude' use, e.g. at 40,000 ft the cabin height was 20,000 ft. This meant the crew was permanently on oxygen and the tea urn boiled at 80 instead of 100, resulting in lukewarm coffee or un-mashed tea!

"Our Commanding Officer was Wing Commander Cooke, who, though normally a technically good pilot was totally mad! My present hearing problems were caused by a Cooke departure from Bodo, Norway. What followed is a true horror story which nearly ended in tragedy. Cooke decided to carry out a steep, low speed climb out, and with rapidly reducing airspeed, lowered the undercarriage 'to blow the slush off'. The Flight Engineer leaped out of his seat and pushed the 'stick' forward, accidentally catching his elbow on the emergency pressurization switch which sent the cabin height from 2,000 feet to minus 1,000 feet. The intercom was blue with expletives, as you might imagine. This incident not only caused agonizing ear pain to all the crew, but imploded the under floor sewage tank. The contents of this froze and subsequently thawed out in Sharjah the following day. Some poor devil had to go under the floor in temperatures of around 110°F to clean up the mess. You might wonder what the co-pilot was thinking while this near tragedy unfolded and can only assume that he felt out ranked (or he could have been asleep). To Cooke's credit, he explained what he had done and praised the engineer's actions, which undoubtedly saved the aircraft from a deep stall, and the crew from oblivion".

1962

On 1 January 1962, "Dev Squadron" (Signals Development Squadron), so long a "hush-hush" unit, at last became official when it received the number plate, badge and history of 151 Squadron, and it continued with the experimental, demonstration and exercise tasks assigned to the former unit; including radar development and research work.

The new unit was engaged with a number of classified duties within the Signals field for which it used a variety of aircraft types. "A" Flight used the Varsity T1, and for a short time Handley Page Hastings TG530 "Iceni", borrowed from 51 Squadron.

"B" Flight used Lincoln B2's and "C" Flight used Canberra B2's. All three types bore the Signals Command legend, 151 Squadron went about its secretive duties, rarely coming into the public eye. The Lincolns continued to participate in service exercises and provided anti-jamming training for ground radar operators, who had to overcome the jamming signals put out by the Lincolns, just one of which, flying at 15,000 feet, could allegedly shut down the entire east coast radar chain.

On 14 March 1962, four officers from 7th Air Division Headquarters of the USAF, visited Watton to attend a 51 Squadron briefing and were given a presentation of the work of the CSE.

Flight International magazine edition 17 May 1962, carried the following brief article on the work carried out by Signals Command: "Control of radio engineering, electronic warfare, telecommunications, plus the calibration

151 Squadron Crest.

and operation of navigational aids. Administering signals units, transmitting and receiving stations, communications and switching centres, ground radio servicing squadrons, and schools for advanced training with radio warfare techniques. The Command controls the Central Communication Centre and Central Signals Establishment. It uses Comet, Canberra and Varsity aircraft for airborne aspects of its work."

In June 1962, all five Lincolns went to RAF Idris in Libya on detachment; and two detached to Gibraltar for exercises with the Royal Navy.

An air defence exercise, Matador II, was held in September, CSE Lincolns were deployed to provide ECM in support of "V" Force attacks. During this exercise CSE Lincolns were ordered to jam a Russian ship.

The Cuban Crisis

During September 1962, USA U2 spy planes discovered that the Soviet Union was building Surface-to-Air Missile (SAM) launch sites in Cuba and there was an increase in the number of Soviet shipping arriving on the island; these were suspected of carrying new supplies of weapons, including missiles, for the communist island.

President Kennedy complained to Khrushchev about these sinister developments and warned him that the United States would not accept the presence of these weapons in their backyard. During the same month, a CIA Agent in Cuba, overheard Fidel Castro's personal pilot talking to another man in a bar, stating that Cuba now had nuclear weapons. U2 spy plane surveillance also showed that unusual activity was taking place at San Christabel, and during October it was confirmed that the Soviet Union was placing long-range missiles in Cuba.

Kennedy then agreed to a naval blockade of the island and put the USAF on high alert for attacks on Cuba and the Soviet Union. One hundred and twenty-five thousand US soldiers were positioned in Florida in readiness for a land invasion of Cuba. Kennedy then announced to the world, and Khrushchev, that if the Soviet ships carrying weapons to Cuba did not turn back, or refused to be searched, a war was likely. The world waited anxiously, but Kennedy had called Khrushchev's bluff, and the latter sent a letter stating that the Soviet Union would be willing to remove missiles from Cuba in exchange for Kennedy's promise that the USA would not invade Cuba. This one and only nuclear confrontation, and the possible annihilation of mankind on the planet, as a result of such action, dissolved tensions. The event which threatened to escalate out of control into a Third World War, frightened both sides, and it marked a change in the development of the "Cold War". Sadly, President Kennedy was assassinated the following year, in November 1963, thus robbing the west of a Great Statesman.

During the autumn of 1962, a meeting was held by the Commandant to discuss redeployment of units from Watton, one of these being 51 Squadron.

On 3 December 1962, Tom was again a Qualified Signals Leader Flying Signals once more, whether this was with 51 Squadron, or 151, the former Development Squadron, it is not known, but most probably with 151.

In February 1963, 151 Squadron's Lincoln RF398 flew to Akrotiri and Idris, and this was possibly the last time a Lincoln went abroad. Flight Lieutenant John Langley was the Pilot of RF398 during March 1963. One exception to the Lincolns coming into the public eye, was when the last three Lincolns made a farewell fly-past over East Anglian stations on 19 March 1963, before being withdrawn from service.

151 Squadron Crew of Lincoln RF398 en route to aircraft.

On 25 May 1963, the Squadron Number 151 was withdrawn from the unit, which then took up a new number, namely 97 Squadron.

After four years without a third Comet, following the loss of XK663 in June 1959, 51 Squadron was to get reinforcements. At the beginning of March 1963, following a lengthy preparation period, Comet C2 (RC) XK695 arrived at Watton to be fitted out with the special equipment necessary to enable it to take up its duties with the squadron. Whilst 51 Squadron's original Comets had square windows along their fuselage sides, this new aircraft had oval windows, a design modification which had arisen following the earlier pressurization accidents. XK695 didn't spend very long at Watton, as it had been announced that in March 1963, 51 Squadron, the RAF's premier Signals Intelligence gathering unit, was to leave CSE Watton and Signals Command to become part of Bomber Command.

From 1 April 1963, 51 Squadron was to operate its three Comet C2(R)'s XK655, XK659, and XK695, along with its three Canberras and one Hastings from RAF

Crew of RF398 standing by their aircraft.

RF398 taking off from RAF Watton for the last time.

Two of the last five Avro Lincoln Bombers used by Signals "Dev" 151 Squadron at RAF Shawbury during 1963 waiting scrapping. In the foreground is RF505.

Avro Lincoln Bomber RF398 of Signals "Dev" 151 Squadron Preserved at the RAF Museum Cosford.

Wyton near Huntingdon in Cambridgeshire. Thus the squadron formerly known as 192, and then 51 Squadron, clothed in secrecy, which operated around the borders of the Warsaw Pact Countries, gathering Signals Intelligence and in the front line of the Cold War whilst other squadrons were practising and training, had now left Watton.

On 12 March 1963, 51 Squadron held its farewell guest night, and it was attended by the AOC in C, Signals Command, Air Vice-Marshal Pretty and other senior officers. I remember polishing Tom's (Dad's) medals, whilst Stella (Mum) pressed his No 1 Uniform, after I had brasso'ed the buttons of his tunic.

Wing Commander Cooke, Officer Commanding 51 Squadron, was to leave the squadron on taking up the post of Provost Marshal, RAF. During the evening he was presented with the tools of his new trade, which included a set of handcuffs, a whistle and a policeman's helmet. During the afternoon, the AOC in C had spent some time with the squadron's personnel. The main party from 51 Squadron left Watton for Wyton on 13 March, leaving a small detachment to finalize all cleaning details; they finally left Watton on 17 March.

Tom, in the meantime, hung up his flying jacket after some twenty-four years active service and moved to RAF West Raynham, in Norfolk, on 22 May 1963, where he became the Families Officer; he was responsible for Welfare and Housing of personnel on the base.

We will now rejoin the narrative of the Special Operator, continued from 1963.

Special Operator's Story Part II

"Early in 1963 there was a major reshuffle in the organization of the RAF, Bomber, Fighter, Coastal and Signals Commands were all amalgamated to form Strike Command, Transport Command became Air Support Command and a lot of smaller airfields were scheduled for closure. Watton was one of these airfields, and we were posted en-bloc to RAF Wyton, four miles outside Huntingdon, and the home of Nos 543 Victor Squadron and No 321 Canberra Squadron. Our sister squadron at Watton, No 151, was disbanded, and the Special Operations joined us on 51 Squadron. Since ninety per cent of the squadron was married and living in married quarters, there was a period of about twelve weeks where we were commuting, whenever possible, between Watton and Wyton, whilst we waited for married quarters to become available at Wyton, but once we had settled in we much preferred our new base and the extra facilities which the 'V' Bomber crews already enjoyed, but which had not been available to us in Signals Command. We were now entitled to pre-flight and post-flight meals in the aircrew 'Feeder' situated in the Operations Block. Also our safety equipment and flying clothing was stored and looked after for us by the Safety Equipment Section. When flying helmets, oxygen masks, oxygen tubes and Mae Wests were required for servicing or inspection, these tasks were automatically carried out for us. Our 'In-Flight Rations' were also provided from the Aircrew Feeder and were much better than we had received at Watton."

No 51 Squadron, as a Special Duties Squadron flying Comet, still had a strong commitment to the West's defence system and a variety of Canberra, on surveillance flights from RAF Wyton in tandem, continued until 1974, when the Comets were replaced by a specialized version of the Nimrod, the R1. During this transition period the aircraft were worked on at Wyton by a Flight Mechanic called Neville "Scotty" Julian, at that time, my wife Jeanne's brother-in-law, who was married to Valerie, Jeanne's sister; this was some twenty-eight years before I came on the scene with Jeanne. Just shows what a small world it is in some circumstances. The Canberras were finally retired some two years later during 1976.

In 1995, 51 Squadron moved to Waddington, after Wyton changed its role from an operational flying RAF Station. Several of the support organizations, (EWOSE) Electronic Warfare Operational Support Establishment and (EWAD) Electronic Warfare and Avionics Detachment, relocated at the same time.

It was only after the end of the Cold War that the Signals Intelligence role of 51 (formerly 192) Squadron was publicly recognized. Signals Intelligence encompasses both Electronic Intelligence (ELINT) and Communications Intelligence (COMINT). Now based at RAF Waddington, in Lincolnshire, 51 Squadron, continues its highly specialized task as part of No 2 Group. The squadron has taken part in many operations the British armed forces have been involved in, including the Falklands War, the first Gulf War, and operations in Kosovo, the war in Iraq in 2003, and currently against the Taliban in Afghanistan. During February 2008, UK press reports suggested that No 51 Squadron had listened in to Taliban insurgents speaking in broad West Yorkshire and West Midlands accents, suggesting that they were British raised, if not British citizens! *The Sun* newspaper headlined their article "Talibrum".

Chapter Ten

"Out to Grass And A Different Landscape"

Tom retired from the Royal Air Force on his forty-third birthday, 2 November 1964, where he had served man and boy for over twenty-three years from June 1939 – taking out the eighteen months he was in civvie street during March 1948 to September 1949. He had survived a long and bitter Second World War, and served in insurgency driven, far off lands, and at Norfolk and Wiltshire bases during the Cold War. What would he turn his long experience and expertise of Air Gunnery, Signalling and Air Navigation to?

For the next ten years the non-winnable Vietnam War raged unabated with Communist North, fighting Democratic South, in a similar scenario to the earlier and smaller Korean War. The United States of America committed many thousands of young men to the cause, and many atrocities were committed by both sides upon the indigenous people of that South-East Asian Peninsula. Communism may have even influenced "The Troubles" in Northern Ireland, 1968-1993. This could well have created a British type Cuban Crisis situation under the guise of Republicanism if the Soviets had gained a grip there. There was certainly US and USSR background involvement.

Upon retirement, Dad (Tom) took his commutation pension lump sum and with it paid off the mortgage on "Excelsior" 8 Brook Road, Dersingham. He concentrated on his deep interest in horticulture, and studied and trained at the Wisbech and Isle of Ely College Horticultural Station and set himself up as a market gardener. During 1965, and before Trevor, my half-brother, emigrated to Australia later that year, Tom also bought two large Western Red Cedar, Dutch light glass greenhouses. Tom designed these to fit as a lean-to against the outbuildings of our home and the three of us constructed it together, including the internal staging for pot plants, trays, etc. Once constructed, Tom set about buying thousands of brown plastic 4inch pots, compost, seeds, plants, etc; and spent the remainder of 1965/66 growing pot plants for commercial sale.

During 1966 he bought a new Bedford Dormobile, removed the rear seating, and replaced it with greenhouse staging. The idea was that when the pot plants had matured "to sale" stage, he would transport them around West Norfolk villages and sell them from the van. These were the days before numerous garden centres had sprung up, and the ingenious idea was to take the product to the buyer. Alas, although Prime Minister Harold McMillan had announced in 1957 "Most of our people have never had it so good!", by 1964 Labour, under Harold

Wilson, had come to power and Britain was trying to balance her books from the severe debt that the Second World War had affected. In November 1967, as the £1 sterling fell from $2.80 to $2.40 US Dollars, a fall of fourteen per cent, Wilson famously announced; "It does not mean that the pound here in Britain, in your pocket or purse, or in your bank, has been devalued." But it did mean just that, and Britain was in a short but deep recession, so there was not the money around to spend on pot plants and the suchlike. By 1970, the economy had started to pick up again, but this was all too late for Tom's enterprise, and ours, like other families, had been finding it hard to make ends meet. With five children still at home and two grand children to bring up, Mum and Dad found it hard going to feed and clothe a total of nine; I had joined the Police Force in 1966 and sent £30 a month home to help out. Tom eventually found employment with the Borough of Kings Lynn and West Norfolk Council, as a Landscape Gardener in their Parks Department; which prided itself on its gardens and floral displays. His office and base was at Hunstanton; he eventually worked his way up to Foreman, then Head Gardener and had a seat on the Town Council.

Tom also rented allotments, which were at that time situated at the bottom of his garden over a brook; these allotments were owned by Sandringham Estate and were sold in the late 1970s as building land for Hanover Court Housing Association accommodation. Tom found new allotments off Bank Road in the village and continued to be virtually self-sufficient in vegetables and fruit, as well as growing for his grown up and "left home children" still in the neighbourhood. The monthly bill slate to Milton the Butcher, Playford the Baker and Parker the Grocer was whittled down considerably, and the family were in the "black" once more. Around the same time, I had a Police House at Gayton and was also virtually self-sufficient.

Tom was also a keen bee-keeper and had numerous hives dotted about West Norfolk in various orchards; the bees pollinated the fruit trees and in return Tom got lots of honey which he sold in jars, with labels on, to various shops and private sales; he had gone from one sort of flying navigation to another,

During 1978, Tom's hectic life of the late 1930s to the mid 1960s, coupled with previous heavy smoking and drinking, finally caught up with him, when he suffered a series of major heart attacks, from which he remarkably made a full recovery and carried on working for the Council. He also did private work, landscaping, patio laying, etc and was also a grave digger for a while. He also suffered from a "slipped disc" and sciatica, and had to lie with a piece of balsa wood underneath his mattress to keep it firm. Other than that, he seemed to shrug off ailments, and when I asked him in later life how he coped with ailments he replied "I just ignore them and they go away".

Tom carried on working for the Council until his retirement age in 1985. Another ex 16 Squadron member, who was an LAC Flight Mechanic (E) in France at the same time as Tom, was W.E "Bob" Laws. Bob Laws lived at 23

An Aircrew Association Meeting during the 1990's; Tom is on the extreme left.

Stella and Tom at Sandringham Flower Show during July 1980; Stella aged 60 and Tom aged 59.

Gelham Court, Dersingham, and as a result of having adjacent allotments in the village of Dersingham, they bumped into each other around 1985. After talking they discovered that they had overlapped on 16 Squadron in 1940, when Bob and he went with the squadron to Bertangles and that Bob had also been on the Royal Flight, re-named The Queen's Flight, as a mechanic during 1955-57. They had never met until Dersingham united them.

On 13 August 1985, Tom and Stella, Tom and Stella (AKA Dad and Mum) celebrated their Fortieth "Ruby" Wedding Anniversary and on the day, both thought that they were going out for a quiet meal with my first wife and I. We had secretly arranged for all of their children and grandchildren to be at a private function room of a Chinese Restaurant in Kings Lynn that we had booked; even Trevor had made it from Australia and Vera from Germany.

In August 1986, Tom and Stella went to see Trevor and Maureen in Australia and they spent over two months with them, touring that continent. Over the next ten years Tom and Stella continued the "purple patch" of their lives, Tom had by this time, three full allotments to tend, and was still active in the various Horticultural Shows and RAF Associations; the latter which he mainly started attending during the 1990s.

During the late 1990s, Stella (Mum) had a series of major strokes, which left her bedridden, incontinent, and with communication problems, she relied completely on Tom for everything, including the call of nature; Tom became her devoted full-time carer.

Tom and Wares at Sandringham House Lake 2001; Tom aged 79 and Wares aged 76.

Over the years, Tom's brother, James Wares, had tried unsuccessfully to trace his brother, but in the new Millennium managed to trace Tom to Dersingham, via RAFA, and in 2001 Wares and Roanah travelled from their home in South Africa and the brothers were reunited in an emotional meeting.

After that initial reunion, both regularly kept in touch with each other and a visit was arranged for 2003 for Tom to do a return trip to them in South Africa. Sadly, following a heart operation, Wares died one month before Tom was due; however the trip went ahead and Tom met Wares' children and grandchildren. Tom also communicated with his cousins, Graham Davidson and Irene Henderson, both from

55 Squadron Association Reunion Dinner RAF College Cranwell 2003.

Galashiels. Tom was still active during 2003 and 2004, he continued to attend various Squadron Association Reunions, including 55 Squadron at Cranwell, 16 Squadron at RAF Marham in 2003, and Yeovilton in 2004 and was due to attend the September 2005 one at St Omer; but that one was not to be.

Tom wrote a quote on the back of this photograph in a letter to his cousin Irene Henderson; "You can tell that I don't wear a monkey suit very often."

In April 2004, Jeanne and I moved from Cambridgeshire to County Durham, and this gave Tom (Dad) the opportunity to come and stay on holiday with us, whilst my sisters looked after Stella (Mum). At that time he obviously knew that his time left

Tom standing outside his old school during June 2004 aged 82. My last photo taken of him.

on earth was short and wanted to re-trail his early life; again keeping this fact from everyone. During June that year, Jeanne and I met Tom off the train at Durham Railway Station and he had three days with us. In that time we went to Newcastle, where he showed us where he lived at 4 Benton Park Road, from 1933 to 1939, and his school at Heaton Manor, where he was educated from 1933 to 1937, the timing of the latter was so appropriate, as the old part of the school was demolished some ten weeks later.

We also went up to the Northumberland Coast and located the village where his paternal grandmother, Agnes Wares, was born and brought up; at Newton-By-The-Sea. Later in the week, I drove Tom up to the Border town of Galashiels, where he had a reunion with his cousins, Irene Henderson, Graham Davidson and George Knox; and before we returned to County Durham he showed me where he had lived, and had gone to school, etc.

Squadron Leader "Del" Padbury, Aircrew Association and former Navigator on Valiant and Victor Squadrons 49 and 55:

"It is said that military aircrew are a peculiar breed, having a mix of justifiable professional pride, a great sense of exuberant humour, team players and an inbred loyalty. But – not Tom Clark. I have been the Chairman of the local Aircrew Association for many years and my members appear to retain the characteristics of the breed. There was one exception – Tom Clark.

"When Tom joined us he was quiet and reserved. When asked for his flying experience, for branch records, he responded 'AEO V Force' and that was that. He was more inclined to talk about his enthusiasm for gardening, being a keen member of the Royal Horticultural Society. I mentioned to Tom that I had a gardening problem and he offered to visit me and give advice. He did so in that quiet voice of his, but then added that he was seriously ill. He was to attend one more meeting before his death.

"This excellent profile on Tom by his son Chris astounded me, for it highlighted a long and valiant service with determination and courage." **Del Padbury, 26 June 2010**. Sadly, Del died on 30 April 2013.

Tom stayed with Irene in Galashiels for a few days, where the four caught up with each others lives from over sixty-five years before, and after a couple more days with Jeanne and me, he returned to Norfolk. During this time Irene tried to persuade Tom to take two oil colour paintings, which had been painted by his father, Charles, and grandfather, David, and which Irene had been given by her "Uncle Charlie" and "Grandfather David"; Tom told Irene that they had been with her all of these years and that she should keep them.

Sadly Irene, who was a spinster, and with no successors, died during December 2008 and she bequeathed to me, not only those two paintings, but three others as well; one has gone to my second cousin Lynn in Edinburgh, one to my youngest sister, and I have kept the three remaining ones, which I will pass on to my daughter and son. So the paintings will have remained within the Clark family for future generations to enjoy.

It was just as well that Tom had such an enjoyable time reminiscing his forgotten childhood in the sunset of his life, as at long last, his body started to feel its age and the tiredness of a long and fruitful life. During the autumn and winter of 2004, Tom's health went into decline and a cancer which had invaded his body, started to take over. It spread from his lungs, into his throat and brain, and sadly on the afternoon of Tuesday, 22 March 2005, Thomas Buchanan Clark; my Father and Friend; died at the age of eighty-three. Exactly three months later, on the morning of Wednesday, 22 June 2005, Stella May Clark; my loving Mother also died, aged eighty-four.

May you both Rest in Peace and the Love of The Lord, Amen

As well as close family tributes paid at Tom's funeral, there was also one from his brother's South African side, sent by his nephew, Graham Clark and Graham's wife, Sue:

"On behalf of your African side of the Clark family who cannot be with their English side of the Clark family today, we have prepared a few words as a tribute to Tom, our beloved brother–in–law, uncle and great uncle. We do wish that we could all be with you as a family today, but as this is not possible, we will be with you in spirit instead. As wife, children and grandchildren of Tom's only sibling James Wares, we would dearly like to pay a tribute to our Tom, whom we did not have the honour of knowing for many years, but nevertheless, in the time that we did share with him, we felt privileged and sincerely enjoyed his companionship and humour.

"Thomas Buchanan and his younger brother, James Wares, were born in Canada to a printer, Charles James Clark and his wife, Elizabeth nee Buchanan. The boys returned to Scotland without their mother and initially grew up in the Border regions of Scotland. The two boys experienced a rather hard childhood. Their mother died when Tom was about eight years old. Wares was left in Galashiels in the care of his paternal grandmother and two maiden aunts, while Tom grew up in the care of uncle Willie Clark and his wife, Mamie, in Edinburgh. The two boys later moved to Newcastle, where their father married Essie Richardson, four months before his death, caused by pneumonia and diabetes mellitus in 1939. This was the initial start of the brothers losing contact, for in that same year Wares left school just before turning fifteen and joined the Scottish Post Office, while Tom joined the Royal Air Force where he remained until 1964.

"Photographs are evidence that he certainly cut a dashing figure and handsome face in his RAF uniform. In 1941, Tom was involved in a serious flying boat accident at Sullom Voe that resulted in visual difficulties. In the meantime, Wares saw active service in the British Army and Royal Navy as a Signaller in North Africa, the Mediterranean and Italy. With demobilization in 1946, Wares went to seek his fortune in Southern Africa. In 1947, Tom visited Wares in what is now, Harare, Zimbabwe. Tom, apparently then with the King's Flight based in Indonesia, but was on an African trip at the time. That was the last they saw of each other or heard from each other for fifty-three years. What we know of Tom in the interim was that in 1953 Tom received the permanent commission of Flight Lieutenant. From 1964–1985 Tom worked as a horticulturist. Most importantly, we know he married Stella and they raised their family of eight children.

"The highlight of Wares' latter years was being reunited with his only brother, Tom. As a family we were delighted to have Dad trace Tom via the Royal Air Force Association in 2000, and even more pleased when Mom and Dad travelled to the UK in 2001 to be reunited with the 'lost' section of the Clark family. The experience was an emotional one for both Wares and Tom. Wares treasured their subsequent contact whether by phone or letter. Tom reciprocated by visiting South Africa. Sadly, following a quadruple bypass operation, Wares passed away a month before the long planned reciprocal visit. However, we as a family had a great time with Tom on his visit and indeed we are sure it was a memorable one for him. I am sure that the two brothers are now reminiscing; we can't help but picture these two brothers – both tall, intelligent, witty, and with a similar brogue and genteel manner, sitting pinting a couple of well brewed ales together by day, while supping a few, well probably more than a few, fine whiskies by night. While Tom also reunites with Trevor, together the two brothers can meet their parents with whom they shared so little time. What does this tell us? Not only is it sad when parents and children have too little time together, but it is also very sad when siblings become estranged. Life's too short and one shouldn't wait until the latter years when it's too late. While Tom sadly leaves his loved ones behind, it is also befitting that he reunites with his other loved ones.

"We (the Graham family part) certainly loved meeting Tom in Kings Lynn when he was the most remarkable host, putting on a lovely family gathering that we thoroughly enjoyed. It was wonderful to meet most of the family and it was an absolute pleasure having Tom to stay in South Africa. Tom was such an easy undemanding guest who enjoyed the outings and travels while here. Gently spoken, but with a terrific and somewhat naughty sense of humour, we had lots of laughs. He certainly was a caring husband as he spent a good deal of his holiday fretting about Stella and her well-being. We just wish we had enjoyed more time getting to know Tom better. And to you our 'English' family, our sincere condolences from each of us in Africa, to Stella, and each and every one of you – our thoughts are very much with you at this sad time. All that is left for us to say is 'au revoir Tom'. We will love and miss you, but more importantly, we shall treasure fond memories of our time together. May your soul rest in everlasting peace in the wonderful place you deserve to be."

There was also a full epitaph on Tom published in 16 Squadron Association "News brief" by "Jimmy" Taylor, outlining his full RAF career and civilian life. An extract of it is published here:

"Flight Lieutenant Thomas B. (Jock/Tom) Clark 1921-2005. Tom Clark – as I knew him in the last few years – was a man of supreme dignity and modesty, most unwilling to talk about himself or his experiences of the Second World War and afterwards; so the following is a sadly incomplete record of what was certainly an unusually varied and exciting career. The fact that he belonged to at least six other squadrons and other associations besides our own, and to numerous civilian ones suggests, still waters running very deep. Tom was one of nature's gentlemen and all who knew him felt they had gained something special from his friendship. Tom was proud of having belonged in 16 Squadron, even for a short but critical time; 16 Squadron, in turn, can be proud of having a man like Tom serving in its ranks; they don't come better than him".

Epilogue

By 1964 when Dad (Tom) retired, I was an eighteen year old adult and too busy with my own life then to reflect on what my father had achieved, and how he had served his adopted country. Tom was a very private and modest person and never the one to court an audience; as the 16 Squadron Association epitaph to him reinforced. I was not made aware of much of his loyal commitment to the Royal Air Force and Great Britain and beyond, until I started researching his career a year after his death in March 2005. I then began piecing together fragments I knew about him, coupled with articles he had submitted to various former Squadron Associations he had served in. Being his eldest biological child, I was aware of some of his post-war work, including being stationed at Waterbeach, Benson, Hong Kong, Singapore, Swanton Morley, Hullavington, Watton and West Raynham. For most of the remainder of his service, from when I was born at the end of 1945, until near his retirement after twenty-five years at the end of 1964, Tom was the stranger who would arrive home now and then from some far flung corner. My youngest sister would often say to Mum, "When's Daddy coming home?"

The only time that Tom opened up a bit was when he was getting ready to go to the various Officers' Mess Dinners, when Mum was pressing his trousers, whilst I put "Brasso" on his brass jacket buttons and medals, and "Silvo" on the remainder. He had this special brass cover called a "button stick" which was about six inches long and two inches wide, with a gap in the centre; which would

Air Ministry Button Stick.

slip under the buttons and protect the jacket material from the "Brasso" whilst I polished with the wadding.

He would then relate some small aspect of his RAF life, relevant to where he would be entertained that night. The other times he would open up a bit was when his tongue was loosened by copious amounts of neat whisky which he frequently consumed whilst off-duty. But then you had to separate his wicked dry humour and "bullshit" from truth. One example, he told all of us as kids that we were related to the North American Red Indians and had them as ancestors! I believed this into late adulthood and he only told me differently during 2003 when I started researching our family history! When I found that his ancestors were all Scottish and challenged him on it, he said it was just something he had told us and didn't realize that we still believed it. I said, "You Bastard! I've always supported and cheered on the Red Indians in movies"; to which he just laughed.

Normally, Tom would rather talk to anyone about his first love, growing plants and landscape gardening, or a forthcoming trip to Chelsea Flower Show/Kew Gardens or some other Royal Horticultural event. He was an avid viewer of BBC2 "Gardener's World" with firstly Ken Burras, Percy Thrower, then onto Peter Seabrooke, Arthur Billitt, Geoff Hamilton and finally Alan Titchmarsh.

There was also a very dark place that Tom would retreat to sometimes when drunk on whisky, and it is clear with hindsight, and having first-hand knowledge of it, that he was suffering from an undiagnosed Post Traumatic Stress Disorder brought about by his numerous life experiences. Including childhood, the war, life threatening incidents like the Sunderland Air Accident and the shooting down of his Baltimore in Italy; coupled with his time as an air-gunner being tasked to defend his aircraft and shooting down enemy aircraft; then the many long dangerous hours flying in the Far East, and later on, espionage duties adjacent to Warsaw Pact countries during the Cold War. All of this pent-up fear, anger, and other emotions, would sometimes explode violently on both my Mother and me from an early age.

However, upon retirement it seemed that a great burden had been lifted from his shoulders and the real Tom emerged as others knew him; a gentle natured, patient and caring human being. In my adult life we became firm friends as well as father/son, the earlier remoteness that I had experienced from childhood had gone.

It just remains for me to say that I am very proud to have had Tom Clark as my Dad and I hope that he is proud of what I have achieved in this book.

Chris Clark
January 2012

Poem: Valhalla

By Peter Morrey

And we shall see them all
In the life that follows this,
Regal warriors crowned in glory now.

Granted peace and heaven's eternal bliss
Unto us their sacrifice endow,
No longer shall the engines drone their way,
No longer shall the bombs scream from the sky,
Ended is the fear of outward flight
Realising death is standing by,
Sacrifice is hard to comprehend.

And yet the flower of youth went out to die,
Silent eyes that scanned the eerie clouds,
Swinging guns still searching in the sky.
Overhead he watches the war torn strife,
Counted all the warriors in the air, and
Awaiting those who fell, with him to share.
Their names are written in the book of Gold,
Inscribed with blood and tears and chilling sweat,
Of these are many tales of valour told,
Names we must revere- Lest We Forget.

Acknowledgements

The following is a list of people/organizations who have contributed in some way to the production of this book and without whom this story would be lacking in detail. I have tried to place them in chronological order of Tom Clark's Service Record and I publicly thank them here;

Air Marshall Richard Frank 'Dick' Garwood – Foreword
Air Historical Branch, Imperial War Museum
RAF Museum
H.J. 'Jimmy' Taylor, 16 Squadron Association
Flight Lieutenant Oliver 'Olly' Jackson, 201 Squadron
Bircham Newton Memorial Fund, 279 Squadron
Peter Gunn, author of *Bircham Newton*
David Jacklin, author of *Up in all Weather*, RAF Docking
Tom Docherty, author of *Dinghy Drop*, 279 Squadron
Peter Jackson for preserving Tom's Italian account
Mike Trenchard, private researcher, The National Archives
Monty Dean, 55 Squadron Association
Ivor Calverley, 55 Squadron Association
Gary West, Secretary of 55 Squadron Association
Alan Hartley, Secretary of 271 Squadron Association
Peter Wentworth, Secretary of 10 Squadron Association
David Burgin. Secretary 24 (XXIV) Squadron Association
Chris Harrison, Member Secretary, The Queen's Flight Association
Mike Prendergast, RAF Benson, The King's Flight Log Books
The Daily Mail for releasing a copy of the photo of The King's Flight Crew, 1951
Air Chief Marshal Sir David Lee, author of *Eastward*, FEAF
Squadron Leader H.A. Probert, author of *History of Changi*
Pamela Wickes, Flight Logs Far East, Transport Wing, V.I.P. Crew
Alan Hotchkiss, Secretary FETW Association
Tony Cunnane, 'Red Arrows', Swanton Morley Course, 1956
Peter Long, author of *In Support of So Many*, RAF Watton
Peter Oakley, 'Special Operator', 51 Squadron
Stanley Haddock, 'Special Operator', 51 Squadron
Phil Mason, Secretary, 51 Squadron Association
Derek 'Del' Padbury, Aircrew Association
Frank Donnelly, Durham Clayport Library

Index